Advance Hotel Engineering

Advance Hotel Engineering

Mahendra Singh Chabbra

RANDOM

RANDOM PUBLICATIONS

NEW DELHI (INDIA)

Advance Hotel Engineering

ISBN 978-93-5111-535-9

Published in 2015 in India by

RANDOM PUBLICATIONS

4376-A/4B, Gali Murari Lal, Ansari Road

New Delhi-110 002

Phone : +9111-43580356, 011-23289044, 011-43142548

e-mail: sales@randompublications.com,

info@randompublications.com, randomexports@gmail.com

Type Setting by : Friends Media, Delhi-110089

Digitally Printed at : Replika Press Pvt. Ltd.

Preface

Hotels constitute major Part of the hospitality industry. For proper management of hotels the Hotel Engineering Department plays very important role along with other constituent departments. Such scope is very comprehensive and includes several activities like inspections adjustments, replacements, repairs, keeping records etc., the broad areas of hotel engineering maintenance work include civil, mechanical, electrical, safety & security, energy and waste management, fire protection etc. It may well be emphasized failure amounts to management failure inane kind of industry. Due such failures, the customers and the working personnel alike shall be irritated and dissatisfied. Engineering department of a hotel has great importance in as much as it provides utility services like electricity, steam, hot water, air-conditioning and refrigeration, maintain engineering and services of various other equipment. Provisions of proper services and proper maintenance affairs in hotels have great impact on the attitude of the guest. Therefore, hotel engineering department has big responsibility in satisfying guest demand and be instrumental in maintaining the profit level of hotels up to reasonable standard.

I would like to thank my team for standing beside me throughout my career and writing this book. My special thanks go to "Random Publications" who have published the book.

– Mahendra Singh Chabbra

Contents

1

Housekeeping Department

The Housekeeping Department is one of the busiest parts in the hotel as far as the variety of functions performed, and number of staff working. It is usually situated at the laundry room or any other convenient place close to Housekeeping Supplies.

The Housekeeping Department is responsible for:

- Neatness and Cleanliness of all guest rooms and most public areas
- Maintenance of recycled and non-recycled cleaning inventories

Some of the functions might however be leased to a concessionaire. In this case, hotel shall still have a housekeeping department but to a minimum number of staff! The Housekeeping Department is headed by an Executive Housekeeper.

The procedure of cleaning guest rooms by the housekeeping department can be summarized in the following way:

- Checkout clerk contacts the Housekeeping Department that a room became vacant and needs cleaning!
- Housekeeping Department updates the room status from occupied to on-change and sends a room maid to clean the room
- Room maid cleans the room and contacts the housekeeping department back about the latest status and condition of the room
- If the room is Out Of Order for any reason, then the Housekeeping Department deducts that room from those available for sale, until either scheduled to be extensively cleaned or post to the confirmation from the Maintenance Department that the deficiency was repaired!
- Housekeeping Department sends their inspectors to check whether the stated room has been cleaned to the hotel standards or not!
- If the room is cleaned to hotel's standards, the Housekeeping Department shall update the room status from On-Change to Clean and Available for Sale and communicate this to the Front Office Department!
- If the room is not cleaned to hotel standards, inspectors communicate to the Housekeeping Department that the room shall be cleaned again!

DEFINITION

Hotel housekeeping departments can be considered hotel ambassadors because of their dedication and responsibility in maintaining the hotel's image. Housekeeping performs detailed work in guest rooms and hotel areas to provide a clean, comfortable environment for hotel guests to enjoy.

Through cleaning and organizing public spaces, housekeeping departments ensure that what the guests see and experience result in a positive impression of the property.

- *Types*: Housekeeping departments include a variety of job titles. The department will generally have a director of housekeeping, sometimes called the executive housekeeper. This employee is responsible for managing the department and its employees. Housekeeping departments also have supervisors who inspect work and several types of line staff, including room attendants, laundry attendants, turn-down attendants and public space attendants. In addition, other housekeeping employees run the department office by answering phones and dispatching attendants. In some hotels, the office personnel are responsible for managing lost and found items.
- *Function*: The primary role of the hotel's housekeeping department is cleaning guest rooms. Housekeeping works closely with front desk operations to communicate when rooms are clean and ready for guests to occupy. Although usually associated with cleaning and sanitizing guest rooms, housekeepers are also responsible for other areas, such as public restrooms, convention space and offices. Housekeeping departments often manage laundry operations, which includes washing linens as well as employee uniforms. At some hotels, housekeepers are responsible for minibar inventory and room service.
- *Size*: The housekeeping department is often the largest employee department in the hotel. The number of employees is relative to the size of the hotel, and may be a combination of full-time hotel employees and temporary leased labour. The number of full-time employees is generally based on the average number of rooms one housekeeper can clean in one shift. The housekeeping department's full size is based on the rooms per housekeeper per day formula, but daily scheduling depends on occupied rooms and/or special projects.
- *Tools*: Room attendants generally use a cart to hold their tools and supplies so they can bring the necessary equipment with them to each room. Carts are stocked with chemicals and cleaning supplies to clean surfaces in guest rooms and bathrooms. The cart also holds a vacuum cleaner, broom and trash bag. Although not brought to every room, carpet shampooers and ozone machines can be brought to rooms that require extra cleaning attention.

- *Schedule*: Hotel housekeeping departments operate 24 hours each day, but the majority of employees work during the day. Day shift housekeepers are typically room attendants who begin cleaning rooms in the morning. The housekeeping schedule revolves around guest occupancy, so housekeeping departments are at their busiest between guest check-out in the morning and check-in in the afternoon. Turn-down attendants are scheduled for evening shifts, so they can perform nightly turn down in guest rooms. Laundry and public space attendants may work any shift.

IMPORTANCE

- Accommodation in hotels tend to be the largest part of the hotel, it is the most revenue generating department, the housekeeping department takes care of all rooms is often largest department in hotels.
- Hotel aims to make environment comfortable and offer specialised service to the guest.
- A health club is a part of facilities of most large hotels especially resort hotels this also include swimming pool and spa facilities.
- Hotel offer guest the choice of specialty restaurant, coffee shop. The bar also sells liquors which generate the revenue of the hotel. They are available in banqueting, meeting and private party facilities.
- House keeping is the department determine to a large extent whether guests are happy during stay and in turn mankind they return to the hotel.
- Housekeeping is the department that deals essentially with cleanliness and all ancillary service attached to that.
- Revenue can be generated from conferencing, meeting, seminar etc.
- The fine accommodation and service are provided to the guest so they are pleased with the hotel. The guest satisfaction is its primary object and the hygiene factor must always be present in the hotel.
- The rooms in hotels are offered as accommodation to travellers/ guest as individual units of bedroom. Some interconnected rooms are also made which will be helpful to the guest and families. Many hotels offer suits to the guest.
- The standard plays an important role in the reputation of the hotels. One feels comfortable only in the environment which is clean and well ordered, so cleanliness is important for health foremost also for well being.
- Hotel offer laundry, dry leaning facilities for guest clothes, shoe polishing facilities also.

- Hotels try to make the ambiance as pleasant as possible by nice colour scheme, attractive furnishing and a well kept efficient staff.
- These days shopping arcade also found in hotels.

In hotels major part of revenue comes from rooms, rooms which is not sold on any night losses revenue forever and reason for poor occupancy can be anything like hygiene factor, cleanliness, lack of modernizing etc. hence main purpose is to improve whole appeal of the room. A guest spend more time alone in his room than any other part of the hotel, so he can check up the cleanliness he wishes to as some of the guest are more health conscious these days.

He may check up dusting, in-depth cleaning and losses confidence if properly not done *e.g.* If drawers are not cleaned he may generally won't feel like putting his clothes down. Decent room supplies are service like quick laundry and dry cleaning service shows guest that hotel is considering his comfort and wishes to please him. not only this from the cleanliness of lobby, public area, restaurant, cloakrooms, the state and cleanliness of uniform the guest can judge a lot about hotel. it can be positive or negative judgement we can conclude that housekeeping department contributes greatly to all guest impression of the hotel.

FUNCTIONS

The extension of the housekeeping function outside the hotel bedroom normally includes cleaning of the bedroom floors and may also include the staircases, public cloakrooms and other public areas of the hotel. Many a times outside agencies are involved in cleaning the public areas such as the lobby and the restaurant area as well as the men's and women's restrooms. This activity is normally carried out at odd hours or at the times when public is not around this area.

The standard of the cleanliness needs to be maintained and it's the duty of the executive housekeeper to see that pre-determined standards of cleanliness are maintained in all the areas of the hotel it be if the fire-exit stairwells and goods lifts or any other public area.

To ensure this, the day of executive housekeepers begin with a round with assistant housekeeper of all such areas which is visited by the public. For this standards need to be set and once the standards are approved, the department shall strive hard to maintain them.

LOST AND FOUND DEPARTMENT

Many a times while cleaning a guest room attendant comes across some personal items of the guest left behind. The value of the personal item can vary from almost nil to thousands of rupees as in the case of Rolex watches, etc. All the objects found while cleanin g the rooms are, thus, handed over by attendants to the floor supervisor, who maintains a list of the found objects against the specific room number.

FIRST AID

- First aid as and when needed by the guests is provided by the housekeeping department which m aintains the first aid kit.

FLORAL ARRANGEMENT

- Fresh floral arrangements all over the hotel are maintained by the housekeeping department. The private areas like guest bedroom or the public areas like the restaurants and the lobby floral arrangements are made by housekeeping department.

LAUNDRY SERVICES

- The laundry services extended to the guest are usually provided by the housekeeping. The laundry to be washed is collected from the guest room and washed, dried and ironed clothes are supplied back to th e guest room. Earlier, all the hotels had in house laundry services but nowadays many hotels have out-sourced this service, both for the hotel linen as well as for the guest laundry.

PURCHASING

- This is one role of the housekeeping department where a lot of money transactions take place. This is one of the important areas which can affect the profitability of the hotel if various products purchased and supplies are not well managed. The primary areas of purchasing that are under the control of the Executive housekeepers are:
  - Bedroom supplies: *e.g.*, laundry bags, breakfast, cards, shoeshine, etc.,
  - Bathroom supplies: *e.g.*, toiletries,
  - Linen: bed sheets and towelling,
  - Tea and coffee making facilities: *e.g.*, tea/coffee sachets, sugar, milk and biscuits,
  - Working replacements: *e.g.*, shower curtains, crockery, glassware, vacuum cleaners, trolleys, etc.,
  - Cleaning supplies: *e.g.*, air freshener, bleach, cleaning product, and
  - Uniforms: *e.g.*, for the room attendants/porters.

It is necessary for the Executive housekeeper to ensure that the supplies and their consumption is monitored.

The Executive housekeeper would have different policies for these two distinct groups of purchasing. The actual consumption of the first group of purchases can be anticipated in line with the hotel occupancy. It is necessary to maintain a stock of these items so that the staff can put up their requisitions on a daily or weekly basis.

The Executive housekeeper is thus required not only to ascertain the demands but also to control the use of consumable products by maintaining properly the invoices and requisition slips. The consumable products are many and if not properly monitored will obviously affect at large the profit statement of the hotel. Today, computers are used for the purpose. "Assets", though not in true sense, like uniforms, etc. are not regularly used up and they do not need to be replaced daily.

But it is the duty of the staff to maintain their uniform and turn up immaculately, daily. Other items like vacuum cleaners, crockery are phased out over a period of time and are recorded as depreciation. Hotel linen is very difficult to manage, as in a large hotel almost 5000 soiled linens are sent for cleaning daily.

To count and counter check the linen from and to the laundry is a herculean task. Moreover, guests also tend to pilfer items like towels from hotels. To keep account of stock and maintain it and when necessary replenish it becomes the priority job for the housekeeping manager

STAFFING

Staffing, which is one of a hotel's most important management functions, is an ongoing challenge because of the high rate of employee and manager turnover. Full-service hotels can experience annual turnover rates in excess of 100 per cent in certain employee classifications. Some managers consider an annual employee turnover rate of 33 per cent low. At this rate, the entire hotel must be completely restaffed every three years. The higher the turnover rate, the larger the number of employees who must be replaced.

For example, if a hotel with 450 employees has a 75 per cent annual turnover rate, it will be completely restaffed every 16 months. Staffing is the responsibility of the human resources department.

In an attempt to reduce employee turnover, hotel and lodging businesses are giving increasing attention to job design, seeking to enhance those job characteristics that give the employee the greatest satisfaction and motivation. Good job design must take into account the needs of employees as well as the demands of the job.

Well-thought-out job design begins when management conducts a job analysis—that is, a thorough evaluation of the specific tasks performed for a particular job and the time required to perform them. Job analysis is an ongoing process, as many jobs change with improvements in technology and pressure to improve product quality. The job analysis is the basis for the job description and job specification.

A job description includes the job title, pay, a brief statement of duties and procedures, working conditions, and hours. The job specification is an outline of the qualifications necessary for a particular job.

In response to the limits of specialization, organizations can redesign jobs to improve coordination, productivity, and product quality while responding to an employee's needs for learning, challenge, variety, increased responsibility, and achievement.

Such job redesign often involves job rotation, the systematic movement of employees from one job to another; job enlargement, an increase in the number of tasks an employee will do in the job; job enrichment, the attempt to give the employee more control over job-related activities; and flextime, a flexible work schedule that permits employee input in establishing work schedules. In team-driven job redesign, a concept similar to job rotation, employees can transfer back and forth among teams that provide different services or products.

Hotels recruit employees from a variety of sources. Newspapers and employee referrals are used to recruit non-skilled hourly employees. Supervisory and management employees generally are recruited through colleges and universities, promotions from within, professional associations, and management recruiters.

Hotels that take more time in making their selections are more successful in retaining employees. Discussions of employee training and development often concentrate on training techniques without giving a full explanation of what a hotel is trying to accomplish.

As training and development impart job skills and educate employees, supervisors, and managers, they also improve current and future employee performance, which affects the bottom line. Effective training includes problem solving, problem analysis, quality measurement and feedback, and team building.

Performance evaluation, also called performance appraisal, is the systematic review of the strengths and weaknesses of an employee's performance. The major difficulty in a performance appraisal is quantifying those strengths and weaknesses. The performance of some jobs is easy to quantify, while for others it is more difficult. An important part of the appraisal process is a well-established job description, so that the employee and the supervisor have similar expectations.

Compensation includes the monetary and non-monetary rewards that managers, supervisors, and employees receive for performing their jobs. In order to set compensation levels, the human resources department must periodically conduct job evaluations, which determine the value of the job to the hotel. Knowledge of the value of the job to the organization and of wage rates for each job classification allows the hotel to establish a fair compensation policy.

JOB DESCRIPTION OF HOUSEKEEPING STAFF

Duties and Responsibilities:

- All Ledgers are to be put up for Joint Directors signature through housekeeping Manager on a quarterly basis.
- Daily use of cleaning agents are to be recorded and the records to be put up for housekeeping managers signature monthly.
- Ensure proper discipline among Housekeepers, Sweepers, Dhobi, and Tailor working in linen department. Make sure that they wear name badges.
- Floor scrubbing Machine is to be taken by other housekeeper only with the permission of the linen housekeeper.
- Floor scrubbing machines are to be chain locked when not in use.
- Any other job given by the housekeeping manager or the senior management staff from time to time.
- Linen and curtains are to be checked for wear and tear quarterly.
- Maintain a sepearate Indent for the cleaning agents used in Laundry and the Indent should be signed by the housekeeping Manager.
- Periodical Maintenance of washing Machine, Ironing Machine, Iron Box, Sewing Machine, and floor scrubbing Machine to be carried out and the record to be maintained.
- Planning and scheduling the standard procedure for cleaning all types of linen to be displayed in laundry and to be followed strictly.
- Responsible for the cleanliness of sweepers uniform.
- Sell all waste materials and deposit the sale proceeds to secretary.
- Supervision and checking the cleanliness of the surrounding area of main hospital.
- Tailoring rates for various items of stitched materials are to be maintained. For any revision in charges prior approval to be taken from secretary.
- Time schedule to be prepared for collection of clean/soiled linen and to be followed strictly.
- Torn or faded linen is to be segregated and to be shown to joint director quarterly. If any item is found unserviceable the same should be written off the ledger getting after the approval of Jt.Director.
- Torn or faded linen is to be used for cleaning purposes.
- Train and Guide the trainees housekeeper posted in linen department.
- Training classes are to be taken for junior housekeepers when required.
- Washing charges for various linen are to be fixed and approval. For any change in the charges, prior approval to be taken from secretary.

Designation – Floor Executive: Housekeeping:

- Control over all keys of all departments in OPDS.

- Disposal of refuse is to be monitored.
- Ensure proper discipline of Housekeepers and sweepers working in out patient department and make sure that they wear name badge.
- Experimenting new techniques and equipments for cleaning.
- Any other job given by the housekeeping manager or the senior management staff from time to time.
- Indenting cleaning agents and equipments and ensure their proper use and keeping records.
- Maintain the Leave list of all sweepers working in main hospital, free hospital, Laico and other supporting areas and day off Roster of sweepers working in OPDs.
- Maintaining the checklist of furniture, electrical plumbing, carpentry and mason work in the OPDs.
- Maintenance details of continuous duties of housekeepers.
- Maintenance of House Keeping department room and attending to phone calls promptly.
- Maintenance of sweepers attendance Register, wage sheets, deployment, control and details for continuous duties.
- Maintenance responsible for the sweepers uniform collected after working hours from the sweepers.
- Make sure the tyre cart is secured and locked after working hours.
- Planning and scheduling the standard procedures in writing for the proper care of all types of floors, walls, windows, furniture, bathrooms, Lavatories and other equipments to be prepared and follows trictly.
- Preparing inventories for furniture and keeping records for their maintenance.
- Reporting and checking of all maintenance work.
- Responsible for the cleaning schedule of freshwater tank, filters, coolers and septic Tanks and the cleaning and due dates are to be displayed in the boards as well as in the Register. The register shall be put up for Housekeeping managers signature every month.
- Supervision and checking the cleanliness of out patient departments and Basement area.
- Supervision of quality maintenance and infection control.
- To develop proper use of cleaning procedures.
- Training and taking classes for juniors

Designation: - Ward Executive: Housekeeping:

- Attending to patients complaints
- Control of all keys of 1st and 2nd Floor
- Development and standardization of newer and improved method of cleaning for better results at lower costs.

- Ensure proper discipline of housekeepers and sweepers in 1st and 2nd floor and make sure the wear name badges.
- Ensure up keep and maintenance of hospital property.
- Any other job that may be assigned by the housekeeping Manager or the senior management staff from time to time.
- Indenting cleaning agents and equipments and ensure their proper use and keeping necessary records.
- Maintain day off roaster of sweepers in 1st and 2nd floor.
- Planning and scheduling the standard procedures in writing for the proper care of all types of floors, walls, windows, furniture, bathrooms, lavatories and other equipments to be placed and to be followed strictly.
- Preparing inventories for 1st and 2nd floor furniture and keeping records for their maintenance.
- Responsible for the sweepers uniform collected after working hours from the sweepers of 1st and 2nd floor.
- Supervision and checking the cleanliness of 1st and 2nd floor.
- Supervision for quality maintenance and infection control.
- Take adequate precautions for controlling cross infections.
- To assist in quality health care and patient care programme.
- Training and taking classes for juniors

Designation – Ward Executive: Housekeeping:

- Attending to patient's complaints.
- Control of all keys of 3rd and 4th floor.
- Development and standardization of newer and improved method of cleaning for better results at lower costs.
- Ensure proper discipline of Housekeepers and sweepers in 3rd and 4th floor and make sure they wear name badges.
- Ensure upkeep and maintenance of hospital property
- Any other job that may be assigned by the housekeeping manager or the senior management staff from time to time.
- Indenting cleaning agents and equipments and ensure their proper use and keeping records.
- Maintain day off roster for sweepers in 3rd and 4th floor.
- Maintaining the checklist of furniture, Electrical, plumbing, Carpenting and Mason works in 3rd and 4th floor.
- Planning and scheduling the standard procedures in writing for the proper care of all types of floors walls, windows, furniture, bathrooms lavatories and other equipments to be placed and to be followed strictly.
- Preparing inventories for 3rd and 4th floor furniture and keeping records for their maintenance.

- Responsible for the sweepers uniform collected after working hours from the sweepers of 3rd and 4th floor.
- Supervision and checking the cleanliness of 3rd and 4th floor.
- Supervision for quality maintenance and infection control.
- Take adequate precautions in controlling cross infections.
- To assist in quality health care and patient care programme
- Training and taking classes for juniors.

Designation – Senior Trainees: Housekeeping:

- Attend all theory and practical classes as per the programme.
- Indenting cleaning agents, equipments and ensure the proper use and maintain their records.
- Planning and scheduling the standard procedures for cleaning in writing and follow strictly.
- Preparing inventories for furniture and keeping records for their maintenance.
- Work under the supervision of executive Linen housekeeper.

ATTRIBUTES AND QUALITIES OF HOUSEKEEPING STAFF

HONESTY

This is a very essential attribute for housekeeping staff, especially Room Attendants, who have access to all guest rooms. Guest belongings, sometimes invaluable are often found lying around in the room. The temptations to thieve are great.

It is only the personal quality of discipline and integrity that checks these temptations:

- *Eye for Detail*: It is one of the greatest qualities that house keeping staff must have. It is with this quality that the finer aspects of housekeeping are taken care of and it is what determines a good service from an average one. This quality enables housekeeping staff to take into consideration the minutest details.
- *Co-Cooperativeness*: Housekeeping staff needs to be co-operating with other departments to achieve more efficiency.
- *Briefing and Scheduling of Staff*: Briefing is that process at the beginning of a work shift which is provided by management to facilitate a two-way communication between management and staff. It is the one time during a shift that all housekeeping staff are together to share information and feelings before they disperse to their work areas.
  - Briefing Schedule:
    - i Personal hygiene and grooming.
    - ii Any new policies and procedures introduced by managcl1lenL must be made out and explained to the staff.

iii At n briefing the duties or each staff member and the areas of accountability are explained. This would mean that staffs are assigned a floor and allotted their number of rooms. The staffs likewise, are told which floors or public areas they are assigned to for cleaning. They are also told which supervisor would be in charge.

iv Briefing is a time which can be used as a training opportunity. Simple tasks may be demonstrated so that they can be practiced under supervision at their work place.

CLEANING A ROOM

Prior to reporting on a 1loor the room attendant already knows the status of a room in her given lot of rooms. The room attendant can prioritize room to be attended to first on the basis of immediate needs. Before entering the room knock at the door firmly with the index finger knuckle announcing clearly" Housekeeping".

When there is no answer, repeat the knock after ten seconds announcing yourself as before. If there is still no answer open the door and knock announcing inside the room "Housekeeping". When there is no reply and one is relatively sure that there is no one in, open the door wide and keep it that way till the entire cleaning cycle in the room is complete.

ROOM CLEANING PROCEDURE

- And centre sashes or windows, close windows.
- Arrange furniture if necessary
- Check the maintenance requirements and report to the department head.
- Clean all the surfaces in single circular motions with a dry cloth. Use a hand dust pan to collect any unwanted matter on the surface without lifting dust in the air Ensure that all surfaces are spotlessly clean. Pay special attention to nooks and corners especially those points that may not obviously be visible to the guests eye.
- Clean lamp shades with a clean dry duster.
- Clean mirror with a dry cloth.
- Clean the bath room.
- Clean the ceiling and air-conditioning vents for cobwebs.
- Collect all loose papers or magazines and stack them neatly on the desk.
- Disinfect telephone mouthpiece with Dettol. Wipe balance of the telephone with a damp cloth, check phone for the dial tone.
- Dust both sides of all room doors, baseboards, window sills, inside and out, bottom

- Dust closet, shelves, hangers and rods. Brush the closet floor.
- Have a last look at the room referring to the checklist for completion of work.
- Switch off the room air-conditioner. Draw all curtains and open the windows for airing the room.
- Switch on the air-conditioning.
- Turn the mattress side-to-side on succeeding days followed by end-to-end turning. Smooth out mattress to air it.
- Use a stiff upholstery brush or vacuum cleaner on upholstered furniture arms, backs and seats.
- Wash the floors.

CLEANING A BATHROOM

- Clean mirror first with dry cloth then with glass cloth and finally with dry cloth.
- Clean the ceiling and air-conditioning vents for cobwebs.
- Cleaning activity starts from the ceiling downwards to the floor.
- Collect all trash in bathroom waste basket and deposit in trash hamper of the maids-cart.
- Finally close the windows shut all lights and close the bathroom doors.
- Floors are cleaned from the wall farthest to the door to the exit.
- Open all exhaust vents.
- Scrub the floor with the prescribed mop and ensure it is dry
- Scrub the toilet bowl and bidet using the special brush or mop and the prescribed sanitizer. The inner rim should be cleaned. Ensure it is dry and spotless inside. Clean the WC from the outside with a sponge till it is sparkling find dry. Clean the lid and toilet seat of the toilet bowl dry and close them.
- Scrub to dry the area next to the wash basin.
- Wipe down tile walls using a sponge or damp cloth. Follow with a dry cloth ensuring that tiles are free of water marks.
- Wipe dry the shower curtain with a sponge.
- Wipe off light bulbs and shades with dry cloth. Check that all bulbs are working.

DIRTY DOZEN

- Air-conditioning ducts and diffuser grills. Under bathroom counters.
- Area above racks
- Behind the WC bowl- the s-trap.
- Beneath the table
- Faucet nozzle filter
- In the toilet roll niche

- Interior surface of drawers
- Rear surface of doors
- Toilet vents
- Top of the door edges and ceiling.
- Top of the picture frames

ROOM MAINTENANCE PROCEDURE

As hose keeping has contact with all rooms and public areas practically in every shift, it is they who detect report and ensure the completion of all maintenance work. This requires close co-ordination with the engineering department.

WEEKLY CLEANING PROCEDURE

In addition to daily cleaning routine, a room attendant normally has some cleaning chores that are of a time-consuming nature. Such items may sometimes be beyond the physical capacity and need the assistance of a skill worker.

Such tasks are:

- Cleaning of window panes
- Polishing of brassware
- Scrubbing of balconies and terraces
- Scrubbing of bathroom tiles
- Vacuuming of under heavy furniture.

CLEANING AND CLEANING MATERIALS

We know that any establishment has to be clean, well maintained and presentable at any given moment of time. But how to ensure well maintained premises? Cleaning is the most important and primary aspect of housekeeping. It is a process of removing dirt, dust and grime by using methods such as dusting, shaking, sweeping, mopping, washing or polishing. There are certain areas you may clean daily, whereas you may clean other areas occasionally or once/twice in a year. Since there are different types of surfaces like wall, counter tops, marble floors, ceramic tiles, wooden chairs, etc, special cleaning agents are used to clean these specific surfaces. As suggested, discuss these various aspects of cleaning as well as the materials and equipments used for cleaning.

MEANING AND IMPORTANCE OF CLEANING

Cleaning involves sweeping floors, dusting furniture and other surfaces, mopping or washing floors, polishing surfaces, objects and accessories, scrubbing tiles, sinks, toilets, disinfecting drains, rearranging cleaned areas and putting things in their specific place. We can say that cleaning is a process of removing dust, dirt or any other undesirable materials like stains, spots, contents of an ashtray, etc.

What happens if cleaning is not done on a regular basis:

- Yes, your house will become the breeding ground of insects such as cockroaches, spiders, ants, flies and mosquitoes. It will look dirty and will be most uncomfortable.
- Living in such circumstances can also lead to diseases such as asthma, bronchitis, etc. Thus, cleaning is necessary for a general presentable appearance and also to ensure good hygienic conditions. What do you understand by dust and dirt?
- 'Dust' collectively refers to the loose particles, which are very easily moved by air and settle on any surface. It is easily removed with the help of a dry cloth.
- 'Dirt' refers to dust which sticks to any surface with the help of moisture or grease. It is more difficult to remove dirt as compared to dust. Dirt has to be removed either with a detergent or any other cleaning agent. Let us now read ahead of some general methods of cleaning.

METHODS OF CLEANING

That dust and dirt can be removed by dusting, mopping etc.

Based on these we can describe the cleaning methods as follows:

- *Dusting*: You are already familiar with the term 'dust'. But how do you remove dust? When any surface is wiped with a piece of dry cloth, it carries the loose dust with it and the process is known as dusting. This should be done with a clean soft cloth.
- *Shaking and Beating*: What happens when you shake a cloth full of dust? Yes, the dust falls out. Similarly when you shake or beat any soft material, like a carpet/rug or a curtain, the dust falls out, making the object dust free to a large extent. This is mostly done in open air so that other things do not get dusty.
- *Sweeping*: When a broom or a brush is used to carry the dust laterally along the room, the process is known as sweeping. While sweeping any vertical surface as walls, you should remember to start from the top and sweep downwards. Similarly for lateral sweeping as for floors, start from one end of the room and move to another, preferably a door, and carry the dust all along or collect in a dust pan. All the movable objects kept on the floor should be lifted, swept under, and kept back in place.
- *Mopping*: You have read that wiping with a dry cloth is dusting, similarly, wiping a surface with a damp cloth is called 'mopping'. The piece of cloth used is known as a 'mop' and is generally coarser than a duster. In this process, both the dust, as well as easily removable dirt, is also removed. Mopping is mostly done on floors. Extra

attention should be paid to nooks and corners otherwise it gets tougher to remove fixed grime later on.

- *Washing*: Sometimes mopping alone is not sufficient to remove dirt. Such surfaces are then scrubbed with the help of a yard broom along with plenty of water. Eventually the dirt loosens and is carried off by water. This process is known as 'washing'. In case of tougher stains or dirt, detergent may be added to the water.
- *Polishing*: When some reagent is rubbed on a surface to bring out the shine, the process is known as polishing and the reagent applied is known as the 'polish'. Similarly, many other objects/ decorative items made of brass, wood, marble etc, may be polished.

CLEANING EQUIPMENTS AND MATERIALS

Let us now learn about the equipment and other materials, which assist us in the process of cleaning. Can you name a few? Let us try to make a list of such equipments.

Equipments

Following are some of the equipments which you will come across during the process of cleaning:

- Brooms- brooms are either soft or hard. The soft ones are used to sweep the floors, whereas the hard ones are used to wash the floors.
- Brushes-are available in various sizes and shapes and are made of different materials. Different brushes are used for specific jobs. Brushes with nylon or plastic bristles are used for cleaning carpets or furniture, round feather brushes are used to remove cobwebs, metal brushes are used to clean wire mesh in the windows. You have special nylon brushes to clean the toilets.
- Buckets or basins- metal or plastic buckets/ basins of suitable sizes are used to carry water, detergents and chemicals so that there are no spills.
- Dust bins-these are available in plastic with a lid. These should be lined with paper so that the garbage does not stick to the surface. They should be emptied and washed daily.
- Dust pans- these are made of either plastic or metal and have flat surfaces, rounded at the sides. After sweeping, dirt and dust is collected directly into these with the help of a broom and carried to a dustbin. Dustpans save sweeping the entire amount of dust from one room to another. Instead, dust can be collected from each room and disposed of simultaneously. Dust pans should be cleaned after use.
- Dusters - These are mostly made of soft cotton, flannel or artificial

feathers mounted on a stick. These are used to clean loose dust and are also used for wiping various surfaces. You should use separate dusters for dusting and wiping surfaces such as dining table, mirrors, kitchen slabs, etc. They should be washed and dried after use.

- Mops- are mostly made of thick, loosely woven cotton cloth. These are used to wipe dust from the floors. These are dipped in clean water and squeezed before wiping the floors. You should change the water after mopping each room or when it gets dirty. You should thoroughly wash the mop and spread it for drying, after use.
- Polishing cloth- these are made of soft absorbent cloth such as flannel. Dry polishing cloth helps to clean and shine the polished surfaces by rubbing them vigorously.
- Vacuum cleaner- it works on electricity and has a fan. This sucks in the dirt and dust from the surfaces and stores it in a disposable bag inside. This bag should be emptied regularly.

Materials

There are many materials and reagents, which help in cleaning, scrubbing and polishing surfaces.

Some of these are commercial preparations for cleaning and you may be already familiar with some of them:

- Water- Water is the simplest cleaning reagent available to us. Some dirt may be loosened and dissolved in it. Although most of the time, some other cleaning agent is also used along with it.
- Detergents- Detergents are available in powder, solid and liquid form.These are used with water to clean various surfaces. The basic ingredients in a detergent are surface active agents, known as surfactants. A detergent may have more ingredients to make it more effective, like alkaline salts, bleaches, foam boosters, germicides and perfumes. The exact nature and use of a detergent will actually vary just as to its ingredients. However, there are a few points which should be kept in mind while choosing a detergent. It should –
  - Be readily soluble in water
  - Be effective in all types of water and produce no scum
  - Have good wetting powers so that the solution penetrates between the object and the dirt particles
  - Have good suspending powers to suspend dislocated dirt and not allow it to settle back
  - Be effective over a wide range of temperatures
  - Be harmless to the object and the skin.
  - Clean quickly
  - Be easily rinsed away

- Abrasives- some of the common abrasives are sand, finely powdered brick, saw dust, wheat bran, emery paper, fine ash, filtered chalk etc. Besides these, steel wool, nylon mesh, coconut fibres are also used to scrub dirt. Their use depends on the surface to be cleaned and the type of dirt to be removed. The extent of cleaning will depend upon the nature of the abrasive used and on the scrubbing action.
- Acids- strong acids are used to clean toilets and are available in crystals or liquid form. Milder forms of acids are also used to clean very dirty tiles. Acids should be rinsed off as soon as possible after use and should be stored away from children. Vinegar and lemon are used to clean stains on metals like brass and copper.
- Alkalis- baking soda and ammonia are used as grease emulsifiers and stain removing agents.
- Bleaches- stains on fabrics are removed by bleaches such as sodium hypochlorite, sodium perborate, hydrogen peroxide, sodium hydrosulphite etc.
- Solvents – solvents such as methylated spirit, carbon tetrachloride, kerosene, petrol etc; are used to remove grease, wax and other stains from the surfaces. You should keep methylated spirit, kerosene, petrol, away from fire as they are inflammable. Carbon tetrachloride is harmful if inhaled.
- Polishes- polishes are used on surfaces such as floors, furniture, leather and even metals. When rubbed on a surface, they provide a protective covering to the surface and produce shine. The object also gets cleaned in the process.

SCHEDULE OF CLEANING

Now the important question is how to do cleaning? You must have observed the cleaning process at your own house. Do you clean your rooms completely by removing all the furniture etc, every day? No, because that would require a lot of time and labour which can not be devoted everyday. Then how to do the cleaning?

For this, it is important to follow a certain schedule of cleaning. Everyday, a general cleaning of the open surfaces like floors, furniture and other such surfaces is required. Once in a while some more time is given to cleaning and you probably move heavy furniture and clean beneath it or beneath the carpets. Maybe once in six months or a year you empty the room completely and give it a complete wash, polish the floors, whitewash the walls, ceiling etc.

Thus we can basically divide cleaning into three types of schedules:

1. Daily clean
2. A weekly clean
3. A spring clean

A daily cleaning would be a general cleaning done every day; a weekly cleaning would be a more thorough cleaning done periodically, depending on the frequency of use. In a guest house, hotel, or a hospital, it may be done once a week or even earlier. Spring cleaning is usually done once a year or when particularly needed. It may be earlier in the case of a hospital.

General Procedure for Daily Cleaning

Let us now see how a room is cleaned daily.

Can you suggest in what order the work should be carried on:

- Brush or vacuum clean the carpet.
- Dust all surfaces including furniture and fixtures.
- In the end, adjust windows, do a general survey to see that everything is in order and to your satisfaction.
- Mop the whole area.
- Once you enter the room, open all windows in order to let the fresh air come in.
- Remove all unwanted objects like tea cups etc., and empty ash trays and dust bins.
- Replace linen wherever required, like in a bedroom, make the bed, in a restaurant cover the tables, in bathrooms, check for towels, soaps etc.
- Sweep the floor.

Similarly the kitchen can also be cleaned in the same way:

- Collect all used utensils from the counters.
- Empty the dustbin, wash, wipe and line it with newspaper.
- Mop or wash the kitchen with a mild disinfectant.
- Sweep the floor.
- Wash all utensils. Drain and store.
- Wipe and clean the gas stove, electrical appliances and the counters.

General Procedure for Weekly Cleaning

You now know that special cleaning is more thorough than daily cleaning.

Let us now see in what order should one work for special cleaning of a room:

- Check and clean thoroughly, all the drawers, furniture, fittings, all hangings or pictures, lights, etc.
- Remove all dirty linen.
- Remove all unwanted objects like trays, teacups, bottles etc. Empty the ash tray and dust bins.
- Remove stains from walls, doors, windows and furniture.
- Replace linen with clean linen
- Start in the same way as in a daily clean – that is, first open all the windows for fresh air.

- Survey the room for any discrepancy and adjust windows as desired.
- Sweep, dust and mop the surfaces.
- Vacuum clean the carpets and other upholstery. If vacuum cleaner is not available, use a brush.
- Wipe, dust or polish table lamps, accessories, telephone, if needed.

In the case of kitchen:

- Change the newspapers.
- Clean the jars and bins.
- Clean the sunmica on the cupboard door panels with a wet cloth.
- Clean the tiles.
- Rearrange the cupboards.
- You can empty out the shelves.

General Procedure for Spring Cleaning

Spring cleaning is done after long intervals, the frequency being as less as once a year. Thus, it may also be called annual cleaning. It is the most thorough cleaning of a room.

Let us now see how a spring cleaning should be done:

- Adjust windows, survey the room to satisfaction.
- Clean carpets thoroughly in the sun or send for dry cleaning. Re-lay it.
- Dust and mop.
- If any maintenance work is required, this is the right time to do it.
- If desired, rearrange the heavy furniture to give a new look.
- If necessary, remove all furniture and furnishings from the room. At least remove soft furnishings like carpets. Clean the cobwebs.
- Polish the furniture, decorative objects and floors.
- Remove all the movable objects including lamp shades, pictures, wall hangings etc., wipe and clean everything.
- Replace everything at the predetermined place, including all furniture and fixtures.
- Sweep the floors.
- Take off all linen, including curtains and remove them from the room.
- Ventilate the room.

In the case of kitchen:

- Clean exhaust fan and light switches.
- Clean the cobwebs.
- Clean tiles with detergent.
- Empty out the kitchen.
- Label and arrange all boxes back in place.
- Replace newspaper lining in cupboards.
- Spray insecticides in corners.

- Spread the pulses, spices, etc out in the sun.
- Tighten any loose screws.
- Wash kitchen counters with hot soapy solution and if needed, polish them.
- Wash the floor.
- Wipe stains on cupboard doors.

HOUSE KEEPING CONTROL DESK

The housekeeping control desk is the central hub of the housekeeping department. This is the area in the department where all information is received and from where messages are conveyed to housekeeping and other staff present in various parts of the hotel.

Thus, the control desk may be considered the nerve centre for to – and – fro communication in the housekeeping department. one of the main functions of the control desk is ensuring smooth coordination between housekeeping and other departments such as maintenance, front office, food and beverages, security, sales and marketing and so on.

The location of control desk is normally adjacent to the Executive Housekeeper's office. This desk is manned 24- hours otherwise the lifeline of housekeeping communication would stop.

ROLE OF CONTROL DESK

- Front office also alerts the desk attendant about the expected and existing crews in the house. So that the rooms can be make ready for the new arriving crew after the departure of existing crew in a very short period of time.
- In most of the hotels, this is the area where housekeeping employees; report for work; collect keys and signing for them; persue the log book get their briefing and at the end of their shift, report back to.
- Its is the control room attendants who receives departure room numbers from the front office and transmits them to the appropriate floor supervisor.
- The control desk attendant receives all the message of the guests such as a request for extra blankets, baby-sitter services, which she transmit to the concerned floor supervisor for further action.
- The control desk receives messages from in house guests over the telephone apart from maintaining the intra and inter –departmental channels of communication. hotel room directories provide the control desk extension number to the guests which they can use if they require housekeeping services.
- The floor supervisor informs the desk attendant once rooms are cleaned and ready for sale and this is updated in the computer so

that front office can easily obtain the information o f the status of room.

- The main physical feature visible in most control desk is the key cabinet. On the wall, where all floor masters keys and store keys are kept under lock and key themselves.
- The role of the housekeeping control desk is to facilitate communication to various parts of hotel. this role can be exercised in many forms which are as follows;
- Another common feature here is a large notice board displaying notices like
  - Room numbers of the groups in the house
  - Room numbers of crews in the house
  - Night cleaning schedule
  - VIPs in the house
  - Weekly cleaning schedules
  - Daily roster of supervisors and staff
  - Any other significant information relating to in-house guest or the hotel staff.
- One of the most important roles of the control desk is maintaining various important records, registers, forms and formats so that they are available and easily accessible for reference to managers and supervisors.

COORDINATION WITH FRONT OFFICE

The control desk acts as the nerve centre for coordination with the other departments in the hotel. the control desk attendants receives the night report, the arrivals and departures list, VIP list, and the list of crews and groups in the house from the front office. Based on these documents, the housekeeping department schedules the workers for cleaning, maintenance and servicing of guestrooms and related areas.

- *7. Night report*: This report, prepared each night by front desk attendant, indicates the rooms occupied that night and ones that are to become check-outs the following day. Based on this report, the executive or assistant housekeeper schedules employees for servicing these rooms. Once the rooms have been cleaned and made ready, the floor supervisor calls the control desk or the front desk directly, releasing the room for sale.
- Apart from the communications the front office needs to depend on housekeeping for the provision of clean uniforms to its staff.
- *Crews in the house*: Sometimes the arrival of a crew and the departure of another crew from the same airline may overlap. In such circumstances, it is important for the allotted rooms to be cleaned within

a short period of time. Thus for this there should be a effective coordination between front office and housekeeping.

- *Flowers*: sometimes the management extends its compliments to a guest with a special gesture of a flower arrangement in the room as recognition of the importance of a person. This requirement of flower arrangements for certain guests is conveyed to housekeeping by the front office on a daily basis.
- *Groups in the house*: The group rooming list must be provided before the group's arrival to the housekeeping as groups tends to move together in terms of arrival, departure, sightseeing tours and meals. Their rooms need to be readied together in view of strict time parameters. Group rooming lists enable the hk department to organize their work and have the group's room ready on time.
- It also helps to gear renovations and spring cleaning to low occupancy periods there by preventing loss of revenue.
- The housekeeping and front office department also coordinate with each other for other important information which require special attention like
- There must be coordination between housekeeping and front office department to share information on occupancy levels which helps to forecast occupancy for the year and makes it easier to draw up a budget, establish par stock levels and estimate required staff strength.
- There should be coordination know about the daily room report and housekeeping discrepancy report.
- There should be coordination to clean front office public areas
- To ensure efficient rooming of guests, both housekeeping and front office must inform each other of changes in a room's status. Knowing whether a room is occupied, vacant, on change, out of order under repair, or similar for proper room management
- VIPs in house: this information is essential so that the staff can take a little extra care and keener precautions in cleaning and supervising VIP rooms.housekeeping can take extra care in cleaning the VIP rooms by equipping the rooms with additional amenities as per the policy of the management. These amenities can be; bathrobe; bath slippers; extra soaps; hangers; and glass tumblers.

COORDINATION WITH ENGINEERING DEPARTMENT

The housekeeping control desk have to coordinate with the engineering department for maintenance request that the room attendants registers while servicing the guest room or in the floor.

- A need for urgent repairs is reported to maintenance over telephone and these requests are usually taken into action immediately.

- Boiler work: this is necessary to maintain a supply of hot water to guestroom.
- Electrical work: air conditioning and heating; fused bulbs, lights and lamps that are not functioning; defective plugs and plug points; short circuits; and faulty geysers, refrigerators, and minibar fall under this category.
- Mechanical work: this entails repair or replacement of any faulty equipment, such as vacuum cleaners, ice-cube machines, and so on.
- Plumbing work: this deals with faulty faucets, showers, drainage systems, water closets, and so on.
- The housekeeping department depends on maintenance to keep things in order.
- There are various heads under which maintenance work is done they are:
- While carrying out their scheduled work, housekeeping employees may find some deficiencies in the hotel facilities, such as faulty electrical plugs, dripping faucets, leaking pipes or malfunctioning air-conditioning units etc.

All maintenance requirements needed on floors are entered in the maintenance register kept in the control desk. The control desk attendant notes down the room number, the maintenance work required and the name of the GRA or the supervisor who called attention to the problem. The desk attendant prepares a maintenance slip in duplicate. She retains the second copy in her book and forwards the first copy to the engineering department.

The engineering department then prepares a 'work order slip' and sends the concerned technician directly to the floor. When the job is completed, a copy of tradesperson's completed 'work order ' is sent to the executive housekeeper for acknowledgement of work completed satisfactorily. If this copy is not sent to the executive housekeeper within an appropriate amount of time, housekeeping issues another 'work order', which signals maintenance to provide a status report on the request repair.

GUEST ROOMS

The guestroom is the main product of a hotel, as it contributes to more than 50 per cent of the total sales, making the profit percentage from room sales very high. The 'sale 'of a room means leasing the room for occupation for 24 hours at a pre-determined cost.

Thus, a room sold on a particular day earns revenue for that day, and then it can be sold again and again. Rooms are sometimes referred to as 'highly perishable commodities' as rooms not sold for the day lose out on the revenue for that day. in addition to earning revenues, guestrooms also have a role in the image-building of the hotel. Guest may stay in a hotel for pleasure, convenience or from necessity. Whatever the reason for the stay, they will always expect a certain standard of service and comfort. the housekeeping staff in particular, have the responsibility of making the guestroom's home away from home' for the guest.

The guestrooms should be neat, hygienic, comfortable, private and safe. The basic necessities in a guestroom are constantly varying. Nowadays these may include internet and Wi-Fi connectivity, channel music, television, temperature control and so on. Guest also expect that they will not be disturbed often and that the location of the rooms would be such that they have a good view. Safety is a key factor with regard to guestrooms-guest would like the guestroom location to be safe and not accessible to one and all. The doors of a guest room should have a double locking system operable from inside, along with strict control measures in the hotel with regard to the handling of guestroom keys and master keys. Fire –exit layouts being placed in the rooms is a necessity as well.

Irrespective of its location, a guestroom should also offer easy access to other guest service areas, such as restaurants, gymnasiums, swimming pools and so on. With clear directions to and from the room or elevator being posted in corridors. The guest would also expect to be able to get in touch with ancillary departments providing other services to guests from the room itself. The various services include- room service. Restaurants, housekeeping, valet and so on should be clearly indicated with explanation and intercom numbers.

RULES ON THE GUEST FLOOR

- A GRA should not knock on the door or try to access a guestroom when the 'do not disturb' card is displayed on the door knob. If the card has been displayed for a long time, the matter should be referred to the supervisor.
- Always accompany the rooms service staff, when they are clearing trays and maintenance staff for repairs, when they enter the room. Because room attendant will be held accountable for any missing guest or hotel property in the room.
- Always follow the procedures of entering a room even if the declared vacant. the procedures includes knocking the door and announcing "housekeeping" to be repeated after 15 seconds if there is no reply for three times. If there is still no answer, it can be assumed that the room is empty and the GRA can then enter and proceed to clean it.
- Conversation among the floor staff must be restricted to a minimum. In case communication is necessary, this must be done in low tones even when guests are not in sight.
- Dump garbage and soiled linen in the designated hampers of the maid's cart. Such items must be away from guest view.

- Guest room doors must be kept wide open when the room is being attended. This notifies the supervisor as to which room is being cleaned and where to reach the room attendant. It is also a protection to the room attendants from the undesirable guests.
- Housekeeping personnel cannot make external calls from the guest rooms. External calls are only permitted from floor telephones as an exception only after receiving permission from the floor supervisor.
- If the guest returns when the room is being cleaned, the room attendants may ask the guest if she can continue or come later.
- In case the guest answers the knock, GRA should introduce himself/ herself and ask if they would like their room serviced. If yes, the GRA should proceed to clean the room. Alternatively, the guests might not want service immediately. In this instance, ask them for a convenient time.
- In spite of following the procedure for entering a room, if the guest is inside either sleeping, or in the bathroom, quickly withdraw door apologizing and shut the door softly.
- It is important to report any suspicious objects like arms and drugs to the floor supervisor. Who may call the security for further inspection.
- Room attendants must greet all guests just as to the time of the day. it is a professional courtesy and creates friendly environment on the floor.
- Room attendants should always reach the floor by the service elevator and enter the floor through the service entrance.the guest elevators are meant for the guest only.
- Staff should be helpful and give readily give required information. Misleading a guest through misinformation must be avoided.
- The floor telephones must be attended promptly.
- The GRA must be in uniform and properly groomed when entering the floor. The moment a room attendant enters the floor, she reflects the image of the property.
- The importance of a guestroom to the guest must be understood and appreciated by all housekeeping staff. Prior to commencing work on the floor, all housekeeping staff, especially room attendants, must follow some floor rules that lends as air of efficiency and least inconvenience to guests. The hotel's management sets these rules and they are communicated to the staff through employee manuals and briefings. The most essential and usual are:
- The passageway must be kept free of equipment, trays or trolleys.
- The room attendant must return the master key to the control desk supervisor at the end of the shift.

- The room attendants should remember that the guest is always right. Arguing with a guest is prohibited. If a guest is being unreasonable they have to refer the guest to the supervisor.
- The staff should always remain calm in front of guest-running about in haste or due to panic must be avoided.
- When accepting any gifts from the guest the staff should also request a letter stating this gift and explaining the guest's action.

CLEANING AGENTS

Cleaning agent in general can be defined as natural or synthetic substances that are used to assist the cleaning process- that is, the removal of dirt and dust and the maintenance of a clean appearance on the surface. The various kinds of cleaning agents used by the housekeeping department staff.

WATER

Water is the probably the most common and widely used cleaning agent as it is easily available. It is useful in rinsing and finishing of cleaning processes. Precaution must be taken to change dirty water with fresh water because it could leave a film of dirt instead of removing it. Warm water dissolves soap more readily than cold water; hence it must be used to remove dirty soap leather. water is of two types, hard water and soft water.soft water is best for cleaning.

Hardness in water is caused by the presence of mineral salts- mostly calcium and magnesium, iron and manganese. The mineral salts reach with soap to form an insoluble precipitate known as soap film or scum. The result is that the soap film does not rise away easily/it tends to remain behind and produces visible deposits on clothing making it stiff. It attaches to the insides of bathtubs and sinks. Caution must be taken that water is soft as no detergent is effective with hard water.Moreover, hard water does not wet the surface well as a precondition for good cleaning action.

DETERGENTS

These are the cleaning agents that, when used in conjunction with water loosen and remove dirt and then hold it in suspension so that the dirt is not re-deposited on the cleaned surface. They can be of two types. Soapy detergents and synthetic detergents.

Basic properties of a good detergent are:

- Be easy to rinse away and be biodegerable.
- Be effective in all rabges of hard water, without producing scum.
- Be effective over a wide range of temperatures.
- Be harmless to the skin and surface to be cleaned.
- Cleanse quickly wit minimum agitation.

- Good emulsifying power – to break up the grease and enable the dirt to be loosened.
- Good suspending power – to suspend the dirt in solution, thus preventing its re- deposition.
- Good wetting power- to lower the surface tension of water and enable the surface of the objects to be thoroughly wet.
- Readily dissolve in water

TOILET CLEANERS

These are strong, concentrated cleaning agents designed to clean and disinfect WCs and urinals. They are available in liquid, powder and crystalline forms. They are acidic in nature as their main function is to remove stubborn stains and limescale.they all contains some form of disinfectant.

- *Crystalline toilet cleaners*: These contain sodium acid sulphate, anionic surfactants, and pine oil.
- *Liquid toilet cleaners*: These contain dilute hydrochloric acid, bleach and pine oil. Adequate protective gear should be worn by the user while using such a toilet cleaner.
- *Powdered toilet cleaners*: These cleaners contain a soluble acidic powder, chlorinated bleach, a fine abrasive and an effervescing agent to help the active ingredient spread in water.

Whatever the from of toilet cleaner used, they should never be mixed with other cleaning agents since harmful gases may be produced in the resulting reaction.

SELECTION OF CLEANING AGENTS

The use of cleaning agent is meant to save time, effort and money. if selected well, all the three objective may be fulfilled.

The following points need to be considered when selecting cleaning agents:

- Composition of the cleaning agents
- Cost effectiveness.
- Ease of use, saving of effort and time.
- odour
- Packing volume and quantities.
- Range of action or versatility
- Shelf life
- The type of spoilage
- The type of surface
- Toxicity or side-effects.

SUPPLEMENTARY HOUSEKEEPING KNOWLEDGE

KEY CONTROL

Key is a specially shaped and designed piece of metal or plastic/ magnetic card used for opening and closing the lock.it is an essential too for lock. In a hotel, it refers to the door lock key, which is primarily concerned for safety of hotel room contents and guest valuables. The responsibility for handling key of the houseguest has always been with front office and housekeeping department. In all large, hotels the information desk holds the responsibility of issuing, retrieving and controlling room keys. Room attendants also handle room keys to prepare guest bedrooms. Hence, it is essential that strict control of keys is maintained regularly.

MANUAL/MECHANICAL KEY SYSTEM

The standard of manual key system in operation comprises of the following:

- Electronic/ Magnetic Key System
- Emergency key
- Grand master key
- Individual guestroom keys.
- Master key
- Sub master key/floor key

CONTROL OF ROOM KEYS

Maintaining a strict control over the guest room keys is the responsibility of the information part. it is very necessary that a strict control be maintained for averting any mishaps. The information assistant keeps the keys into the correct slots of the key rack/ pigeon hole.

For the security of both guest and the hotel, room keys issuing system must be very efficiently operated and controlled.the theft, loss or unauthorized duplication of keys could have serious security implication.

The system of key control is as follows:

- A logbook or control sheet can be used to monitor the distribution of keys.
- The keys of inter-connecting rooms should be kept secure and scheduled.
- a regular inventory of keys should be carried out, and missing or damaged key should be reported immediately to the concerned authority.
- Guests should be requested to handle their key cautiously.
- Guests should be urged to drop the keys at the 'key drop slot' maintained at front desk each time they leave the premises upon their departure or for their own personal reasons.
- Identification should be sought and verified, if necessary, prior to issuing a key to a guest.
- key should always be placed in the correct hook/ slot of the rack
- Key should be retrieved from the guests at time of check out.

- Keys should not be handed over to unauthorized personnel.
- Know the different types of keys in circulation within the hotel.
- The master keys, when not in use, should be secured in a safe place.

PEST CONTROL

Pest conrol is a programme of eradicating pests. Pests are removed through pesticides.a pesticide is called a chemical used to control or eliminate pests. Insects are probably the larger pests.many insects transmit diseases such as malaria and typhus.some insects destroy or cause heavy damage to valuable vegetation. Other common pests include bacteria, fungi, rats and such weeds as poison ivy and ragweed.

Manufacturers use various chemicals in making pesticides:

- A pest is any organism that competes with humans, domestic animals. Or desirable plants for food or water.
- Eradication: Destroying an entire pest population.
- Injures humans, domestic animals, desirable plants, structures or possessions
- Pest control goals
- Prevention: Keeping a pest from becoming a problem
- Suppression: Reducing pest numbers or damage to an acceptable level.
- Transmits diseases and annoys humans or domestic animals.

SAFETY AND SECURITY

Safety and security are concepts often used interchangeably, and it should be understood that both are means of safeguarding human and physical assets. The tern 'safety' is with reference to such things as disasters, emergencies, fire prevention and protection, and conditions that provide for freedom from injury and prevent damage to property. The tern 'security' is used with reference to freedom from fear, anxiety, and doubts concerning humans as well as protection thefts of guest, employee, or hotel property.

WORK-ENVIRONMENT SAFETY AND JOB-SAFETY ANALYSIS

The management of any place of work are legally bound to provide a hazard-free environment to their employees. The nature of work that the housekeeping staffs are involved in is such that employees may easily become accident-prone if they are careless with equipment, chemicals, or procedures.

Safety Management Programmes

The overall objective of a safety management programme is to eliminate hazards before they cause any serious accidents.

- Conduct periodic in-house safety inspections.

- Establish a safety committee.
- Investigate and analyses all accidents and injuries.
- Maintain accurate safety records.
- Make departmental heads aware of the nature and variety of hazards.
- Motivate staff members to be safety conscious.
- Practice safety management and monitor follow-ups.
- Review the effectiveness of your own safety management programme.
- Review work procedures and inspect work areas for safety hazards.
- Train staff members to implement safety consciousness.

SAFETY AWARENESS AND ACCIDENT PREVENTION

Safety awareness should be an ongoing programme at all establishments The management of all establishments should be aware of the laws concerning safe work environments and should be provided to all staff in order to raise awareness about safety. All employees should be aware of the potential hazards in their respective departments. All heads of departments must ensure that employees follow safe job procedures, correct unsafe conditions immediately, and take adequate time to do the job so that accidents are not caused due to haste.

The executive housekeeper should develop a comprehensive list of safety rules to be followed by all housekeeping employees. This can be part of the 'housekeeping safety manual'.

The following guidelines can be followed for the prevention of accidents:

- Always dry hands before touching plugs, sockets, and electrical fittings.
- Always follow instructions when using any cleaning equipment.
- Clean away broken glass carefully.
- Dispose of rubbish carefully.
- Keep floors clean and dry.
- Label cleaning agents clearly.
- Mark faulty equipment as 'out of order'.
- Never place cigarette butts of sharp objects in the trash bag on the room attendants' carts.
- Open and shut doors carefully.
- Place warning and safety signs around the area while cleaning.
- Replace caps on cleaning chemicals immediately and securely after dispensing.

Procedures to Follow in Case of an Accident:

- Either administer first aid or get help from trained personnel.
- Fill in accident report form and hand it over to the manager concerned.
- Report the matter immediately to the manager concerned.
- Transport the victim immediately to a hospital, if required. If the

injury is serious, call an ambulance for the same. Follow all necessary first-aid measures until the ambulance arrives.

- When a guest or employee has met with an accident at the hotel, the procedure followed should be as follows:
- With the help of another person, check if the victim requires any assistance.

HOTEL SERVICE FOR OVERNIGHT ROOMS

- *Ease Pressure*: What's the first thing that comes to your mind when you think of the word hospitality? Is it a semi-clean home with an open-door policy? Is it a chicken spaghetti casserole on its way out the door for a sick friend? Hospitality can be all of above and none of the above. Often hospitality is confused with perfection. Perfection seeks to impress; hospitality seeks to put another's needs before your own. The word "hospitable" is derived from the word hospital, which means a charitable institution, a repair shop, a hospice or a shelter. Hospitality provides a shelter for the soul, a healing for the spirit. Ultimately this is what we offer when we open our home in the true spirit of love or when we offer our time, gifts or talents outside of our home to reach others. If hospitality comes down to love and kindness, one of the ways we are kind to ourselves is by doing our best to stay healthy. If you're like most women, you probably don't sleep enough. You eat the crust off the peanut butter and jelly sandwiches as you feed your kids and run in a frenzy to "keep it together" each day. We have too much to lose by not being our best selves. Be kind to yourself so you have the energy to be kind to others. Keep in mind that home sometimes can be the hardest place to extend hospitable kindnesses. Often at home, we're tired, overworked and grumpy. When we let our hair down, it has lots of tangles! Our goal is to freely give love and kindness to others, and our starting point is at home. Work together to solve issues, plan together to serve and listen to each other's concerns. Personal care of you+family+friends = the foundation for hospitality. For many of us, our friends are like our extended family. Life without them would just be dull. We need that connection to ease our soul. A deep heart-to-heart talk with a cherished friend feels as comforting and soothing as a super-soft, oversized sweatshirt on a chilly day. Friends are important. A good friend is one who understands your world, the difficulties and triumphs. Thinking of my favourite friends always makes me smile because of all the love, laughter, tears, prayers and cherished moments. Hospitality begins with us sharing our hearts. It blossoms by us loving our families and cherishing our friends. The key to accomplishing hospitality is easier than you think: an open door, a cup of coffee and listening ears. Happy hospitality. Often our planned visits revolve around food. We meet at restaurants, at each other's homes for dinner or at a yogurt shop for a treat. Life loses its richness without the opportunity to live it with friends. Have you scheduled time with friends lately? They offer joy, share the burdens and lighten the load. Patients who travel to Aberdeen Royal Infirmary for an operation the next day, or who need to stay for long-term treatment, will all be able to make use of the facility. NHS Grampian believes the hotel, which will be built in the hospital grounds, will ensure better treatment for those who need it. Dr Roelf Dijkhuizen, medical director with the health board, said: 'We want a facility where people who make use of hospital services can stay overnight. The most obvious example would be someone who comes from the islands and is waiting for a flight home. 'Another would be a cancer patient who needs treatment that is only available in the hospital over three consecutive days. At the moment, we have to ask them to stay in hospital for those days, but with a hotel we can provide much more convenient and private accommodation at a much lower cost.' The hotel will be built in partnership with a private contractor. Aberdeen Royal Infirmary is seen as the perfect site for the development because it takes in patients from such a large area. At present, anyone travelling from Orkney and Shetland for a non-urgent operation is put up overnight in a fully staffed ward. Health bosses are growing concerned that this is taking away beds from patients who desperately need treatment. They feel the freeing-up of the beds will ensure better levels of care for patients on the wards. The facility will operate in the same way as a normal hotel but people using Aberdeen Royal Infirmary services will be put up free of charge. Patients with relatives could also make use of it, as well as visiting health officials. Dr Dijkhuizen added: ' If we invite colleagues from the U.S. to visit for a conference, we don't have to give away all the profit to another hotel. We could put them up here. 'This would be good for the hotel company and good for the NHS if we put the contract together properly.' But Aberdeen MSP Brian Adam is sceptical and has raised his concerns with NHS Grampian. He said: 'I am not sure developing a hotel is the greatest use of NHS land, property or energies. 'I think the fact they are calling it a hotel shows that these days the health service is all about privatising as many services as possible.' Reported customer tips averaged about half the cash earnings of waiters and waitresses in hotels and motels studied by the Bureau of Labour Statistics during July through September 1983. The survey, covering

23 metropolitan areas, found employer-paid wages making up the balance. In most areas, these wages averaged between $2 and $3 an hour, largely reflecting the tip allowance employers can apply towards meeting the Federal minimum wage of $3.35 an hour. Customer tips also contributed substantially to the earnings of several other occupational groups. For waiter and waitress assistant, tips commonly averaged 16 to 22 per cent of their earnings, 44 to 57 per cent for bell persons, 25 to 40 per cent for public bartenders, and less than 20 per cent for service usually had the highest employer-paid wages, ranging from $3.99 an hour in Dallas — Fort Worth to $10.16 in Las Vegas. Public bartenders, receiving tips to a greater extent than service bartenders, had wages averaging from $3.55 an hour in Miami to $9.83 in San Francisco-Oakland. Although service bartenders, who prepare drinks for waiters and waitresses to serve, usually averaged more in wages than public bartenders, this pattern was reversed when tips were included in the comparisons. Similar patterns occurred between other occupations, including waiters and waitresses and their assistants. For example, table waiters and waitresses in full-course restaurants averaged less in wages than their assistants in each area surveyed — usually by 30 to 60 per cent. When tips were included in the comparisons, waiters and waitresses averaged more — usually by 40 to 70 per cent. Paid holidays, most commonly 6 to 8 days annually, were provided to at least three-fourths of the non-supervisory, non-office workers in each area studied. At least nine-tenths of the workers in each area were also covered by paid vacations, typically 1 week after 1 year of service, 2 weeks after 2 years, and 3 weeks after 10 years. Life, hospitalization, surgical, basic medical, and major medical insurance, were available to three-fourths or more of the workers in nearly all areas. Retirement pension plans were available to a majority of workers in 10 of the 23 areas. Also, food and beverage service workers typically received at least one free meal a day. The 2,050 establishments within scope of the survey employed a total of 356,000 workers during July through September 1983. Of this total, non-supervisory, non-office employees represented five-sixths of the workforce. Nearly one-half of these workers were concentrated in Las Vegas, Atlantic City, New York, Los Angeles — Long Beach, and Chicago. Corresponding employment in the remaining 18 areas ranged from about 14,000 in Dallas-Fort Worth, San Francisco — Oakland, and Washington to 1,750 in Buffalo. Nearly three-fifths each of the food service and other non-office workers were employed in hotels and motels with collective bargaining agreements covering a majority of such workers. The proportions,

however, varied widely by area. For example, virtually all of the workers in Atlantic City were covered by labour-management agreements, but no establishment visited in Houston or Memphis had union agreements covering a majority of their workers. The Service Employees International Union and the Hotel and Restaurant Employees Union, both AFL — CIO affiliates, were the major unions.

- *Service Encounter*: As the services sector becomes a larger component of our national economy, it becomes increasingly critical that the management of service operations is addressed systematically. One concern is the interaction of service employees and the technology making up the job design. Effectively matching job design and technology leads to effective service encounters, while mismatches cause short-run or long run problems for the organization. Organizational mismatches between job design and supporting infrastructure, specifically the information technology selected, can give rise to the use and exercise of judgement and discretion by service encounter employees that from the viewpoint of the organization or the customer is extraordinary, conflicted, or perverse. Perverse judgements debilitate the organization and degrade the quality of the service encounter. Conflicted and extraordinary, judgements ultimately debilitate the organization and may degrade the quality of the service encounter if some customers should perceive others as having received preferential treatment. This paper explores dynamics in managing operations, technology, and human resources that give rise to the exercise of such judgements with the intent to construct a conceptual framework that will explain such judgements and the behaviours that issue from them. The importance of the service encounter to a service organization is well documented in the operations management and marketing literature. This encounter is often the only point of contact the customer has with the organization. It is the context in which the organization provides the customer with what is presumably of value. The customer assesses the value of what the service organization provides on the basis of how adequately it provides explicit and implicit benefits that meet customer needs and expectations. It is thus incumbent upon a service organization to insure that its customer contact personnel are sufficiently supported through appropriate job design, training, and supporting infrastructure that can include an appropriate information technology. This better insures that the organization's customer contact personnel represent it in the best possible way to its customers. Job design defines the extent to which customer contact personnel must exercise judgement in meeting customer needs.

Ideally, the organization's infrastructure is sufficient to support the conformance of job design to customer needs. This paper will explore dynamics in managing operations, technology, and human resources that give rise to the exercise of problematic judgements with the intent to construct a conceptual framework that will explain such judgements and the behaviours that issue from them. The authors have identified three types of problematic judgements that they label perverse, conflicted, and extraordinary judgements. Perverse judgements debilitate the organization and degrade the quality of the service encounter. Conflicted and extraordinary judgements ultimately debilitate the organization and may degrade the quality of the service encounter if some customers should perceive others as having received preferential treatment. A conceptual framework that provides an adequate understanding of the dynamics that prompt such judgements being made permits more effective planning of the service encounter, the discovery and analysis of the nature of service quality gaps, and suggests actions that can be taken to close those gaps. In cases where these judgements occur, remedial actions can be taken that have both operational and strategic implications. Such a framework can benefit both the organization and the customers it serves. This is divided into five parts. This review provides the motivation for critiquing the quality of service encounters as a technology management and subsequent organizational design issue. This part will touch on the increasingly important role of services in societal economies, the focus on the training of customer contact personnel at the expense of attending to the organizational infrastructure that supports those encounters, and how the introduction of IT into a service organization impacts its infrastructure.

- *The Role of Services in the Economy*: The evolutionary course societal economies appear to follow involves a movement towards increasing organizational complexity. Technological innovations result in increased productivity and diversity in the extractive and manufacturing sectors of an economy which result in shifts of the labour force into other sectors. This shift is made possible only because of a simultaneous accompanying increase and expanding diversity of business, trade, infrastructure, social/personal, and public administration services. Without the direct and indirect linkages that exist between the material goods producing sectors and these service sub-sectors, increased productivity and diversity in the goods producing sectors would not be viable. Adequately performing this increasingly complex function has resulted in the percentage of the U.S. workforce allocated to services steadily increasing at a modest exponential rate in this century. Since the 1960's, services have accounted for more than half of that labour force with no indication that the continued growth in this proportion has passed an inflection point. By 1995, service industries accounted for 75 per cent of GDP and 78 per cent of employment. Therefore, it becomes increasingly important that services be the focus of critical attention for the purpose of evaluating their functional effectiveness and efficiency. If not clone, our understanding of services for this time and the future may prove inadequate. Eventually, this inadequacy will lead to their practical mismanagement and the degradation of the effectiveness and efficiency required of services to contribute towards the realization of healthy activity of an evolving economy.

- *Focus on the Service Encounter*: Addressing the concerns for service quality and effectiveness has been done in several different ways. The most basic way is to analyse the service encounter, the interaction between the customer and the service delivery or customer contact personnel. Research on service encounters may focus on perceptions of the persons involved in the exchange. Hartline and Ferrell devised a model that addressed the management of service encounter employees based on the perceptions of the three groups that had previously been studied separately; managers, employees and customers. Their literature review and the literature search this paper's authors conducted inductively suggest that the preponderance of studies exploring service quality and effectiveness have limited themselves to issues related to micromanaging service encounters.
- *Business Strategy*: Organizational strategy begins wish the organization's mission statement that identifies what service the organization provides. This implies an interaction between the target market segment and the service provided and an interaction between technology and personnel employed to produce and deliver the service and how the service package is designed. The design of a job consists of what customer encounter personnel are expected to do based upon their skills and qualifications and organizational constraints. These expectations cannot, however, be divorced from the technology through which customer encounter personnel act. A service is produced as a response to an existing market that it can opportunistically enter, as an instrument that calls new kinds of markets into being, or as a combination of both. The Internet auction company, eBay, is a recent example of such a combination. On-line auctioning existed prior to eBay's appearance. However, eBay took on-line auctioning several steps beyond what already existed to an interactive environment and redefined customer expectations. As a

result, eBay has virtually monopolized the on-line auctions industry and has dramatically expanded the industry's market in which it is the dominant player, attracting new customers while holding its old ones. The nature of services is such that their production and consumption is simultaneous. Consequently, the production and delivery of a service constitute its encounter with the customer whose expectations are standards against which the efficacy of the service is evaluated. How the production and delivery of the service are designed into the service package is therefore, critical. The technology selected for the service package plays a part in that design. On the one hand, the service package is first designed to which a suitable and available technology is then attached. Such is the case, for example, with fast foods where IT systems are employed to open transactions and communicate customer orders to the back room. IT may be employed in the back room to monitor operations and bring the transactions to a close. On the other hand, technology may restrict how decision makers would like to design their service packages or it can open up the design of a package so as to include heretofore infeasible possibilities by which competitive advantages can be pursued. Such is the case, for example, in tele radiology. Recent developments in IT and standardization in the way imaging equipment generates its images has made it technologically possible to physically decouple radiologists from the images they must read. As a result, access to radiological services has become decidedly more timely and widespread for potential customers than heretofore thought possible. Such developments have created opportunities to redesign the initial service package and revise customer expectations by reinforcing initial diagnoses with second and third opinions and exploiting subspecialization skills while at the same time, reducing the turn-around time to patient consultation.

- *Service Package Design*: The widely accepted means of categorizing service organizations is through the use of typologies. One of the most widely used typologies is Lovelock's that strategically profiles a service package. Of particular interest to the authors of this Study is Lovelock's typology that juxtaposes customization of services with [+ or -] exercise of judgement and discretion by customer contact personnel in meeting individual customer needs. A barber, for example, is expected to provide the customer more customised services than a home pest exterminator who has a finite set of programme modules from which to select and much less judgement to exercise. Like the barber, an attorney also performs a customised service but the attorney must use and exercise judgement and discretion that exceeds the judgement and discretion a barber uses and exercises and certainly exceeds the judgement and discretion the home pest exterminator must use and exercise. It is expected that similar services will position themselves similarly in Lovelock's typologies. Technological innovations in service production and delivery can, however, lead to typological repositionings of a service operation and a consequent revision and redesign of its profile and service package. One must assume that such redesign of the service package is done to derive some competitive advantage or at least prevent the service operation from being competitively disadvantaged. The various technologies an organization chooses to employ therefore interact with all the typologies that strategically profile it and contribute to the design of the organization's service package. The specific interaction between the employment of IT and the extent to which customer contact personnel are empowered or not empowered to use and exercise judgement and discretion to meet customer needs during the service encounter is this study's object of analysis. Working down the main diagonal of Lovelock's typology of customization and discretion, the more standardized the service, the less use and exercise of judgement and discretion by customer contact personnel is necessary. The more customised the service, the more use and exercise of judgement and discretion by customer contact personnel is necessary. In most cases customer contact personnel are the sole points of contact customers have with an organization providing them the service they seek. Their evaluations of it and decisions about future patronization of it are largely determined by how customer contact personnel manage to present the organization during service encounters. Thus, how the judgement and discretion customer contact personnel are empowered or not empowered to use and exercise and the IT they employ interact in the design of the service encounter can be decisive if the organization is to attract and hold its customers. The extent of judgement and discretion customer contact personnel are expected to use and exercise understandably varies from service to service. However, what about situations that do not precisely conform to a given service for which the technology has been designed? Judgement and discretion used and exercised by customer contact personnel in such situations is important for at least two reasons. First, decisions including judgement and discretion or the lack of them may affirm or contradict organizational objective or policies. Furthermore, unacceptable decisions issuing there from will result in positive or negative encounters from the customer's viewpoint. These decisions may be particularly important in achieving a service recovery when a service failure has occurred or is imminent. A service operation employs IT in order to increase and improve service efficiency and effectiveness in a way that is consistent with its competitive strategy. Fitzsimmons suggests that IT accomplishes this by creating another entry barrier, generating revenue, creating a database upon which empirically based decisions can be made, and enhancing productivity. Customer contact personnel draw on and contribute to such a resource when they access IT to support their service encounter activity. Their access to the IT system can, however, vary. They may be restricted with respect to the range of information they can browse. They may also be restricted with the respect to the range of information they can input. Fast food customer contact personnel can browse virtually no range of information and the range of information they input into the system is restricted to the orders they take. Their job can be characterized as being almost completely circumscribed by the technology associated with their job. A customer wants, for example, a taco with allowable modifications. A predetermined closed set of intermediate steps is synchronic with the outcome. The employee merely selects predetermined and technologically constrained choices, as one would push a stop or start button on a machine. Airline ticket counter personnel must, on the other hand, be able to browse routings, schedules, and ticket information for the entire industry in order to input the orders they take. The outcome of the order is something separate from the subset of intermediate steps that achieve it. Airline ticket counter personnel must create that subset. They use IT to expedite the construction and creation of that subset. The IT they employ does not therefore, so nearly circumscribe their jobs as with the fast food order taker. Job design for service employees has been categorized as a "production line" approach or an "empowerment" approach. The production line approach, as its name implies, is based on a Tayloristic view. It is based on four tenets — simple tasks, clear division of labour, substitution of equipment and systems for employees, and little decision-making discretion of employees. This design seeks to gain customer satisfaction through efficiency, consistency, and low costs. The empowerment approach, on the other hand, allows employees to make decisions that in the production orientation would be reserved for higher-level management. In such settings, jobs are less simple and more broadly defined and employees are given more latitude. In order for employees in such a design to be effective, they must have access to needed information, knowledge about how to use the information, and sufficient power to meet customer requests during the service encounter. The production line approach gains its low costs through consistency, which can be translated into lack of personal service. This means that as the service encounter is standardized, the choice of actions possible by the service provider is limited. Attempts to provide personalized service in such a setting would drive up costs and violate the competitive advantage of the firm. In addition, while the customer receiving the personal service may be more satisfied, other customers who are receiving slower service because of it may be disgruntled. The empowerment design is slower, less efficient and more expensive to operate. It requires careful selection and extensive training of employees. This design could put a firm at a competitive disadvantage from a cost standpoint servicing encounters of a routine form. Companies must clearly define their business strategy and know the environment and the customer base they pursue in making a decision concerning job design for their employees.

2

Hospitality Maintenance and Engineering

ESTABLISHING THE COLLECTIVE MODEL

Interest in employment, now the preserve of many individuals, but not all, in western economies, derives from the fact that'Work dominates the lives of men and women ... the management of employees both individually and collectively remains a central feature of organisational life'. Before beginning an examination of employment relations in the HI, it is useful to outline the historical development of employment relations and their relevance as a field of study, thereby introducing the reader to some of the key terms used throughout the book.

Hyman academic interest in employment relations was prompted when the potential stability of social order was put under threat by militant behaviour among a growing number of unionized industrial manual workers, who were no longer prepared to tolerate very bad terms and conditions of employment. This challenge to social order, which began in the late nineteenth century, was met by two responses.

First, the social welfare reformers, in keeping with their predecessors who had successfully campaigned for health and safety legislation earlier in the nineteenth century, urged legal intervention to improve the conditions under which work was performed and the terms under which it was undertaken. They achieved limited success, notably the introduction of minimum wages in four manufacturing industries in 1906.

The second and main response, which was to characterize public policy on employment relations until 1979, was that voluntary collective bargaining provided the best means to secure order within employer-employee relations. Collective bargaining is a process whereby employers and trade unions negotiate the substantive terms and conditions of employment, such as pay and hours of work, and procedural agreements that facilitate the resolution of disputes between the parties.

Industrial relations, the term in usage at the time, focused on the institutions of collective bargaining in fixing these'rules' of employment, largely within male-dominated manufacturing environments. Collective agreements were not legally enforceable. While public services such as the health service, the railways and the coal mines came to assume importance in industrial relations following the mass nationalization programme after the Second World War, private services remained the'Cinderella' of British industrial relations. Even though the growth of private services such as retailing and hospitality opened up more employment opportunities for women, whose main work opportunities had been in domestic service in the earlier part of the century, unregulated, female service work was deemed not to be part of industrial relations.

Even so, the lack of collective bargaining arrangements prompted the Labour government to extend the scope of minimum wage legislation to embrace these sectors. Thus in 1945 the newly named wages councils, a form of'state-sponsored' collective bargaining, were able to fix remuneration and paid holidays for many'unprotected' workers in private services.

COLLECTIVE CONSENSUS AND A MORE ACTIVE STATE

Greater state intervention in employment matters was a response by both Conservative and Labour governments to the mounting economic difficulties of the 1960s, *e.g.* statutory and voluntary incomes policies. State intervention also constituted a response to the perceived failure of voluntary collective bargaining to provide an effective regulatory mechanism for social order and social welfare, notably to protect the interests of the low-paid, many of whom were women. This perceived breakdown prompted the government to appoint a Royal Commission in 1965, the Donovan Commission, to investigate the state of employer-worker relations, in order to recommend how the'system' could be reformed.

The Donovan prescription sought to maintain voluntarism, and placed the onus on employers to improve the rules of employment, and to introduce more formal procedures for the resolution of disputes. Donovan's prescription was not universal, because it could not be applied to large parts of private services comprising small, informally managed, non-union workplaces, where female and part-time employment was concentrated. A different approach based on legal intervention in employment relations began to develop, based on employment protection for individual employees.

Early employment protection rights of the 1960s included the right to a written statement of terms and conditions of employment, statutory redundancy pay and equal pay.

Workers lacking the protection of a trade union and with no recourse to formal workplace procedures could resolve an employment dispute, which is those in scope of the law, by going to an industrial tribunal.

The 1970s represented a significant turning point for legal intervention in employment relations. Britain joined the European Economic Community in 1972. This heralded the start of a wide-ranging programme designed to establish a floor of new rights relating to matters including unfair dismissal, maternity leave, sex and race discrimination and health and safety at work.

The main beneficiaries were to be those working in private services. Events of the 1980s and early 1990s effectively killed the model of voluntary collective bargaining. In pursuit of an overriding objective to deregulate the labour market and employment, successive Conservative governments systematically dismantled institutions deemed to interfere with the free working of the labour market, notably the trade unions and wages councils.

Paradoxically, in spite of the government's antipathy to the EU's social action programme and subsequent opt out of the social chapter, the EU continued to influence British employment relations in a significant way. Rulings from the European Court of Justice obliged Britain to introduce new legislation, *e.g.* the transfer of undertakings or the amendment of existing legislation relating to equal pay and sex discrimination.

The floor of employment rights was both strengthened and extended. Managers reasserted the right to manage increasingly flexible and non-standard workers under the banner of'managerialism', in workplaces that might be labelled'bleak houses'. An alternative version of management thinking stressed the benefits of'commitment' over'control'. Both approaches came to signify the two variants of HRM.'Soft' HRM emphasized fostering commitment, improving quality and developing the human resource, whereas'hard' HRM was contingent and calculating in its utilization of the human resource.

If organizations were to survive the effects of adverse economic conditions, globalization and increasing competition, the imperative was to integrate HRM within business strategy. The impact of HRM on industrial relations was widely debated. Other key issues in the wider academic debate included the extent of continuity and change in industrial relations, the sharp decline in trade union membership, the impact of deregulation and whether employment relations could be re-regulated.

NEW LABOUR: NEW HOPE?

By the mid-1990s individual relationships were catapulted firmly to the forefront of analysis of the employment relationship. Recognition of this change had been apparent from WIRS in 1990, perhaps most notably within the HI. HI managers are free to exercise a high degree of managerial prerogative in the absence of unorganized labour, termed'unbridled individualism'. The election of a Labour government for the first time in nearly 20 years in 1997 raised expectations that there would be a new agenda for employment relations, although Heery's assessment was that'it is extremely doubtful whether New

Labour will issue in a new industrial relations'. New Labour's stakeholder economy is based on fairness and partnership. Fairness at work is to be achieved in two ways.

The government signed up to the EU social chapter and set about introducing a new floor of minimum employment standards, including a National Minimum Wage, and family-friendly measures. Social partnership between employers and workers is designed to foster a more consensual and cooperative relationship between employers and employees. The Low Pay Commission whose first task was to recommend the initial rate of the NMW, provides an early manifestation of social partnership comprising employer, worker and independent representatives. Although many of the Conservatives' trade union reforms remain in place, the introduction of statutory trade union recognition procedures might help reverse the steep decline in trade union membership.

By the time of WERS in 1998 the system of collective representation had crumbled'to such an extent that it no longer represented the dominant model'. In reality employment relations could conform to different and diverse patterns. Private service establishments employing 25 or more employees were numerically more important than private sector manufacturing and the public sector put together. Their share of employment increased from 26 per cent in 1980 to 44 per cent in 1998, reinforcing the point that alternative ways to view and reform employment relations were long overdue, particularly in circumstances of'bleak house' or'black hole' employment. Although we find these terms wanting in respect of the HI, they highlight the relevance of the industry as a unit of analysis. Consequently we shall show how these types of workplaces throw up major problems for employment relations reform.

Agenda for the Twenty-first Century

In calling for a new industrial relations paradigm, Ackers now argues that the new problem of social order focuses on links between employment and society, and that such a link provides an explicit ethical framework for policies like social partnership. He rejects the traditional industrial relations notion of workers as unattached individuals in their out-of-work lives, and argues that industrial relations can no longer ignore issues of work-life balance and corporate social responsibility. Indeed social concerns underpin'Fairness at Work' and the'Welfare to Work' programme, and family-friendly issues are a new addition to WERS.

Hence a new definition of industrial relations as neo-pluralism: Employment relations are the study of the social institutions involved in the normative regulation of the employment relationship and business's interaction with other stakeholders in society. Thus Ackers rejects as inappropriate Kelly's industrial relations paradigm for the twenty-first century, which derives from a redefinition of Marxism based on socialism, workers' mobilization, economic militancy and strikes, and organized labour. Edwards identifies three pressing issues in contemporary employment relations:'high commitment' or'high involvement' work systems, the international context and economic performance.

The first, although interesting, is very rarely found anywhere in Britain. Its alternative of'low skills' and'low wages' strikes right at the heart of much hospitality employment. This links to economic performance, where the absence of collective bargaining is likely to have contributed to income inequality and the perpetuation of low pay in the HI, although pay may be subsidized by the state through social security and taxation. The further subsidy of low pay through tips as a defensible employment practice is a matter of conjecture. We shall also explore if particular employment relations practices can be linked to successful performance outcomes.

The international context and its implications for employment relations in the HI are considered below and in subsequent chapters. A fourth pressing issue can be added. Employment relations discourse needs to recognize that prejudice and bias have been built into much of the theoretical and practical analysis, thus distorting its perspective. Gender is not the only example, but may be the most obvious. In spite of an increasing interest in what may be described as'women's issues', such as (un)equal pay and employment opportunities, family-friendly policies and sexual harassment, one major barrier to understanding employment relations is an assumption that they are gender neutral.

The argument is that adding women's issues to the agenda is simply not good enough. Management, trade unions and the state are not gender neutral, and therefore we need to recognize the gendered characteristics of the employment relationship and work and integrate this into our understanding of the field of employment relations. Other'omissions' include age, ethnicity and the role of customers.

We shall explore these issues throughout the book where it is possible or relevant to do so. All these issues were placed under review in The Future of Work Programme launched by the ESRC in 1998. The Programme has supported 27 projects designed to rectify gaps in our understanding and improve the quality of information available to the policy-makers in the UK. Topics under investigation have included the future of unskilled work, business re-engineering and performance, the changing position of ethnic minorities and women in the labour market, the future for trade unions and the changing nature of the employment relationship.

EMPLOYMENT RELATIONS IN THE HOSPITALITY INDUSTRY

Three terms denote the relations between managers and workers in the employment relationship-industrial relations, employee relations and employment relations. These terms are often used interchangeably, but can also convey subtle differences of meaning. They may coincide with other fields of academic enquiry and practical activity concerned with'people management', namely personnel management and HRM. Edwards provides an insightful analysis of the employment relationship, taking as his starting point the distinction made by Fox and Flanders between market relations and managerial relations. At the root is an economic exchange between capital and labour, in which the price of labour is set as a contract of employment. In this economic exchange between the buyer and seller of labour, the parties do not share equal power resources.

In common law the employer has the right to command and the employee has a duty to obey. The commodity at the heart of the bargain is the worker's labour power. The employer will seek to maximize control over that'labour process' in order to generate a surplus as profit. The employment relationship, as an exchange and in recognition of its broader context, has also been termed the effort-reward bargain:'an economic, social and political relationship, for which employees provide manual and mental labour in return for rewards allotted by employers'. Labour only becomes useful if it can be persuaded by management to work, but this is only the beginning. Workers must demonstrate commitment, continue working to the required standards, and not deviate from those standards.

In other words workers must follow'rules', otherwise management may need to deploy corrective or punitive measures via the disciplinary procedure. Bonamy and May argue that a weakening of employment relationships since the 1970s has given rise to the emergence of employment as a service relationship. This relationship demands increased recognition of the professional qualities of the'autonomous' worker, which poses problems of incompatibility with an employment contract built upon subordination. Pay is determined by time worked, whilst idle time due to poor organization and absenteeism is reduced. This is manifested in new forms of employment contract, externalization of employment to agencies and the sub-contracting of activities. Edwards notes that, if we were starting from scratch, 'employment relations' might be the best label.

Employment relations do not rule out all variants within the employment relationship including:

- Trade unions and formal collective bargaining;
- Individually based management/workforce relations conducted informally;
- Managerialism;
- More democratic and highly participative non-union relations;
- Men, women and disadvantaged groups;
- Employees and workers, including atypical workers and the self-employed.

Further:

- Employment relations is the main term used in the WERS sourcebook;
- Industrial tribunals have been renamed employment tribunals;
- The cornerstone of New Labour's industrial relations policy is the Employment Relations Act 1999.

A necessary departure for this book, as noted earlier, is to relocate the nexus of the employment relationship to include a relatively ignored third actor in the employment relationship-the customer. The notion of the customer in the employment relationship has been increasingly incorporated into the sociology of work, but less so in employment relations. Front-line workers, such as receptionists and servers in bars and restaurants, have to serve two'masters': their superior manager and the customer. Individual workers can have a simultaneous and coterminous employment relationship with the organization and the customer.

Organizations in services are best seen as inverted pyramids, with most workers in direct customer contact. Direct service workers engage directly with customers in an exchange that carries both economic and social connotations.

Their ability to deliver successfully hinges upon a social relationship with indirect service workers, whose actions are also instrumental to the provision of good customer service, *e.g.* an enjoyable meal or clean bedrooms. Indirect service workers are not in regular customer contact, so customer influence may be more economic than social. Hence, customers cannot be excluded from an analysis of the employment relationship.

An earlier definition has been revised:

- Employee relations in hotels and catering are about the management of employment and work relationships between managers and workers and, sometimes, customers; it also covers contemporary employment and work practices.
- Before exploring the facets of the employment relationship, we need to outline why our attitude towards things influences the way in which we see any given situation, and how it.
- Triplets watch a local football match from adjoining seats, getting an almost identical view of the game. The result is United 5 City 1. One triplet is deliriously happy, the second feels very low, while the third is able to provide a balanced analysis of events, conceding that the result was a fair one, although two of United's goals were the result of dubious refereeing and City deserved more than a single goal.
- Why did their particular attitude affect their view of the game?

Fox proposed two frames of reference as a means by which'the problems of industrial relations can be seen realistically and laid more open to solution'.

The unitary perspective is a'management ideology' built on the belief that everyone in the organization shares the same goals, and that'conflict' is pathological and derives from deviance. Trade unions are seen as an intrusion, competing with management for worker loyalty.

Fox's main argument was that the unitary perspective was a naive and unrealistic frame of reference that might'distort reality and thereby prejudice solutions'. Yet in reality many managers do perceive their organizations in unitary terms, regarding themselves as the sole source of authority. Unitarism has underpinned the'human relations school' of management, including Mayo, Likert, McGregor, Schein and Herzberg, and reasserted itself in'managerialism' and HRM. Fox suggested that the more realistic approach to managing people was to recognize that organizations are pluralistic, comprising various groups, each with their own basis of authority and sets of interests.

The'rules' of employment are not just the preserve of management. A new pay rate set by management will not necessarily be seen as fair by workers, creating an issue of potential dispute. Therefore conflict or differences between individuals and groups are inevitable. Management should recognize this inevitability, and find the ways and means to regulate such differences. An institutional approach-collective bargaining between employers and trade unions, and the development of formal procedures to deal with disputes about pay, grievances and discipline-was considered to be the most appropriate solution. However, this is flawed to the extent that it implies both parties to the bargain have equal power resources at their disposal.

Later Fox revised his thinking and added a third perspective of radicalism, prompted by a wave of'shop floor' discontent and'wildcat' strikes at workplace level. Such worker behaviour was perceived as a reaction against exploitative and oppressive employers whose sole aim was to maximize profit. Conflict was caused by the economic disparity of society as a whole, with the principal disparity between capital and labour-employers who own and manage the means of production and workers who have their capital to sell.

This view underpins the labour process approach. This approach stresses the contradiction of managerial goals, with regulation and control having to be balanced by the need to gain workers' consent. Even today Edwards argues that unitarism cannot be written off as naive and outdated any more than radicalism because of the apparent disappearance of discontent. Ackers' neo-pluralism refocuses the employment relationship beyond the workplace by connecting the old pluralist and voluntary frames of reference with new questions raised by contemporary society. The health of society is put first, encouraging industrial relations policy initiatives that are driven by social concerns, not just a business agenda. Further he argues that the employment relationship bears hidden ethical considerations of trust and responsibility in relation to human beings.

As we shall show, both managers and workers in a variety of work and employment situations in the HI do see their workplaces in unitary terms, but this does not necessarily infer the absence of conflict. Areas of potential dispute, conflict and difference do exist between managers and workers, between managers and other managers, and between workers and customers, demonstrating that workplaces are pluralistic. In cases where workers'fiddle' or'pilfer' from their employer, the nature of their behaviour is more in keeping with a radical perspective.

Thus it is possible to observe facets of unitarism, pluralism and radicalism in the same employment relationship in which management, for the most part, remains the more powerful.

Even so, areas of common interest self-evidently exist otherwise all these relationships would break down. Consent provides the basis for resolving conflict and achieving cooperation. Cooperation is built on trust between individuals engendered at workplace level rather than through elaborate organizational mechanisms.

Yet securing workers' consent is neither a straightforward nor certain process. Therefore, a mix of overt and covert conflict and cooperation underpins all employment relationships and, as we shall argue, workplace harmony owes more to pragmatic acceptance and accommodation among the parties in the employment relationship than to ideological belief.

THE RULES OF EMPLOYMENT AND POWER RELATIONS

We have already noted that the employment relationship is underpinned by rules, hence the continuing validity of Clegg's definition of industrial relations as'The study of the rules governing employment' which Edwards explains in more detail: This does not limit the subject to the collective relations between managements and trade unions, for a rule can derive from other sources, and there are rules governing non-union groups; nor does it restrict analysis to one sector, for it covers all paid forms of employment. A rule is a social institution involving two or more parties which may have its basis in law, a written collective agreement, an unwritten agreement, a unilateral decree or merely an understanding that has the force of custom. In non-union settings, as much as union ones, rules determine rates of pay, hours of work, job descriptions and many other aspects of employment. The subject is about the ways in which the employment relationship is regulated. To regulate means to control, to adapt or adjust continuously or to adjust by rule.

MANAGERIAL ISSUES

While rules may be the substantive rules of employment, *e.g.* pay and conditions of employment, implicit in the notion of rules affecting people is the concept of behaviour. Management's job is to control and direct workers' behaviour to perform work to the desired standards, and thereby ensure that the rules of employment are adhered to.

Four key issues arise:

1. Rules are not always absolute and may be gendered.
2. Managerial control of workers' behaviour is underpinned by a power relationship.
3. This power relationship is unequal and may be gendered.
4. Managers have a choice of means to maximize control.

The first point is that one should caution against perceiving rules in too absolute a sense. At one end of the spectrum rules embodied in the law of the land provide a good example of formal rules. Any breach may incur very severe penalties, *e.g.* health and safety. In a workplace setting rules in practice may derive from informal understandings that can in one set of circumstances be interpreted by the worker as a permissive concession or in a different set of circumstances as something to be observed at all costs. Strawberries as a worker's perquisite during the Wimbledon lawn tennis championship are a good example. Experienced workers know that taking home unwanted strawberries is'permitted' during busy periods. When fewer staff are needed, increased managerial surveillance will be deployed to dismiss staff caught in possession of company property.

Rule-learning is part of what Polanyi refers to as'tacit skills'. As argued elsewhere:

Tacit skills, such as learning to deal with customers, are learnt in and through the very act of doing, often involving trial and error and not from following a body of procedurally-designed rules. They are seen as an interpretive achievement of the user as to how the'rules' fit the task in hand. By mastery of the rules comes the power to extend them.

This example embracing the customer provides a developmental point to Edwards' observation that rule-making is difficult, and that rules have to be interpreted in action for them to have any real meaning. Specifically in the labour contract this is because the worker's ability to work is only realised as useful labour in the course of carrying out that work, hence'a rule is a complex social institution'.

In service work physical appearance and'personality', or'aesthetic labour', are an implicit part of the employment contract. Only female flight attendants, not their male colleagues, are subjected to regular weigh-ins to ensure they comply to specified weight: height ratios. This demonstrates clearly how a rule may be gendered.

The second point to note is that the very essence of management seeking to control workers' behaviour is underpinned by a power relationship. Power is the capacity to pursue one's own interests individually and collectively, involving the capacity to oppose the actions of others and to pursue one's own objectives, and is embedded in continuing relationships. This does not mean power has to be exercised by either party in an overt sense. The threat of power may be sufficient to maintain broadly consensual employment relationships, such that any disputes or differences are resolved amicably without recourse to either party seeking to deploy sanctions against the other. The third point assumes a power inequality in the employment relationship. Self-evidently an employer is more powerful than an individual worker. The employer's ability to terminate a worker's services is likely to be more detrimental to the worker than to the employer, in spite of employment protection legislation.

Yet the individual behaviours of workers, such as high labour turnover, may be detrimental to an employer, even though they are not concerted. When workers combine collectively, with or without the backing of a trade union, there is some tilt in the balance of power, because collective sanctions may be imposed against the employer. Ultimately the outcome of the process by which each side seeks to gain concessions will depend on the relative power of the parties. For example, a plentiful supply of suitable workers in the labour market makes existing workers more readily dispensable and replaceable on the employer's terms. The opposite would be true for workers with scarce skills who can command high wages.

As Wajcman argues, gender relations are power-based and women's subordination in the workforce and workplace owes as much to trade unions as it does to managers. Spradley and Mann provide a graphic account of how the subordination of one group of female workers was brought about by another group of male workers who were the custodians of the male proprietor's trust. The male bartenders controlled the orders, and sought to make the cocktail waitresses' job difficult by giving orders in an inconsistent and confusing way. Any mistakes became the waitresses' responsibility, even if they had been caused by the bartenders. Such was the power of the bartenders that pleasing them became more important than pleasing the customers.

The fourth point is that managers have a choice of means to maximize control over workers. Friedman's'direct control' is a variant of Taylorism. Management is responsible for planning, designing and organizing the labour process, while cheap, unskilled workers perform standardized, simple repetitive tasks. Fast food is a good case in point, and also epitomizes McDonaldization, a social critique of how contemporary society and culture are being shaped by rationalist scientific management. While Taylorism sought to control the organization of work, McDonaldization is based on rationalization, replication, standardization of products and service, and quantification. In this low trust strategy worker behaviour is controlled through the use of standardized scripts in the service encounter.

In Friedman's alternative of'responsible autonomy', a high trust approach, managers delegate control to relatively privileged skilled workers who may already have elements of job control and discretion. The objective is to get workers to identify with the competitive aims of the organization so they will behave responsibly with minimum supervision. An obvious example of where such an approach might be used is in a luxury hotel, but it is also associated with empowerment and much customer-service work. As we shall argue and implied in the example of cocktail waitresses, these and other similar approaches including'hard' and'soft' HRM provide a useful framework for analysis, but are not necessarily alternatives.

The history of hotel internationalization has been characterized by American chains that secure control and integration through highly standardized procedures and manuals of operational procedures. Yet a'soft' focus on the service encounter as the driver of competitive advantage necessitates developing a culture of customised service. Mass customization illustrated by Burger King's have it your way' slogan as a challenge to McDonald's hold on the market is proposed as an alternative paradigm to McDonaldization.

WORKERS AND CUSTOMERS

Other tensions within the employment relationship impinge upon the rules of employment and power relationships. If management is about the achievement of organizational goals through people it can be argued that managers will be successful to the extent that these goals coincide with the aims and aspirations of those people, be they workers or customers. This'matching' of broadly reciprocal needs between employers and workers may be referred to as a'psychological contract', or set of contracts. It suggests managers and workers can share goals, but this is not at all straightforward. There is not a necessarily clearcut distinction between boss and worker, or a'them and us' scenario. Further we must also account for a psychological contract with customers.

Two key points are noteworthy:

1. Organizations comprise people and are, therefore, social organizations.
2. People, as social animals, may behave in unpredictable ways.

Workers

Human beings do not necessarily behave consistently or predictably, even in the same sets of circumstances. People are citizens and customers as well as employees, and these multiple identities bring different and sometimes conflicting expectations of the organization.

This makes the management of the employment relationship an uncertain process within which there is a blend of contradictory principles around the need to control and to gain the consent of workers. Workers may seek to regain control individually or collectively when they perceive that management has operated outside the rules.

At that point workers' consent has been withdrawn and management will need to find ways to restore order and regain consent. In Lucas workers' individual response to organizational rules is seen in three main ways-to conform or be deviant in employment, or to terminate their employment. These responses are similar to Marchington's'getting on','getting by' and'getting back'. These are behaviours deployed in circumstances where customer care and service quality are dependent on workers' use of their tacit skills, which contain both technical and attitudinal elements.

Limiting the definition of tacit skills to employer-employee relations is too narrow. Marchington overlooked how workers exhibit their tacit skills in ways other than in respect of their relationship with the employer, notably the customer. The point that'getting back','getting by' and'getting on' are as much resistance strategies in the labour process as coping mechanisms is developed.

At workplace level personal relationships are likely to be closely connected to morale and success. Managers often'muck in' when required. In small workplaces the existence of a single leader, often the owner, may serve to inspire loyalty from the workforce, but it is not a one-way process, as workers' respect has to be earned.

Is it realistic to suggest that Mina, Jo and Sadie, who wait on table in the restaurant, share all the same goals as their boss? The hotel may not be doing very well, so there may be mutual concern for the survival of the business. Yet these ladies' main goal may be to serve their customers cheerfully and effectively, while at the same time enjoying some social banter among themselves and with their customers in the process of earning a reasonable wage.

Customers

Within the triadic employment relationship a simultaneous and coterminous relationship with the organization and the customer directly impinges on how workers carry out their work, and such interactions may be rewarding or stressful. The consequent effect on workers' performance may have positive or negative implications for the rules of employment: what they can earn, their prospects of promotion or actually keeping their job. Unequivocally the worker-customer relationship affects the rules governing employment and workplace behaviour.

But so do employer-customer relationships, hence the employment relationship embodies a triadic set of power relations. This relationship embodies a socio-economic exchange, and is not simply an economic exchange around the price of labour. Fox provides a useful starting point, since he noted that organizations are social organizations and how people behave is a crucial issue in the employment relationship. Even Edwards' point that'a rule is a complex social institution' does not adequately encapsulate our position. The main justification for widening the scope of this relationship derives from the fact that the service encounter is the interaction of the producer and consumer of services, and is a more complex phenomenon where financial considerations are interwoven with social ones. In hospitality the social function of service work derives from the provision of a'home away from home'.

The service encounter entails'emotion work'-the assumption of a social-self, which effectively masks the individual's own personal dispositions to act, including the need to smile and be pleasant in an uninvolved way. We have already noted that'aesthetic' and sexual labour may also be inherent in service work. It is the'normalizing' social role of service labour that distinguishes it from other wage labour. Service work cannot be understood in terms of economic rationality alone.

Examination must be based on the supposition that service work is the intended outcome of a necessarily social process in which some social interaction occurs between one or more producers and one or more consumers. The relations between three groups of people-managers, workers and customers-embody the potential for contradiction between, on the one hand, uncertainty, unpredictability, conflict and difference and, on the other hand, consent, team effort and concerted performance. The practical benefit this book seeks to convey accrues from an understanding of the nature and scope of the rules of employment in this triadic employment relationship, and how it is regulated, primarily at workplace level.

THE EMPLOYMENT RELATIONSHIP IN A WIDER CONTEXT

This chapter concludes by considering some key external contextual influences on workplace employment relationships at two levels-internationally and, in more detail, nationally in Britain.

The International Context

The national context of British employment relations increasingly needs to be understood within a much wider international context.

Three international dimensions have particular resonance for this book:

- International competition has created more open economies that have attracted investment from foreign-owned businesses. For example the French-owned groups Accor and Envergure have respectively opened hotels within their Novotel and Campanile brands in the United Kingdom.
- On a larger scale American multinational corporations have created world brands. McDonald's, Burger King, KFC and Marriott are among those that are now household names in many countries across the world.
- Spin-offs from European integration, especially on employment law

in Britain, have provided an important underpinning to the employment relationship in the HI.

Foreign investment and MNCs are clearly important factors underpinning the expansion of hospitality and tourism not only in Britain but also in developing countries. Examples of'better' employment practices, in so far as they may exist in the British HI, have been associated with foreign-owned businesses. Aspects of the American model of employment relations, that is non-union and market-driven, may seem to reflect some aspects of observed employment relations practice in the British HI, but the similarity has been overstated.

The United States has substantially more legal regulation than Britain, which has benefited American HI workers, while the trade unions are not entirely powerless-issues we highlight in later chapters. The European model based on social partnership designed to forge a common agenda between capital and labour is considerably more diverse and different across the member states than is often acknowledged. While we cannot expect it to reflect current developments in HI employment relations in most British workplaces, it has not necessarily produced wholesale benefits for HI workers across the EU either.

The British experience is not necessarily mirrored in other countries across the world. Differences in other countries' institutional arrangements and cultural considerations are among the factors that will affect their employment relations systems. Detailed comparison with other countries is beyond the scope of this book, but key instances of international employment relations within hospitality and tourism are cited throughout the remaining chapters.

THE BRITISH CONTEXT

Workplace employment relationships cannot be immune from wider economic, social, legal and political contextual influences. Contemporary examples, which may be influential in Britain today. The distinctions between these sets of influences are not always clear-cut as they can be interrelated.

The State

Although we have already touched upon some aspects of the state's interest in employment relations, we need to examine its role in a little more detail. The state is not a single or cohesive body, and comprises a number of institutions that have an interest in the employment relationship, whose objectives do not necessarily coincide. Parliament is the legislature, government ministers form the executive, the judiciary enforces the law, and civil servants are the administrators.

The state sponsors specialist agencies in the field of employment, and has done so since the end of the nineteenth century. Three government departments impinge on employment relations within a much wider brief. The most important is the DTI, which has overall responsibility for employment relations, small firms and competitiveness. The Employment Relations directorate is responsible for developing policy and legislation affecting individual workers and trade unions, EU legislation, promoting partnership and best practice, regulation of employment tribunals and the dates of public holidays. The DTI publishes consultation documents, research papers, practical guidance on how to implement employment legislation and regulations, and codes of practice on matters such as picketing.

The Department for Education and Skills is responsible for developing the skills of young people and adults. he Department for Work and Pensions delivers support and advice in areas of work and work-related benefits, including New Deal, sickness and accidents at work, and retirement. Although publicly funded, other state agencies and bodies are independent of government because they are controlled and managed by their own executive. The main institutions discussed later in the book are ACAS, the Central Arbitration Committee and employment tribunals. The Equal Opportunities Commission, Commission for Racial Equality and Disability Rights Commission each have overall responsibility for specific types of anti-discrimination or equal opportunities legislation.

The Health and Safety Commission and Health and Safety Executive have responsibility for health, safety and welfare legislation. Their roles include the publication of codes of practice. Other bodies assist with the enforcement of minimum employment standards. The Inland Revenue's powers include obtaining information from employers, issuing enforcement notices requiring employers to pay the NMW and imposing penalties on employers not observing the NMW. Environmental Health Officers are responsible for the enforcement of health and safety standards. Many other institutions, some of which may have a political bias, offer a mixture of fact and opinion on employment relations. National bodies, which take either an employer or management view, include the Confederation of British Industry, the Institute of Directors, and the Chartered Institute of Personnel and Development. The British Hospitality Association, Restaurant Association, the British Beer and Pub Association the Hotel, Catering and International Management Association and the British Institute of Innkeeping are specific to the HI. The HtF, formerly the HI's National Training Organisation is recognized by government as the employer-led voice on all issues relating to hospitality training, education and qualifications.

The HtF also carries out research, and produces useful statistical information about the labour market. The Trades Union Congress Institute of Employment Rights and the Low Pay Network serve to defend workers' interests. The HCIMA can also be regarded as having a worker perspective since, as the professional body of hospitality managers; it serves to defend their interests as well as disseminating good management practice. Three large unions have special sections for hospitality workers: the General, Municipal and Boilermakers' Union, the Transport and General Workers Union and the Union of Shop, Distributive and Allied Workers. The National Association of Licensed House Managers was self-standing for many years, but has recently become part of the TGWU.

3

Improves Security System in Hotel

TRAINING

Although many systems are user-friendly, employee training is important. Most vendors offer free on-site training after installation. Training includes basic information on the proper way to programme and use card keys, maintenance tips, and a discussion on how to change batteries. For an extra charge of between $100 and $300 per employee, vendors usually provide additional training at their facilities.

Those sessions offer more detailed information about the system's hardware and software so that employees have a better understanding of how the system works. To control costs-which also include transportation, lodging, and meals-the additional training should be limited to those employees who will be directly responsible for fixing minor problems with the system. It is also possible to negotiate a lower price for the additional training. The Westin Hotel in Boston sent two employees to Wisconsin for additional training when its system was installed in 1995.

The employees-the assistant director of security and the front office manager-used the information they learned in the two-day class to train other employees.

The hotel's security manager negotiated with the vendor to include the additional training for free. Electronic locks provide many advantages to the security manager. Lost card keys present little worry, while the lock's memory helps narrow the list of potential suspects in a crime. Before buying a lock, however, the security manager must thoroughly research each system, talk to vendor references, and negotiate a purchase agreement that ensures the company will get the most for its money.

LOCKING IN HOTEL SECURITY

Choosing an electronic lock system is one of the most important tasks a hotel security manager can perform. These systems not only improve security, they save the security department time and money in the long run.

With electronic locks, the security staff no longer has to spend hours each week rotating key cores between guest rooms-and keeping detailed logs to record which cores were moved to which rooms. In addition, card keys can be programmed to function only during designated time periods; lost cards can be inactivated with a few strokes of a computer keyboard; and locks can keep track of card holders who enter a room, a feature that helps security identify potential suspects during a room theft investigation.

When purchasing an electronic lock system, the security manager must decide how many functions the card needs to perform; how much memory the lock should have; and what type of training programmes are offered by the vendor. In addition, the security manager should check each vendor's references for potential system problems and, when a system has been chosen, write a purchase and warranty agreement that gives the hotel the most for its investment.

STAFF DUTIES

Card keys are an effective way of assigning duties to the hotel staff. Each employee is assigned a specific card. The card is then activated only for areas where the employee is authorized to enter. For example, if a housekeeper is responsible for twenty rooms on the third floor, his or her card will only open the doors to those rooms during the employee's shift.

LOCATION

In addition, cards can be programmed to access other parts of the hotel, such as the pool, health club, or parking facility. For top executives or other VIPs, the card can be programmed to access special elevators that take them to the concierge's lounge or private meeting rooms.

Cards can also be programmed to work like a credit card, used to charge a meal at the hotel restaurant or merchandise at the gift shop to the guest's room.

THE CARD

Most hotel access cards use magnetic stripe technology. These cards are either swiped through or inserted into the lock's reader. Cards can be programmed to handle several functions, depending on the hotel's needs. The following are some of the basic features a card key can perform.

TIME

Cards can be programmed at the front desk to work only during the time the guest plans to stay at the hotel. For example, a card might be programmed to work from Monday at 12 noon, when the guest first arrives, until Friday at 10 a.m., the guest's checkout time.

PRICE

Cards range in price from about nine cents to thirty cents per card, depending on the number of features that can be programmed onto the magnetic stripe. This is far lower than the estimated $7.75 it costs for one set of hard keys and key tags.

SPARES

When buying cards, it is important to have enough spares so that lost keys can be replaced and backup cards can be made. During a power outage, for example, the front desk will not be able to use its PC and card encoder to programme cards for arriving guests. If the hotel does not have preprogrammed backup key cards for this situation, it risks losing business to more prepared establishments.

At the Westin Hotel in Boston, for example, security has programmed three backup cards for each of the building's 800 rooms. The cards are kept in a secured blackout kit that is kept in a vault and used for emergency purposes only.

THE LOCK

The individual electronic lock is the heart of the system. It consists of a card reader and memory, a regular mortise lock, and a deadbolt. The security manager should consider several factors when purchasing a lock, including the lock's memory capacity, its power source, and its compliance with federal guidelines.

MEMORY

The various systems on the market today are able to record between 100 and 300 room entries. Each time a card is inserted or swiped through the reader, the memory documents the specific card that was used as well as the date and time of the entry.

This is important for investigations of a theft, when the security manager can retrieve data from the lock's memory by using a hand-held interrogator that plugs into the lock. The information can then be used to determine who entered the room near the estimated time of the theft. Memory capability can have a significant effect on the lock's price.

Locks at the lower end cost between $25 and $35 each; those that can document 200 to 250 card entries may cost between $40 and $55; and locks with a 300-event memory run as much as $100 per unit. To determine how much memory the hotel should have in its lock, the security manager must know the hotel's occupancy rate. A popular hotel that is sold out most nights will have a large number of room entries each day and therefore will need a lock with more memory. Hotels in smaller markets may have several rooms unoccupied each night and can opt for a less expensive lock with less memory. In addition, the security manager should consider the crime rate of the area and the hotel's liability exposure should a room theft go unresolved. In 1995, the 800-room Westin Hotel purchased locks that documented up to 100 entries.

This decision was based on several factors. First, the hotel does not sell out every night, meaning that some rooms might be unoccupied for one night or more each week; second, the crime rate in that section of Boston is relatively low and the hotel has experienced few thefts; third, the hotel investigates reported theft within forty-eight hours-well within each lock's memory capacity. In addition, Massachusetts law limits liability claims against hotels to $300, regardless of the value of the loss.

BATTERY POWER

Many of the systems on the market are self-contained battery-operated units. Battery-powered locks are more reliable and much less expensive than locks that are hard-wired to a central computer-which can cost twice or three times more because the wiring has to be installed throughout the building. In addition, hard-wired locks sometimes fail during power outages. Batteries-usually AA or lithium-typically last three years. It is helpful to purchase a lock that has a function indicator on the front panel that tells management when a lock's battery is low and whether the lock is malfunctioning. The Westin's locks have a function indicator with three lights: green means the battery is functioning properly, red means the battery is dead, and flashing red and yellow lights mean the battery is low.

A solid yellow light indicates another problem with the lock. When the yellow light is on, the security staff runs a diagnostic test on the lock by plugging a laptop computer into the lock and getting a readout of the specific problem. For example, the lock will report that its battery is running low or that the door's latch is not working properly.

The security manager should also determine how the battery is replaced. Some older systems require the lock to be removed from the door and replaced with a new one. The used lock is taken back to the vendor's shop, where a new battery is installed. With newer systems, the AA or lithium batteries can be replaced right at the door in just a few minutes. Some models have a battery pack that is simply removed from the side of the lock. Others require that the building engineer unscrew a back panel and remove individual batteries. Both procedures are simple.

ADA

When purchasing electronic locks, the security manager will likely get a complete package that includes the lock, the cards, and door handles. The security manager should ensure that the electronic system's door handles comply with the Americans with Disabilities Act (ADA). Under ADA, hotels must equip a percentage of their guest rooms with door levers that can be opened by a disabled person. For example, a hotel must replace some doorknobs with handles that could be pushed down easily by someone who does not have a hand or who has lost fingers.

HARDWARE

Although electronically activated, electronic locks rely on hardware such as a mortise lock and a deadbolt to secure the door. The security manager must decide whether he or she wants a system with a manual or an automatic deadbolt. Used for years, the manual deadbolt is locked by someone physically turning a switch or pushing a button on the door. Newer electronic lock systems, however, come with deadbolts that automatically engage when the door is closed.

The locks automatically release when either a card key is inserted into the lock or when the door's inside lever is pushed down. Automatic deadbolts add security because they do not rely on a person remembering to set the deadbolt.

However, there is a danger that if the lock malfunctions, the deadbolt will prevent security from getting into a room without completely disassembling the lock or breaking down the door. In addition to the deadbolt issue, the security manager must decide whether to integrate the new electronic lock system with the hotel's existing mortise locks or have the vendor install new hardware. This decision should be based on the age of the existing mortise locks. A locking device older than ten years may not interface well with the new electronic system.

This could lead to malfunctions or delays in releasing the lock. Installing new mortise locks with the electronic system can add anywhere from $10 to $20 per door to the cost of the project.

However, a security manager could face months of frustration if, after installing a $200,000 electronic lock system, the old hardware begins to malfunction. To cut down on the added cost, a hotel security manager could negotiate to have the vendor buy the old mortise locks that are removed from the doors during the installation of the new system. This was done at the Westin Hotel, which reduced the cost of the project by $8,000.

SPARES

Most vendors provide spare locks as part of the purchase price. The number of spares can vary, but it usually equals two per cent of the total number of locks purchased. For example, if a hotel buys 100 locks, it will receive two spares, or 102 locks. This number should be sufficient because electronic locks do not break down often. Nevertheless, even with spare locks, the security manager should negotiate a strong service agreement that requires the vendor to replace or repair locks that malfunction.

In most cases, vendors will give a one-year warranty in which broken locks are replaced or repaired at no charge as long as the lock malfunctioned on its own and was not broken by a hotel employee or guest. The Westin Hotel negotiated a three-year warranty. The agreement should also include a turnaround time clause that requires the vendor to respond to requests for repairs in a short time period. This actual turnaround time will depend on how close the vendor or its subcontractors are to the hotel. There are so many subcontractors in Boston that the average turnaround time is two hours.

INTERROGATOR

The interrogator, which is used to collect information stored in the electronic lock's memory, is a hand-held device about the size of a calculator. The interrogator is plugged into the lock via a cable. (The cable comes attached to the interrogator and cannot be removed.) The device collects the information from the lock and eventually downloads that data onto a computer hard drive. The security manager can then view the information on the computer screen or hook it to a printer to make a hard copy. The interrogator can be used to collect all the entries stored in the lock's memory or just those recorded within a certain time period. In addition, a security manager can use the data collector to diagnose a problem lock.

For example, a lock will tell the interrogator that its battery is running low or that there is a problem with its memory chip. Although not part of the basic package, the interrogator is a vital part of an electronic lock system. The security manager should consider having two interrogators because the unit's cable can break easily.

The interrogator costs about $300 to $850. Check-in operation. In general, the electronic lock companies have made the front desk equipment user-friendly. Most systems consist of either a laptop or PC connected to a card encoder, a small box where card keys are programmed.

The computers prompt hotel employees through the check-in/card programming process by asking for a guest's name and address, the guest's room number, and the time of check-in and scheduled check-out. This information is then transferred to the encoder, which transfers it onto a card. The security manager should make sure that the electronic lock's front desk computer can interface with other systems at the hotel.

This will enable the hotel to programme card keys for purposes other than to enter a guest room. For example, guests could use their access cards to buy a meal at the hotel restaurant. The card would be swiped through a computer at the restaurant, which would transfer the billing information to the front desk system so that it could be applied to the customer's room charges. While this feature is convenient for guests, it poses some security concerns for the hotel. For example, a lost or stolen card that has not been reported to the hotel could be used to purchase a meal or merchandise from the hotel restaurant or gift shop.

This is a bigger concern than the card being used to break into a guest's room because room numbers are not printed on cards. The security manager should also check the front desk computer's memory capacity. The systems on the market today can store the names and addresses of between 3,000 and 10,000 customers.

Larger hotels will require the higher end of this spectrum. This information can be helpful during an investigation. It can also be used by the hotel's marketing department to develop mailing lists for promotions. The central PC of an electronic lock system will cost between $6,000 and $15,000, depending on the system's memory, speed, and interfacing ability.

REFERENCES

Before choosing a lock, the security manager should visit other hotels that are using the system to see if they are happy with it. Most security managers are willing to give an unbiased explanation of how their system works. The security staff at the Westin visited several hotels in the area before choosing a system.

The tours lasted one to eight hours and helped the staff determine which lock would be best for its property.

PURCHASE AGREEMENT

Once a system has been chosen, the security manager should negotiate a purchase agreement that includes a strong warranty, free software upgrades, and other issues.

Large hotels will have considerably more bargaining power than smaller properties and should use their leverage to get the most from the vendor. Vendors who are trying to break into a market are often willing to provide services beyond their basic sales package. At the very least, the security manager should explore these options.

PAYMENT PLAN

Most agreements require a down payment of about one-quarter or one-third of the total cost.

The balance is covered only after the installation is complete and each lock has been tested. The security and engineering staff at the Westin Hotel checked every lock before signing the final work order. In addition to testing a lock with a card key, the staff also checked for scratches on the outside of the locks, something that can impair the physical appearance of a hotel property.

SOFTWARE UPGRADES

The security manager should negotiate for free software upgrades from the vendor.

This feature is important since software can change rapidly. A hotel that periodically gets upgrades will have most of the latest features that are developed by the vendor.

The security staff at the Westin began asking about free upgrades before it chose a vendor. The security manager asked each vendor if any new developments were on the drawing board and told each company that free upgrades would be a major factor in which vendor the hotel eventually chose.

Only one of the three vendors under consideration offered free software upgrades. That vendor was eventually chosen by the hotel.

INSTALLATION

A good vendor should be able to install locks within a fairly short time period. For example, it took only four weeks to install 800 locks at the Westin Hotel.

The installation should be done during slow seasons to minimize inconvenience to guests. The security manager should also schedule the installation by sections that can be closed off to guests.

For example, the Westin did the project in January when few people visit Boston.

As a result, entire floors could be closed to guests during the installation period. Once the locks had been installed and tested on each floor, the floor would be open for business. This allowed the hotel staff to see how guests would respond to the locks while the vendor's technicians were still on the property.

When a guest had a problem with a lock, the technician was responsible for fixing it immediately. A hotel engineer accompanied the technician to watch how minor repairs were made. Locks that experienced major problems were removed from the door and replaced. Only a handful of locks malfunctioned.

WARRANTY

Most vendors offer a one-year warranty in which they promise to replace for free hardware and software that malfunctions. The Westin Hotel was able to negotiate a three-year warranty.

The hotel made the extended warranty an important factor in its decision to buy the system it chose. The hotel knew it had considerable leverage because of its large size and because the vendor was eager to break into the lucrative Boston market.

It was also important that the vendor agreed to fix or replace broken locks within two hours at no additional cost. The Westin did not want to wait a day or longer for service during its busy season. Each day a lock is broken is a day a room cannot be rented. In some cases, however, there may be no local vendor who is close enough to visit the hotel and repair a lock in such a short time period. When the lock's vendor is located in another city, the security manager should negotiate a deal under which the vendor agrees to pay for all overnight mail charges so the lock can be repaired or replaced as soon as possible.

4

Refrigeration and Air Conditioning

REFRIGERATION SYSTEMS

REFRIGERATION AND HEATING EQUIPMENT

Multifactor productivity gains averaged 1.5 per cent per year over the 1967-94 period; to comply with Federal legislation, the industry shifted from chlorofluorocarbons, an important input in the production process, to environmentally safer substitutes Multifactor productivity in the refrigeration and heating equipment industry increased at an average annual rate of 1.5 per cent over the 1967-94 period.

This industry's output includes air conditioners, refrigeration equipment and systems, electric heat pumps, furnaces, refrigerated display cases, soda fountains, beer dispensers, and snowmaking machinery. Multifactor productivity is a measure used to analyse the overall economic efficiency of an industry. It relates the growth of the industry's output to the growth rate of the combined inputs of labour, capital, and intermediate purchases.

An important input for the refrigeration and heating equipment industry had been chlorofluorocarbons, a chemical compound used since the 1930s. By Federal enactment, however, CFC'S were phased out because they were linked to depletion of the ozone layer in the atmosphere. As a result, the industry has had to allocate a substantial amount of resources to the transition away from CFC'S. This article examines detailed productivity, output, and input data in the manufacture of refrigeration and heating equipment to provide measures of multifactor productivity growth over a 27-year period. Special emphasis is placed on the "productivity falloff" that began in 1973. The article also includes descriptions of recent production technology, new designs and methods of manufacturing, and market influences that could influence industry output and input.

PRODUCTIVITY

Since 1984, the Bureau of Labour Statistics has published an index of output per employee hour, or labour productivity, for the refrigeration and heating equipment industry. Labour productivity relates output to the input of labour, while multifactor productivity relates output to the combined inputs of labour, capital, and intermediate purchases. Labour productivity does not measure the exact contribution of labour, but reflects many influences that affect the use of labour, such as changing technology; economies of scale; substitution of inputs of capital and intermediate purchases for labour; managerial skills; and the level of experience and education of the workforce.

While the multifactor productivity measure reflects many of these influences, it does not reflect changes in capital relative to labour and in intermediate purchases relative to labour. Labour productivity in the industry increased at an average annual rate of 1.7 per cent over the entire period studied, while in total manufacturing the rate was 2.7 per cent. Over the same period, multifactor productivity rose 1.5 per cent per year in the industry, while in the total manufacturing sector of the economy, it advanced 1.1 per cent per year. The 1.5-per cent rate of growth in multifactor productivity resulted from a 3.6-per cent average annual increase in output and a 2.1-per cent average annual gain in combined inputs.

Analysing the 1967-94 period in more detail, we find that labour productivity rose rapidly, at 5.2 per cent per year, while multifactor productivity increased 3.6 per cent per year during 1967-73. Multifactor and related productivity measures in the refrigeration and heating equipment industry, average annual rates of change, 1967-94 Each measure presented in this is computed independently. Therefore, multifactor productivity, the capital effect, and the intermediate purchase effect might not sum exactly to output per hour, due to rounding. The capital effect is the change in the ratio of capital to labour, multiplied by the share of capital costs in the total cost of output. The intermediate purchases effect is the change in the ratio of intermediate purchases to labour, multiplied by the share of intermediate purchases costs in the total cost of output.

The refrigeration and heating equipment industry did not escape the productivity falloff that affected most manufacturing industries between 1973 and 1979. Both labour productivity and multifactor productivity growth rates fell sharply from the 1967-73 period to the 1973-79 periods. Labour productivity dropped 0.3 per cent per year for the latter period, down from a 5.2-per cent per year increase for the 1967-73 period.

Multifactor productivity growth fell from an annual rate of increase of 3.6 per cent to a 1.9-per cent rate for the same periods-a slowdown considerably smaller than the 5.5-percentage-point falloff that occurred in labour productivity. For the 1979-94 period, labour productivity growth recovered from the 0.3-per cent-per-year decrease during 1973-79 to post a 1.1-per cent average annual increase.

Multifactor productivity growth was subdued, rising just 0.6 per cent each year after 1979. The influence of capital on output per employee hour, referred to as the "capital effect," is measured as the change in the capital-labour ratio multiplied by the share of capital costs in total costs of output. Analogous to the capital effect is the "intermediate purchases effect" which is derived by multiplying change in the intermediate purchases-labour ratio by the share of intermediate purchases in the total cost of output Labour productivity growth equals the sum of these two effects plus multifactor productivity growth.

For the entire 196794 period, the capital effect was 0.0 per cent per year, while the intermediate purchases effect averaged 0.1 per cent annually. Although the capital effect and the intermediate purchases effect were negligible for the entire period studied, they did vary in the subperiods. During 1967-73, the capital effect contributed 0.2 percentage point to the growth rate of labour productivity and the intermediate purchases effect contributed 1.3 percentage points.

For the period 1973-79, the capital effect equaled-0.1 per cent on average, while the intermediate purchases effect declined 3.3 percentage points, to 2.0 per cent per year. During the 1979-94 periods, the capital effect decreased slightly to a-O.1-per cent average annual rate, while the intermediate purchases effect increased, to 0.6 per cent per year.

TECHNOLOGY CHANGE

Production techniques and, hence, rates of productivity, in this industry have been affected by new technology from a product's start to finish. With the introduction of new methods, the industry strives to reduce wasted materials, decrease rejected finished parts and products, and diminish labour requirements. Computer-aided design assists an engineer in designing a new product by taking over repetitive tasks, warning of inconsistencies in measurement, and increasing the designer's usable memory many times over by storing almost unlimited data.

Computer-aided manufacture guarantees that an engineer's specifications are carried out to degrees of accuracy that were impossible before the advent of microprocessor-controlled production equipment.

Engineering firms developing new heating and cooling products have embraced CAD technology. These systems allow a shop to get more work, of a more complex nature, from fewer engineers. The systems can even be programmed by senior engineers to coach the less experienced, to ensure that all work meets design, cost, and productively standards set by the firm. Designing any new product or component usually involves several stages, at which modifications are tested within the CAD environment.

This is the point at which a CAD system saves significant labour hours and material. The "brain" of these systems can modify drawings and actually test the modifications in minutes, making it unnecessary to completely redraw the component, or to manufacture one version to test a change. Most CAD systems can scrutinize a component for noise, vibration, stress, buckling, and fatigue. Computer-aided manufacturing has allowed a plant in Indiana to make finished motor vehicle air conditioners from raw castings, with almost no manual handling. The plant, which makes compressors for cars and light trucks, has 5 miles of conveyors-all monitored and controlled by six microprocessors.

Together, the conveyors take up almost 200,000 square feet of plant space. Production processes that once were performed as separate operations, and often manually, are now integrated into a "system approach." Many of the new technologies introduced into this industry are aimed at improving control of processes such as metal cutting and bending. Precise cutting of metal not only reduces waste, but also is essential "down the line," where automated equipment requires very close tolerances. A Minnesota plant uses machine vision modules to detect any flaws on metal to be used to make freezer coils.

The vision modules detect irregularities and direct controllers to reverse the flow of the material and cut off the flawed portion. This reduces labour and material requirements while producing fewer defective products. The plant also has been able to switch to a lighter gauge steel. This is because the new drives improve handling to such an extent that the material is less likely to be damaged. Environmental concerns will continue to alter the designs and methods of manufacturing in the refrigeration and heating equipment industry for some time. Meanwhile, engineers and designers have begun discussing and practicing the "design for disassembly" concept in this, and other industries as well.

The goal of this concept is to construct a product so that it can be easily disassembled into its component parts for simplified recycling. At present, the recycling of refrigeration and heating equipment is limited because of the large quantities of labour needed to take the equipment apart. This new theory of design will require yet newer technologies of the industry and of its suppliers of intermediate inputs.

OUTPUT

Changes in output in the refrigeration and heating equipment industry respond to many variables, including new residential and non-residential construction, renovation of existing structures, automobile sales, Federal legislation regarding the environment, and the general health of the economy. For the entire 1967-94 period, output in the industry increased 3.6 per cent each year on average, compared with a 2.5-per cent average annual increase for all manufacturing.

This industry is highly cyclical, with sharp swings in output: the sharpest increase occurred during 1972, when it posted a 32.5-per cent jump in output; the deepest drop took place in 1975, bringing output down 35.5 per cent from the previous year. Two industries, motor vehicles and equipment and building construction, dominate the demand for refrigeration and heating equipment.

For 23 of the 27 years between 1967 and 1994, changes in output in the industry move in the same direction as changes in output of the motor vehicles and equipment industry. The relationship between new construction and the demand for new refrigeration and heating equipment also is strong. A significant market for the industry's output is retrofit and reconstruction. This involves work on commercial buildings intended to upgrade cooling and heating equipment to meet new standards, increase the appeal of unleashed space, and reduce indoor environmental problems.

The trend for the retrofit and reconstruction market appears to be upward. Specifically, legislation at the Federal level, which began the CFC phaseout schedule, will spur the demand for retrofit and replacement. In the United States, there are more than 130 million motor vehicle air conditioners, 5 million commercial refrigeration systems, and 80 thousand air-conditioning units for commercial and institutional buildings running on CFC'S.

Many of these components will have to be replaced or retrofitted. For many of the establishments in this industry, international sales represent as much as 35 per cent of total revenues. In 1993, the value of U.S. imports of refrigeration and heating equipment increased almost 8 per cent, while the value of the exports of this industry increased 12 per cent.

Exports will continue to increase due to the economic and social changes taking place in Eastern Europe and the former Soviet Union. More significant is the liberalization of trade made possible by the North American Free Trade Agreement of 1994.

This should create excellent opportunities for the industry to expand its exports to Canada and Mexico. The refrigeration and heating equipment industry is currently experiencing a boom in the production of one of its products. Shipments of air conditioning systems for institutional and commercial buildings have grown dramatically.

These units, called chillers, are needed to replace older, less efficient systems that rely on CFC'S. A survey by the Air Conditioning and Refrigeration Institute, "U.S. shipments of chillers to building owners around the world jumped 32 per cent in 1995 to a record 9,444 units, of which about 40 per cent were used in America to replace CFC chillers..."

Moreover, this surge will continue for several more years because the institute's survey also showed that, "...65,375 or 82 per cent of...chillers in the U.S. were still using CFCS on January 1, [1996] when a ban on CFC production went into effect." Only a few years ago, the outlook for this industry was not encouraging. At the time, producers complained of the potential for equipment shutdowns, the need for employee layoffs, and low inventories. This was primarily due to legislation requiring stringent cutbacks of CFC compounds before the replacements had been invented. Research and development, however, have led to the design of efficient CFC-free refrigeration and air conditioning products, which has helped increase the demand for the industry's output.

Inputs

Over the entire 1967-94 period, labour input increased 1.9 per cent per year, on average. Again, this hides the divergence between pre-and post-1973 trends for the industry. From 1967 to 1973, labour input in SIC 3585 grew at an average annual rate of 7.9 per cent, but from 1973 to 1979, it increased just 0.1 per cent per year. In the final period, 1979-94, employee hours edged up 0.4 per cent each year, on average. In 1967, there were 81,500 people employed by the refrigeration and heating equipment industry. The average hourly earnings for production workers in the industry at that time were $2.93, compared with $2.82 for all manufacturing.

In that same year, 70 per cent of all industry employees were production workers, compared with 74 per cent in all manufacturing. In 1994, the level of employment reached more than 130,000-an impressive recovery from the 1991 level of 115,000 employees. By 1994, average hourly earnings of production workers were $11.80 in the industry, compared with $11.62 in all manufacturing. In 1995, employment in the industry had swelled to a new peak of 139,000. This is in stark contrast to employment in the total manufacturing sector, which last peaked in 1979. Employment levels in the next few years could surpass the 1995 peak for the reasons discussed earlier.

As measured in BLS multifactor productivity studies, capital is the flow of services derived from the equipment, structures finished goods, work-in-process, and materials and supplies inventories that are kept on hand in the firm, as well as the land on which plants are located. Financial assets are not included in the measure.

Capital services in the refrigeration and heating equipment industry grew at an average annual rate of 2.2 per cent between 1967 and 1994. Reflecting the industry's tremendous growth through the early 1970s, capital services averaged a 9.8-per cent annual increase during the 1967-73 period. However, gains slowed sharply after 1973, to just 0.1 per cent per year during 1973-79. This slowdown continued for the 197994 period with capital services increasing at the same rate of 0.1 per cent.

From 1967 to 1994, measures of the services of capital structures and land moved similarly to that for total capital, increasing at average annual rates of 2.0 and 2.7 per cent, respectively. That for equipment rose even faster, at an average annual rate of 4.9 per cent. Inventories were steady at 0.0 per cent per year, on average. In the first interval, 1967-73, equipment services rose almost 13 per cent each year, then fell off to a gain of 4.4 per cent annually during

1973-79. Between 1979 and 1994, these services grew even more slowly, at an annual rate of 2.1 per cent.

While inventories as a whole were cyclical for this industry, when viewed in more detail, a different picture emerges. For unitary products, particularly window air conditioning units, inventories change with the seasons and the severity of seasons. A summer that is cooler than average would leave inventories higher than average for the year. Also, the suppliers of materials to the industry sometimes offer incentives, such as attractive financing, that will induce manufacturers to stock up on inventory. For the component products, such as industrial and commercial heating/cooling units for whole buildings, there generally is no inventory. The product itself is so specialized that the materials are not ordered until the buyer has committed to the purchase. In 13 years, the services of structures declined; these annual reductions never exceeded 2 per cent.

For the entire period, 1967-94, the measure for structures increased 2.0 per cent each year, on average. However, the overall increase masks the high pre-1973 gain of 8.8 per cent each year and the drop-off to just a 0.2-per cent gain each year after 1973. Intermediate purchases. Intermediate purchases consist of the raw materials, energy and purchased services used in the production of the industry's output. Materials make up more than 90 per cent of the value of intermediate purchases for the refrigeration and heating equipment industry, with services ranging from 6 per cent to 9 per cent of that value, and fuels and electricity, the remainder. The input of intermediate purchases increased 2.2 per cent each year, on average, between 1967 and 1994, but this overall rate hides the large difference between the pre-1973 and the post-1973 periods. During 1967-73, input of intermediate purchases increased by more than 10 per cent each year, on average, but in 1973-79, this component decreased 3.5 per cent per year. The 1979-94 intervals showed a cessation of the downward trend of the use of intermediate inputs, with an average annual increase of 1.4 per cent each year. The use of intermediate purchases generally follows that of output.

However, when output is increasing faster than the use of intermediate purchases, the result is a gain in intermediate purchases productivity. From 1967 to 1994, intermediate purchases productivity gained 1.4 per cent each year, on average. The rates of change in intermediate purchases productivity were 3.0 per cent for the 1967-73 period, and 3.5 per cent for the 1973-79 period. The last period, 1979-94, shows a complete slowdown in the growth of this measure, to an average 0.0 per cent per year. The price of intermediate purchases for the refrigeration and heating equipment industry increased S. 1 per cent, on average, between 1967 and 1994. Producers are continually trying to discover ways of substituting one group of inputs for another, to reduce the cost of a given level of output.

A rise in price encourages substitution away from the relatively costly input for a cheaper alternative. In this industry, from 1967-73, the price of materials was increasing only 4.4 per cent each year, on average, while the cost of labour was increasing 7.8 per cent per year. The intermediate purchases effect was an average 1.3 per cent annually between 1967 and 1973. In the second period, 1973-79, this trend was reversed as labour became relatively inexpensive while materials became more costly.

The intermediate purchases effect declined to an average-2.0 per cent per year in this interval. The last period shows the prices of materials and labour increasing at more equal annual average rates. The intermediate purchases effect was closer to zero, at an average annual rate of 0.6 per cent each year, because less incentive for substitution existed in this period. The 1992 Census of Manufactures details almost 40 categories of materials for the heating, air conditioning, and refrigeration equipment industry. Motors and generators made up the largest portion of the total value of these materials at 13 per cent. The second and third largest shares were for carbon steel and automatic temperature controls.

Refrigerant gases accounted for less than 1 per cent of the value of materials consumed by this industry in 1992, but this understates their importance to refrigeration and heating equipment manufacturers. CFC'S were used as an evaporative agent in many refrigeration and mobile-air conditioning applications. They also were used as a blowing agent to form the insulation that keeps the cold air inside the refrigerated space.

CFC'S are very good at both of these functions. Being large, stable compounds, they have a very low thermal conductivity figure and are non-toxic, non-flammable, and non-corrosive. As insulation, CFC'S were blown into liquid plastic and forced, under pressure, into cavities between the walls of appliances.

There, they served as insulators and a stress member of the cabinet itself. Because CFC molecules are large, they do not escape readily through the solidified plastic, as oxygen or carbon dioxide would. The low thermal conductivity of CFC-based insulation allows the compressor to run less often, reducing the energy used by the product. The use of CFC-based insulation increased in the 1970s, so that manufacturers could comply with new regulations regarding the efficiency of their products.

The refrigeration and heating equipment industry's inputs and output are regulated, to varying degrees, by the Montreal Protocol; and the U.S. Clean Air Act Amendments, National Appliance Energy Conservation Act, Energy Policy Act, and Toxic Substances Control Act.

The refrigeration and heating equipment industry began using CFC'S as inputs in the production process in the 1930s. Decades later, the Montreal Protocol and Clean Air Act Amendments mandated that the industry substitute away from these materials to safeguard the atmosphere. Although the costs of developing the substitutes themselves were borne chiefly by the industrial inorganic chemicals industry, the refrigeration and heating equipment industry required new manufacturing techniques, because the ozone-safe coolants are not perfect substitutes for the originals. Production workers had to be trained to use the new materials, which are toxic, corrosive, and combustible-characteristics that CFC'S do not share. To handle these substitute coolants, new compressor, seal, and blower technology needed to be devised.

The development and adoption of these technologies used resources that might otherwise have gone towards improving efficiency in the production process.

This could help explain the slowdown in multifactor productivity growth in the industry during the post-1979 period. After rising 3.6 per cent per year between 1967 and 1973 and 1.9 per cent per year between 1973 and 1979, multifactor productivity increased at an average annual rate of just 0.6 per cent in the 1979-94 period. Initially, the industry substituted hydrochlorofluorocarbons for CFC'S in the production process; HCFC'S do only 2 per cent to 10 per cent as much damage to the ozone layer as CFC'S.

However, their use is to become limited by the year 2003. The industry is already replacing these second-generation coolants with the third, hydrofluorocarbons.

HFC'S do no damage to the ozone layer but they are a greenhouse gas and may become limited-use inputs in the future. The fourth-generation coolant may not be a chemical at all. Thermoacoustic cooling is a recent discovery in which sound and inert gas cool an enclosed space. The refrigeration and heating equipment industry will continue to face challenges arising from the need for safer coolants in its products; meeting those challenges might restrain productivity growth in the near future.

Output per hour, or labour productivity, in the refrigeration and heating equipment industry increased at an average annual rate of 1.7 per cent between 1967 and 1994. Multifactor productivity for the same period gained 1.5 per cent. The industry experienced rapid growth in output and in both labour productivity and multifactor productivity between 1967 and 1973. A dramatic slowdown in all three measures occurred between 1973 and 1979, after which labour productivity rebounded somewhat.

A major market for this industry's products is in retrofit and reconstruction activities, which have grown consistently in recent years, in part because of legislation at the Federal level. Exports represent a significant portion of the quantity demanded of this industry. Some establishments generate more than 35 per cent of revenues from exports. Finally, a difficult challenge has been met by the refrigeration and heating equipment industry in that substitutes have had to be developed for a group of critical inputs, first chlorofluorocarbons, and then hydrochlorofluorocarbons.

PRODUCTIVITY IN REFRIGERATION EQUIPMENT, AND FURNACES

Output per employee hour in the manufacture of air conditioning, refrigeration, and warm-air heating equipment rose at an average annual rate of 1.3 per cent between 1967 and 1982, compared with 2.4 per cent a year for all of manufacturing. Output climbed 3.4 per cent a year during the period, and employee hours, 2.1 per cent. Strong expansion in the demand for the industry's residential, commercial, and industrial products, and rapid diffusion of basic improvements in metalworking technologies were among factors underlying the rising productivity trend. The improvement in the industry's productivity occurred mostly in the earlier part of the period reviewed. After 1973, output per employee hour did not change, as shown by the following tabulation of average annual rates of change:

- The industry's productivity rate for the 1967-73 period was 50 per cent again as high as for manufacturing, but thereafter the trends in the two rate diverged. Year-to-year swings in the industry's productivity were comparatively moderate. These swings ranged between a 9-per cent increase in 1972 and a 16-per cent decrease in 1972. Year-to-year increases in productivity outnumbered decreases by 12 to 2. In the years when productivity dropped, output dipped less than employee hours. Tnus, in 1975 and 1980, productivity declined 16 per cent and 7 per cent while output dipped 34 per cent and 16 per cent, and employee hours, 22 per cent and 10 per cent. In 1974, productivity rose as a 6-per cent decline in output was outdistanced by a 9-per cent decline in employee hours. Output and demand

The manufacture of air conditioning and refrigeration equipment and of warm-air furnaces involves the production of heat transfer apparatus for residential, commercial, and industrial applications, as well as for hospitals, marine vessels, freight and passenger vehicles, and many specialized applications. Heat transfer equipment here includes unitary air conditioners; room air conditioners; commercial refrigeration equipment; as well as heat pumps and dehumidifiers. The industry, in addition, manufactures compressors and condensers, not only for its own final output, but also for home refrigerators The industry's output rose at an average annual rate of 3.4 per cent between 1967 and 1982. The rate for the earlier part of the period ran four times higher than that for all manufacturing, but dropped below the all-manufacturing rate during 1973-82:

- Among reasons underlying the industry's output growth, and underpinning it after 1973, have been exports. As a proportion of value of shipments, exports by the industry nearly doubled between the earlier and the later period studied here-from 8 per cent to 14 per cent. For manufacturing as a whole, the export share in the value of shipments increased less markedly-from 6 per cent in 1972 to 10 per cent in 1980.

The much slowed expansion in the industry's output from 1973 forward corresponds to trends in the output of its major product groups, which in turn parallel the trends in underlying demand from the industry' most important markets.

Thus, the production of heat transfer equipment other than unitary or room air conditioners or warm-air furnaces increased at a rate nearly 10 times higher over the 1967-73 periods than during the 1973-82 span. The increase in the rate had resulted largely from strong demand for motor vehicle air conditioners. Such demand was associated with an increase in motor vehicle output of close to 6 per cent a year in 1967-73. The subsequent tapering of output growth mirrored a falling-off in the annual rate of motor vehicle output by-1.0 per cent for 1973-82. Likewise, output rates of growth of unitary air conditioners and commercial refrigeration equipment slowed after 1973; for warm air furnaces, the rate declined.

This pattern was linked largely to developments in construction. The average annual rate of change in the constant-dollar value of new residential housing construction, for example, declined from around 9 per cent for 1967-73 to 2 per cent thereafter; that for commercial structures, from 15 per cent to 9 per cent; and that for hospitals turned from a 5-per cent annual gain to a 4-per cent annual decrease. Only industrial construction evidenced a contrary trend, with a 10-per cent annual decline in the earlier period giving way to a 3.5-per cent annual rise after 1973. Leaving aside the medium-term swings, the industry's output has been sustained over the longer run by rapidly growing use of central and room air conditioning in homes, as well as more gradual increases in offices and other commercial space, hospitals, and probably in factories.

Increases in the size of homes and other structures generated the shift in demand from room air conditioners to central systems and spurred the demand for warm-air furnaces, which function through the same air circulation system as central air conditioners. In the middle and late 1960's, 28 per cent of all new homes were equipped with central air conditioners; that proportion rose to 43 per cent between 1970 and 1975, and to 66 per cent by 1982. Square footage per new home, to which the size of heat transfer equipment is linked, increased 9 per cent between the mid-1960's and the early 1980's. The proportion of homes wired for room air conditioners more than doubled between the mid-1960's and the mid-1970's, to 53 per cent, but it did not rise much thereafter. Warm-air ducted heating systems in occupied housing units rose by about one-third between 1970 and 1975, but by only 7 per cent between 1975 and 1980. For offices, shopping centres, and hospitals, pertinent data on air conditioning and forced warm-air systems are available only fore some recent years.

A survey conducted in the early 1970's, 91 per cent of all commercial office buildings had central air conditioning, and 67 per cent had forced-air heating systems. For shopping centres, the comparable figures were close to 100 per cent in 1977; and for hospitals and nursing homes, they read 97 per cent and 56 per cent in 1975. These data suggest that industry output is sustained not only by the net increase in such structures, but from replacement and retrofitting with more energy-efficient equipment as well. In 1981, for example, more than half of total residential expenditures on air conditioning and heating systems were for replacement. Furthermore, the introduction of more energy-efficient heat transfer equipment since about 1975 has also bolstered output.

For the same wattage per hour of electric energy input, higher equipment output capacities, as measured in British Thermal Units, have been achieved. Thus, in 1976, the Air Conditioning and Refrigeration Institute listed 56 per cent of new unitary air conditioners as having energy efficiency ratios of between 6.5 and 7.4, and 18 per cent with ratios of 7.5 to 8.4. By 1981, the proportion of the lower efficiency units had shrunk to 37 per cent, while that of the higher efficiency equipment had expanded to 35 per cent. Employment in the air conditioning, refrigeration, and warm-air heating equipment industry numbered 129,000 persons in mid-1984. It rose 32 per cent between 1967 and 1982, or at an average annual rate of 2.2 per cent. Employment reached a peak of 130,000 persons in 1979, and subsequently retreated. This decline was attributable to a 21-per cent contraction in production worker jobs between 1979 and 1982, as compared with a 9-per cent loss in non-production worker jobs. Over the longer term, trends in employee hours displayed patterns of acceleration and retardation similar to those noted for production and output trends. Employee hours in the industry rose during the first 6 years of the review period at an average annual rate much greater than for all manufacturing. Subsequently the rate plummeted:

- Production workers accounted for 70 per cent of total employment, which was the same proportion in both 1967 and 1982-non-production workers made up the balance. The number of women workers more than doubled over the period, raising their proportion of total employment from 14 per cent to 21 per cent. Underlying this increase may have been a shift in the skill composition of the industry's workers to more assembly-type jobs. The rise in the industry's average hourly earnings also slowed relative to the manufacturing average. In 1967, the former was 104 per cent of the latter, compared with 96 per cent in 1981.

Overtime ran somewhat below the manufacturing average during the review period, suggesting that firms in the industry were inclined to hire new production workers, rather than assign overtime when the workload exceeded certain limits. Turnover rates nonetheless lagged; over the 1967-81 span, they averaged 89 per cent of the manufacturing average for accessions, and 91 per cent of that for separations. Thus, it appears that employment stability was somewhat greater in the industry than in manufacturing generally. The skill composition of the industry's workforce differs from that for manufacturing as a whole.

In 1980, craft workers accounted for 17 per cent of total industry employment, compared with 19 per cent for all manufacturing.

Operatives, however, accounted for a significantly larger proportion-48 per cent, compared with 43 per cent. The larger component of operatives stemmed from the proportionately greater number of assembly workers in the industry than in all manufacturing.

The proportion of metalworking operatives in the industry was more than twice as high as for manufacturing generally. By contrast, the occupational distribution of white-collar workers was similar to that for manufacturing.

Professional and technical workers made up 8 per cent of the industry's workforce; clerical workers, 12 per cent; and managers and administrators, 5 per cent. Investment in plant and equipment Like manufacturing establishments generally, the air conditioning, refrigeration, and warm-air heating equipment industry installed new production equipment at a fairly high rate over the 1967-81 periods.

However, unlike other manufacturing establishments, firms in the industry spent at a much higher rate during the earlier than the latter part of the review period. For all manufacturing, the reverse held true:

- The industry's high rate of capital spending in the early part of the period resulted from pressures on capacity, related to high output growth rates. With the abatement of output growth after 1973, fixed investment slowed.

The proportion of total fixed investment spent on equipment is as follows:

- The comparatively high proportion of expenditures for equipment is reflected in the data on the modernization of the industry's metalworking machinery, as reported by the American Machinist. The rates shown, however, obscure large year-to-year fluctuations in the industry's capital spending. This instability was far more marked for the industry than for manufacturing generally. For example, in 1975, the industry's plant and equipment expenditures plummeted 41 per cent and in 1977, they soared 56 per cent. Manufacturing recorded a 9-per cent drop, and a 21-per cent rise for the same 2 years.

Fixed assets per employee in the industry were 79 per cent of the manufacturing average in 1980, compared with 76 per cent during 1972 and 1974-76. The rise in the ratio partially reflected the cumulative effects of earlier equipment installations and new plant construction on the value of the industry's fixed assets. More efficient technology Air conditioning and refrigeration equipment essentially consists of a compressor driven by an electric motor, and two coils-the condenser, in which the refrigerant is compressed to a liquid, and the evaporator, in which the refrigerant expands into the gaseous state, enabling it to absorb heat from the space being cooled.

The heat is transferred from the environment with the aid of fins, mounted upon the evaporator coil. Warm-air furnaces built by the industry are mostly gas-fueled forced-air devices. They include a combustion chamber and a motor-driven blower. The sheet metal housing that shields the equipment is manufactured by the industry, but controls and motors normally are not. Advances in the manufacture of air conditioners, refrigeration equipment, and warm-air furnaces have been linked chiefly to technological progress in metalworking machinery, welding, methods of storage and transfer of parts, and assembly. The are also related to improvements in product design.

The production of air conditioners, refrigeration equipment, and warm-air furnaces basically involves the cutting and forming of metal, as well as welding, brazing, and soldering of components. Efforts to improve efficiency usually focus upon these operations, and on plant layout. Auxiliary operations, such as materials handling, painting, testing, and packaging have received increased attention in recent years. The most recent American Machinist inventory of metal-working equipment indicates that, in 1983, 30 per cent of all metalcutting and metalforming machine tools used in the industry were at most 10 years old. In 1968, the proportion was the same for metalcutting tools, but only 25 per cent for metalforming tools.

The industry has steadily improved its metalworking equipment, by and large maintaining the same proportion of new equipment during 1973-83 as during 1958-68. The higher end of the age distribution, however, shows an increase in the proportion of older metalworking equipment in the industry. The share of metalcutting machine tools 20 years and older rose from 25 per cent in 1968 to 32 per cent in 1983, and the share of metalforming tools, from 25 per cent to 37 per cent. However, the relative increase in older machine tools cannot be readily interpreted as a loss in efficiency, inasmuch as the American Machinist inventory does not take into account the retrofitting of older machines with up-to-date components and control devices.

The efficiency of the industry's metalworking equipment has been significantly enhanced by an 11-fold rise in the number of numerically controlled machine tools. In 1983, NC machine tools accounted for 13 per cent and 17 per cent of metalcutting and metalforming tools 9 years old or less. In 1968, when NC machine tools were not yet widely diffused, the proportions were less than 1 per cent.

The percentage increase in the number of NC tools understates the increase in the output capabilities which the installation of such tools spells. The American Machinist, the number of machine tools in all metalworking industries declined from 16 per 1,000 population in 1968 to fewer than 10 in

1983. "This represents in part the greater productivity of machine tools, in part the simplification of design of many products, so that less machining is required."

This statement also applies to the industry reviewed here: the number of machine tools in the industry's shops dropped by one-third between 1968 and 1983, while output more than doubled. Thus, the output capability of metalworking equipment in the industry rose nearly threefold over the study period, with that rise likely to be largely attributable to NC-equipped machine tools. Examples of how improved metalworking technology has helped to raise output per hour may be drawn from the sheet metal operations in the industry's larger shops, and from the fabrication of some of the major components of its products. In punching sheet metal, templates were conventionally affixed to the press so as to obtain required shapes.

Templates have been increasingly replaced, however, by taped instructions fed to the press, which greatly speeds output and ensures greater precision of the finished shape. Setup time of the press has been reduced to as little as one-twentieth of the conventional operation. In a related operation, the press, after the sheet metal blank has been placed automatically, is programmed to select 1 of up to 30 built-in punching tools from its turret, and to activate the tool selected. Bending of metal parts has likewise been increasingly automated, the bending apparatus being preset to several sequential settings Setup time here has declined to an estimated 10 per cent of what it had been prior to automation.

Despite their being automated, these metalworking processes continue to require close monitoring by trained operators. The operator may monitor two or more machines at the same time, or may be engaged in such auxiliary tasks as placing and removing work pieces. Some of the more advanced shops in the industry feature such machine tools as high-capacity drills, which may drill all the holes in an air conditioning compressor vessel in one or two operations. Older drilling machines, still widely in use, have much lower capacity and speed. Automatic tool wear adjustment is normally also a feature of NC machine tools, but at times this feature is not desired or used.

Replacement of a tool bit is then left to the discretion of the operator assigned to monitor the entire machining process. In small-lot production, loading and unloading the work piece may be done manually. Improved productivity in the fabrication of air conditioning equipment components during the review period is exemplified by the coil manufacturing process. The coil is the heart of the heat exchanger.

The refrigerant is pumped through it to absorb heat from the surrounding space. The coil originates as tubing on a large roll. In the more advance shops, the rolled tubing is automatically straightened, cut to length as specified in, and controlled by, a taped programme, and automatically bent to the shape of a U. This operation has come to be performed by one person, where 10 years or so ago, four persons were required to shear the tube manually and insert it into a bending device. The U-shaped coil is inserted into a nest of aluminum fins. The fins aid in absorbing heat from the refrigerant. The fabrication of fins is usually highly mechanized, precut aluminum blanks being punched to form them, and to accommodate the coils. Numerically controlled punch presses featuring up to 27 spindles are used in the larger shops.

However, the number of blanks that may be punched at a time is limited because punching tends to break rather than cut the metal, and breaking forms rims that cannot be tolerated. Where fins are produced in quantity, punch presses may not be numerically controlled, because longer setup times are usually justified by the longer runs. Loading and unloading of the punch presses has usually been mechanized in the larger plants, so that the fins emerge stacked as nests.

The coils are then inserted manually. Manual insertion is still preferred because it prevents "binding." The operator can readily control the pressure he exerts in inserting the individual coils, which is not the case for mechanical insertion where undue pressure may damage the coil. The coils are then brazed together or soldered to form a continuous loop. Brazing or soldering is still performed by means of hand-operated devices to ensure leak proof joints and the continuity of the loop, so as not to "blind-alley" them).

The fabrication of reciprocating compressors provides other examples of the reduction in unit labour requirements which the industry seeks. Compressors, driven by electric motors function to increase the density of the refrigerant to the liquid state. Basically, the reciprocating compressor consists of a piston sitting on a rod connected to the motor; and a cyclinder, against the head of which the piston moves, compressing the refrigerant. Where compressor components are produced in quantity, multistation machinery arranged in circular form has come to be used.

Yet, loading and unloading of the workpiece, and transferring it between groups of dial machinery, is still widely done manually. Some establishments began to install automatic transfer lines towards the end of the review period, affording automatic positioning of the workpiece, as well as automation of most other metalworking operations. Transfer lines require usually one-half or less of the labour per unit of the more conventional equipment; so-called "uptime," that is the time during which the machinery is fully operation, is estimated to be 20 per cent higher.

Changes in product design have, in some instances been combined with technological advances. Thus, a cylindrically shaped air conditioning machine has been developed that permits several hundred feet of continual coil to be wrapped around a mandrel in one mechanical process. This increases the heat transfer area, hence the efficiency of the machine. It also minimizes the jointing of coil ends and thus, the leakage of refrigerant. Fins consist of many hundreds of tiny aluminum pieces glued to the tubing's surface. Unit labour requirements in mounting such tubing are estimated at 20 to 30 per cent of those for the manual insertion of U-shaped coils into nests of fins and the fabrication of such fins. Product design and technological advance have also been combined in the case of a thermostatic valve body for automotive air conditioning.

After the valve body was redesigned, it could be fabricated by means of a 43-spindle metalworking machine which combines automatic indexing, milling, drilling, counter boring, tapping, and other operations. Material costs were reduced, assembly facilitated, and quality improved. The machine replaced as many as 11 standard machines run by 30 workers. A fundamental design change in air conditioning equipment and warm-air furnaces during the review period made them more energy-efficient.

The relevant design changes usually involved finer tolerances, hence greater precision machining, especially of compressor components. Precision machining in turn has been facilitated by-and has spurred the adoption of-NC metalworking machinery. Functional testing, furthermore, has been upgraded by such electronic devices as automatic calibration stations, which can be programmed for many settings at a time, and which require little attendance. Assembly appears also to have been improved by the better "fit-up" of the more precisely machine components.

Industry structure Industry concentration increased over the period reviewed; in 1977, the 8 largest companies accounted for 51 per cent of the industry's value of shipments, compared with an estimated 45 per cent in 1967. The 20 largest companies accounted for 67 per cent of the value of shipments in 1977, as against 62 per cent in 1967. Moreover, the concentration ratio for 1967 was higher than for 1963.

These increases suggest underlying growth over time in economies of scale, a factor that usually engenders productivity improvement. Employment, too, was concentrated in the larger establishments. In 1977, 50 per cent of the industry's employees worked in 31 of the 860 establishments classified in the industry. At the lower end of the employment size stratification, just over 10 per cent of all employees in the industry worked in 75 per cent of all establishments. It is noteworthy that the size distribution of capital expenditures closely followed the size distribution of employment-such that, for example, nearly one-half of all such expenditures were made by only 4 per cent of all establishments in the industry.In line with the increase in concentration ratios, the larger establishments raised their share of the industry's total employment over time.

Outlook Continued productivity improvement is indicated for the industry. As the American Machinist inventory of metalworking equipment in the industry suggests, diffusion of NC machine tools is far from complete. If past trends in diffusion persist, productivity gains are likely to be generated. Moreover, the larger, more advanced shops plan to install flexible manufacturing systems, which will make small-lot production of larger air conditioning, refrigeration, and heating equipment more efficient. One establishment, which is installing a FM system to produce reciprocal compressors, expects direct labour requirements to be reduced by more than 80 per cent, as compared with conventional production methods. Another establishment, which produces large evaporators in lots of less than 100, also plans to fabricate them by FM methods. Such evaporators require up to 5,000 different metal shapes. In combination with NC machine tools, plant management expects FM to save up to 50 per cent in unit labour requirements, cut lead time by nearly one-half, and cope with declining lot size and more exacting tolerances more efficiently.

Management also foresees significant savings in materials and inventory costs. The cutting of steel, a large-scale operation in the bigger shops, should also become progressively more automated. The cutting and punching of steel is often still done by an operator using templates and judging by sight how to minimize waste in laying them out. Templates an d operator judgement have begun to be replaced by computer-instructed cutting machines, where the computer calculates the most economical distribution of cuts. Templates and operator judgement have begun to be replaced by computer-instructed cutting machines, where the computer calculates the most economical distribution of cuts. The computer memory also records odd pieces of steel that might be used in future work.

With template labour and layout estimation by an operator eliminated, five times as much steel may be processed in the same period as previously. Also, material savings of up to 60 per cent are expected. In welding operations, robots are increasingly being used, but for complex surfaces, skilled welders who may be subject to certification are still necessary. The use of a certified welder is frequently required by a code authority, such as the American Society of Mechanical Engineers, or by a customer, such as the U.S. Navy.

Plant managers generally expect more versatile robots, which sense the complexities of the surfaces to be joined, to become available. But the laborsaving potential of such robots hinges upon the extent to which code requirements are modified. The efficiency of auxiliary operations in the industry is also likely to improve. Thus, while many plants feature partially automated storage of parts and components, work stations are still usually supplied by means of manually operated carts or small trucks.

Some plants in the industry which produce in quantity expect to install fully automated storage and delivery systems that convey parts to work stations upon command. Management in one such plant expects labour savings of 50 to 75 per cent, compared with the partially automated system, as well as the near elimination of damage from multiple handling. The occupational composition of the industry's employment is not expected to change very much during the 1980's, except for growth in the proportions of engineers, engineering and science technicians, and computer specialists. Employment in these occupational categories has been projected by the Bureau of Labour Statistics to rise 27 per cent between 1980 and 1990, compared with a 15-per cent increase for employment in the industry as a whole. The proportion of craftworkers and operatives has been projected to remain unchanged.

The projections signify increased reliance upon engineers and technicians in designing and monitoring more efficient production processes. The projections do not, however, indicate an accelerating trend towards either "deskilling" craftworkers or displacing operatives. In 1990, craftworkers will constitute an estimated 16 per cent of total industry employment, and operatives, 48 per cent-the same as in 1980. The proportion of professional, technical, and related workers in the industry is estimated to rise from 8 per cent to just under 9 per cent.

AIR CONDITIONING SYSTEMS

THE ROLE OF EXPERT SYSTEMS

As more and more companies strive to become competitive, the philosophy and concept of total quality management has been receiving increased attention by practitioners as well as academic researchers. The Council on Competitiveness in its report "Building on Baldrige: American Quality for the 21st Century," states that while there is no fixed definition of quality, the Baldrige Award Criteria defines a framework for TQM. It also suggests that the Baldrige Award Programme, having galvanized U.S. quality efforts, is positioned to become the vehicle to stimulate and coordinate efforts to expand quality as a national priority.

The focus of this paper is on two elements of this framework: information and analysis, and process management. Specifically, this paper will briefly review the role of information and analysis in organizations operating under the total quality management model and will examine in detail the role of expert systems in supporting and improving the management of processes. Many believe that information and analysis is critical to an organization's survival. In the words of Tracy Omdahl, a Baldrige Award examiner, "Without information and analysis, a company is blind, deaf, and mute to the world around it; it will not be a competitor and will probably not survive the adverse business environments of the 1990s". Curt Reiman, director of the Baldrige Award Programme suggests that "as chief information officers dig into the Baldrige Award Criteria they may be shocked to see all the [TQM] trails that lead to their doors, because information is the air that quality breathes". Carlson and McNurlin echo this observation and suggest that new partnerships are developing between functional managers and IS services as TQM programmes are realizing that they need new information systems to support them.

In this paper, the authors, using a TQM model adopted from the Baldrige Criteria, will:

- Review the critical role of information and analysis in TQM organizations; and
- Examine in detail the role of ESs in four areas of process management. Numerous examples obtained through a survey will be presented.

THE ROLE OF INFORMATION AND ANALYSIS IN TQM ORGANIZATIONS

As a basis of our discussion of the role of information and analysis in TQM environments, we have adopted the model of the Malcolm Baldrige National Quality Award. This is unquestionably the most prestigious quality award in the U.S., and its rigour and comprehensiveness are well recognized. Juran, the Baldrige Award Criteria compose the most widely accepted definition of what is included in TQM.

In the Driver the senior executive leadership sets directions, creates values, expectations, and systems to pursue the two basic aims of the organizational goal: excellence in customer and marketplace performance and in business performance.

The pursuit of the goal is accomplished through the system which translates the leadership's direction into goals, objectives, and critical success factors through strategic planning; develops the necessary processes; creates the appropriate human resources; and aligns the processes and human resources to the strategic directions through information and analysis. The key role of information and analysis is made abundantly clear in the Baldrige Criteria: "Information and Analysis is the focal point within the criteria for all key information to drive the improvement of overall performance and company competitiveness.

In simplest terms, Category 2.0 is the "brain centre" for the alignment of a company's information system with its strategic directions. The category addresses the information and analysis requirements for performance improvement based upon the improvement of key processes...." This key role of information and analysis is clearly depicted, which shows category 2.0 connecting all parts and permeating the entire framework.

The information and analysis category in the Baldrige Criteria is subdivided into three items: 2.1 Management of Information and Data; 2.2 Competitive Comparisons and Benchmarking; and 2.3 Analysis and Use of Company-level Data. Item 2.1 which is the focus of our paper, addresses the company's selection and management of information and data to support overall business goals with primary emphasis on supporting process management and performance improvement. As such, item 2.1 represents a key foundation for a performance-oriented company.

ROLE OF EXPERT SYSTEMS IN MANAGING PROCESSES

Executive information systems, expert systems, and decision support systems can be utilized in supporting strategic planning of total quality management, human resources management, and supporting top management leadership. Franz and Foster have developed a decision support and expert system called the total quality management system to assist management in the design of an integrated TQM programme and in developing a TQM strategy. Need for executive information systems in TQM organizations has been analysed by Eom, Karathanos, and Stough.

As suggested, examine how and to which areas expert systems can be deployed in TQM organizations to effectively manage TQM processes. Needless to say, all these management support systems must be built on the sound foundations of other information systems, including quality databases, to continuously update quality-related information and computer-controlled quality measurement systems to compute various quality measurement routines. The Baldrige Award Criteria, the process management category examines how key processes are designed, effectively managed, and improved to achieve higher performance.

The Baldrige Criteria subdivide this overall area into four items as follows:

1. Design and Introduction of Products and Services
2. *Process Management*: Product and Service Production and Delivery
3. *Process Management*: Support Services
4. Management of Supplier Performance

These four items are briefly described in this part, and real-world examples of operational expert system implementations in each of the four process management areas are presented. These examples were obtained from a survey by Eom. The survey compiled a bibliography of 441 operational ES applications based on several previous surveys in books and the following three on-line databases-ABI/INFORM, Management Contents, and INSPEC. The survey, which provides a macro view of ES use in business between 1980 and 1993, offers ample evidence suggesting that expert systems are an innovative technology for helping knowledge workers manages problems in many domains. Many ESs have profound impacts, shrinking the time for tasks from days to hours, minutes, or seconds. Non-quantifiable benefits include improved customer satisfaction, improved quality of products and services, and accurate and consistent decision making. Few business areas are untouched by ESs, which have become indispensable tools for effective management.

DESIGN AND INTRODUCTION OF PRODUCTS AND SERVICES

This item asks a company to describe:

- How products, services, and production/delivery processes are designed including how customer requirements are translated into product and service design requirements; how products and services design requirements are translated into efficient and effective production/delivery processes, including an appropriate measurement plan; and how all requirements associated with products, services, and production/delivery processes are addressed early in design by all appropriate company units, suppliers, and partners to ensure integration, coordination, and capability.

- How product, service, and production/delivery process designs are reviewed or tested in detail to ensure trouble-free and rapid introduction.
- How designs and design processes are evaluated and improved to achieve better product and service quality, time to market, and production and delivery process effectiveness.
- ES Translate Customer Requirements into design requirements and thereby improve the Design and Introduction of Quality Products and Services.

Expert systems are used to automate the design of numerous products such as aerospace vehicles, air cylinders, automobiles and numerous automotive parts, computer systems, drug formulations, electronic chips, elevator systems, optical lenses, etc. In the service industry, ESs are being used to design financial products that combine swaps and options in different currencies to procure capital with minimum risk and with interest. One important reason for the use of ESs here is that they can translate customer requirements into design requirements.

Customer needs and product specifications change and in turn, must be translated into changes in engineering design. ESs can help not only design components faster in response to changing customer needs, but also help improve quality to exceed the customer's expectation. For example, Nippon Steel, the world's largest, developed and implemented the quality-design expert system to meet the increasingly complex customer demands concerning increased quality, different product size, new product order made of a new material or new dimensions, fast delivery time, and so on.

The QDES is built on several reasoning methods such as design based on the most similar past case, evaluations with uncertain knowledge, and learning by experience. The QDES has brought several significant benefits: the design cycle time has been reduced by 85 per cent, and the accuracy of design is 30 per cent improved.

The system has also been used as an on-the-job training tool. Many product design expert systems are targeted to companies that sell complex, option-rich products, such as computer and capital-equipment manufacturers, and to those that sell standard products that can be purchased in a variety of sizes and materials, such as window, door, and furniture manufacturers. Many such expert systems ensure customers get correctly priced and specified products by translating user requirements into quotations and orders. EzXpert, an example of such configurator expert systems, puts a salesperson through a question-and-answer session and prompts the salesperson to enter customer requirements information such as performance specifications, dimensions, and product options.

PROCESS MANAGEMENT-PRODUCT AND SERVICE PRODUCTION AND DELIVERY

This item asks a company to describe:

- How the company maintains the performance of key production and delivery processes to ensure that such processes meet design requirements addressed in item 5.1, including the key processes and their principal requirements; and the measurement plan and how measurements or observations are used to maintain process performance.
- How processes are evaluated and improved to improve products and services and to achieve better performance, including cycle time. Include how each of the following is used or considered: process analysis and research; benchmarking; alternative technology; and information from customers within and outside the company.
- ESs can increase productivity in automating manufacturing process from process planning to controlling production systems.

ESs are increasingly used to increase productivity in automating many production functions: process planning, capacity planning, facility layout planning, design, diagnosis and troubleshooting, monitoring, and controlling production and operations management systems. Process planning is a major bottleneck in the integration of computer aided design and computer aided manufacturing. Expert systems are used to automate process planning, which consists of selecting the assembly sequence, generating a corresponding process plan, and identifying the resources needed. Such ESs bridge CAD and CAM systems by automatically converting the design specification of a product into a process plan without human intervention.

In real-time process control, ESs are widely used to autonomously handle elementary assembly operations, automatic cell control, and stochastic control problems.

For example, General Motors has used an expert engineering design system, Dexpert, to design and manufacture a component of custom motors used in windshield wipers, door locks, and other items, which resulted in faster, higher-quality design, and substantial increase of the life expectancy of a motor. Statistical process control has been a long tradition in manufacturing industry.

This method relies on identifying the usual process variability and exceptional or abnormal variations in a process signal. Distinguishing these two types of variations is a probabilistic decision that demands knowledge of the normal process variability.

In a complex manufacturing process, such as aluminum sheet rolling, several process variables need to be examined simultaneously-equipment performance, operator procedures, environmental factors, product properties, etc. Alcoa Technical Centre developed an expert system called Prosaic, which combines statistical process control theory with the knowledge of process to manage the complex aluminum manufacturing process consistently. Real-time expert systems monitor hundreds or thousands of variables concurrently, respond predictably within a few seconds, and reason under pressure in such process-control situations as the emergency management of nuclear reactors. As ES-related technologies evolve, as suggested, see real-time process-control expert systems that can respond within milliseconds.

ESS CAN INCREASE PRODUCTIVITY IN MANAGING MANUFACTURING LOGISTICS AND IN MANAGING PHYSICAL DISTRIBUTION OF PRODUCTS

Managing manufacturing logistics is an important part of manufacturing process management. Essential goals of process management in TQM organization include how the performance of key production or delivery processes should be managed to increase product throughput, ensure on-time delivery of products, and improve quality.

Due to the ever-increasing technical complexity of manufacturing processes, industry has emphasized manufacturing logistics and information systems as a key to achieving these goals. Manufacturing logistics is concerned with "the moving, supplying, and processing of lots as they are transformed from raw materials into finished goods." IBM developed the Logistics Management Systems [LMS], a real-time, transaction-based, knowledge-based decision support and expert systems, to schedule, monitor, and control the manufacturing flow of the company's semiconductor facility near Burlington, Vermont.

The benefits of the LMS include an increase in product output of about 35 per cent and savings of about $10 million in capital expenditure. In addition to the case of IBM, there are many more examples of ESs in managing manufacturing logistics. Digital Equipment Corporation, for example, developed a system called Movers to control industrial robots that deliver work-in-progress items. Unisys, USA implemented a system, LIMA to quickly develop a plan for maintaining inventory levels of manufacturing parts.

In the area of physical distribution, the French National Railway Company in France developed and deployed an ES, CARAIBE, to generate rotation and maintenance schedules of freight cars. Ship Planning System at the Port of Singapore's terminal has been an effective tool for planning, discharging, and loading of container ships. A large number of applications were reported in managing railway traffic. For example, Gare de l'Est in Paris developed an expert system, GESPI, for railway traffic planning in a large station. Other interesting applications include the DOLRS, which was jointly developed by Target Stores and IBM in scheduling shipments to the distribution centres.

ESs are used in diagnosing problems in many products such as air conditioning systems, aluminum corrosion, appliances, robots, automobile engines, inertial navigation systems, computerized numerical control machines, direct-access storage devices, electrical and mechanical equipment, hydraulic systems, gas-turbine generators, industrial equipment, personal computer boards, printers, rotating machinery, Space Shuttle, transformers, telephone trunk lines, toothpaste tube machines, turbomachinery, textile machinery, and Xerox copiers.

PROCESS MANAGEMENT-SUPPORT SERVICES

This item asks a company to describe:

- *How key support service processes are designed, including*: how key requirements are determined or set; how these requirements are translated into efficient and effective processes, including operational requirements and an appropriate measurement plan; and how all requirements are addressed early in design by all appropriate company units to ensure integration, coordination, and capability.
- How the company maintains the performance of key support service processes to ensure that such processes meet design requirements, including: the key processes and their principal requirements; and the measurement plan and how measurements are used to maintain process performance.
- How processes are evaluated and improved to achieve better performance, including cycle time, addressing how each of the following is used or considered: process analysis and research; benchmarking; use of alternative technology; and information from customers within and outside the company.

ESS INCREASE PRODUCTIVITY IN MANAGING PROCESS OF SUPPORT SERVICES

Support services encompass a wide array of functions such as accounting and finance, management information systems, supplies, legal services, plant and facilities management, research and development, and administrative services. In accounting and auditing, ESs are used to plan corporate income taxes, transfer prices, sales taxes, and excise taxes, and to plan and automate audits. They are also used in planning personal finances and multinational corporations' income tax. In the area of finance, ESs are used for analysing commercial loan applications appraising residential property, evaluating investment proposals, interpreting financial statements, reviewing and granting credit, processing credit-card applications, authorizing purchases, analysing financial risks, planning personal finances, processing interbank transactions, budgeting capital, predicting financial health and bankruptcy, underwriting insurance policies, and monitoring the stock market.

In information systems, ESs are used in the design of logical databases, telecommunication systems, knowledge based systems, and software prototypes. In the area of legal services, ESs review procedures for complying with the U.K. value added tax laws and for processing pensions under different state and local government tax laws; identify, organize and document legal requirements for commercial mortgage loan transactions; and render advice on the legal aspects of trade transactions between the U.S. and Canada. In research and development, expert systems have also been used to analyse, design, and construct information systems for scheduling and staffing development projects; to evaluate industrial investment projects and such business proposals as new product development, major strategic investments, and buying or leasing equipment; to estimate project development costs; and to answer technical questions from system developers.

SUPPLIER QUALITY

This item asks a company to describe:

- The company's requirements and how they are communicated to suppliers, including: a brief summary of the principal requirements for key suppliers, the measures or indicators associated with these requirements, and the expected performance levels; how the company determines whether or not its requirements are met by suppliers; and how performance information is fed back to suppliers.
- How the company evaluates and improves its management of supplier relationships and performance, including current actions and plans to achieve the following: improve suppliers' abilities to meet requirements; improve the company's own procurement processes, including provide feedback sought from suppliers and other units within the company and how such feedback is used; and minimize costs associated with inspection, test, audit, or other approaches used to track and verify supplier performance.

Management of supplier quality is another area of concern for process management. The term "supplier" broadly refers to distributors, dealers, warranty repair services, transportation concerns, contractors, and franchises as well as service suppliers such as health care, training, and education. In this area, Ford Motor Company developed the ESCAPE system to assist in the validation process of over 80,000 incoming warranty claims every night submitted by Ford dealers around the world. The ESCAPE system in combination with programming languages such as COBOL verifies vehicle type, production date, mileage, parts and labour costs and other data for a particular type of warranty cover.

MAJOR BENEFITS OF EXPERT SYSTEMS

Numerous benefits of expert systems include increased productivity, consistent outputs, and improved quality. A survey by Eom identified many different levels of effects of expert systems in increasing physical or mental capabilities, ranging from a tenfold productivity increase to a 484-fold increase. There is no quick fix to become the best-of-the-best in any industry.

No single factor is sufficient to assure the success of a TQM programme. This article has reviewed the critical role of information and analysis in TQM organizations and examined in detail the role of ESs in four areas of process management.

Numerous examples obtained through a survey have been presented. We have shown that ESs are indeed a revolutionary tool that extend physical and mental limitations drastically. Several hours or several days of hard work can be performed by ESs to shrink the completion time of the given tasks to several seconds, as the Dun and Bradstreet example showed. The growth of ES utilization shown by the survey could not have happened without reasonable returns on investments. In view of the strategic value of ESs, it is time to think about how your organization harnesses this technology to gain a competitive edge. ES can be integrated with conventional systems through the creation of hybrid systems.

An ES can be combined with an existing conventional system, or other emerging technologies such as multimedia systems, artificial neural networks, pattern recognition and image processing systems, and so on. Integrating ESs into TQM information systems is crucial to effectively manage the organization's processes under dynamic business conditions. To realise these enormous benefits from ESs, top management must commit investment to this emerging technology.

5

Managing Processes Foreign Exchange in Hospitality

QUALITY IN HOTELS

Ad hoc training and quality control have been common in hotels for centuries. Systematic training, as explained in the previous section, is a prerequisite to implementing a quality assurance management system. Ad hoc training is merely unplanned training and ad hoc quality control is mostly a post-process checking action. These are not adequate to ensure quality standards to achieve ISO 9002 certification. A few hotels have, in the past, implemented steps to introduce "quality circles", essentially a Japanese concept with proven results in Japanese or similar cultures.

Dube et al. (2000) carried out an extensive review of the quality of lodging operations in the United States and noted that functional areas such as human resources, operations, corporate management and marketing receive more attention from management of hotels. They also noted that in the deluxe segment of hotels, the majority of best practices involved operations and human resources. Enz and Siguan (2000) examined thirteen champions in the lodging industry and analysed their best practices.

The service-quality "champions" employed a variety of approaches, frequently in combination. Some of the "champions", for example, worked on weaving key tenets into the fabric of the organization in an effort to disseminate service excellence standards and ingrain employees with them. Others focused on empowering employees to provide whatever service the employee deemed necessary to create guest satisfaction. Ritz-Carlton Hotels, for example, empowers all employees to spend up to US$2,000 to solve a guest problem, if needed. Although such initiatives are noted from hotels in different parts of the world to ensure quality service to guests, the popularity of ISO 9002 in the global hospitality industry has not been a phenomenal success. Up to late 1998, only 865 ISO 9002 certificates were issued to hotels and restaurants worldwide (ISO, 1998).

HOTEL OPERATIONS

Maintaining standardization and required quality in the hospitality industry is very complex. A usual hotel has two main operations: rooms division (bell desk, guest services, reception, business centre, telephone switchboard, rooms, suites, laundry, public areas, etc.) and food and beverage operations (kitchen, restaurant, bars, night clubs, banquet and conference facilities, room service, minibars, kitchen stewarding, etc.).

The other departments (marketing, finance, human resources, engineering, security, computer systems, etc.) provide essential support services to rooms division and food and beverage operations. It is generally accepted that food and beverage operation is the most complex operation in a hotel. This is because it includes departments and sections where the quality of products and services is more visible, more difficult to maintain and can easily affect a hotel's image.

Apart from the quality of food and beverage products, longer operating hours, better quality linen, cutlery, crockery, glassware, design, wider choice of food and beverage items, better quality print of menu cards and beverage lists, more tasteful décor, better operating equipment, better tailored uniforms and better calibre of staff (in general) can be noticed in restaurants situated in five-star hotels in comparison with hotels of lower grades. The food and beverage service in five-star hotels has become more complex and challenging owing to the important fact that this class of clientele certainly pay much more money and in return expect a different and better service/ product.

A survey carried out a few years ago revealed that waiting staff thought that expert serving techniques were the most important features of their work. The customers surveyed, on the other hand, indicated that what they valued most in a waiter was a smiling, agreeable, welcoming blend of social qualities. This does not mean that techniques are not important, since many guests appreciate a high level of practical skills and expect a fully professional service. However, the waiting staff who merchandise a "meal experience" must cultivate friendliness, good manners and the relevant social skills.

The quality of food and beverage service is a combination of predictions and characteristics on which an individual assesses whether the service will give satisfaction each time it is used, based on the guest's own set of values. A quality standard in food and beverage operations is a combination of characteristics accepted by the consensus of market segments as being appropriate to provide satisfaction for their particular purposes.

Therefore, it is important to base policy decisions with regard to quality standards of food and beverage service in a hotel or restaurant on identified and anticipated specific customer needs through research. Hospitality organizations seeking to ensure the continuous quality of their service processes should embark on quality assurance management systems. Only through a systematic process can a hotel achieve a globally accepted quality standard.

QUALITY ASSURANCE

Terms such as five-star, deluxe, high standards, good service, and fair value for money mean totally different things to different people and are therefore meaningless until they are defined in clear, precise terms. Yet expensive hotel investments and crucial marketing decisions are often described with these phrases.

Potential quality can be affected by technical and behavioural factors within organizations and from the environment. It is important to determine the variables that can be manipulated to control these factors, such as design of service process, selection, training, supervision, communication, peer relationships and rewards to ensure sustained quality assurance in hotels.

LE MERIDIEN JAMAICA PEGASUS HOTEL

In October 1998, the largest and premier business hotel in Jamaica, Le Meridien Jamaica Pegasus, became the first hotel in the Caribbean to achieve certification to ISO 9002 Quality Management Standards. This property, referred to as the Pegasus, has 350 rooms and at that time had 400 employees. A unique characteristic of the hotel is the exceptionally long years of service by many senior employees. In 1998 the average length of service to the Pegasus was sixteen years by the first line managers and nine years by the second line managers.

The hotel has four restaurants, two bars, a large ballroom, nine meeting rooms, a gym, two tennis courts, two swimming pools, a jogging track and a shopping arcade. The Pegasus opened in 1972 and has been managed by the same hotel company, Forte Plc. in the United Kingdom, for the last twenty-nine years. During this period, owing to changes within the managing company, the Pegasus underwent two name changes; in 1992 as "Forte Grand" and in 1997 as "Le Meridien". The second rebranding was more crucial, as to reach Le Meridien standards the hotel had to do considerable upgrading and staff training.

In addition to the challenging rebranding process in 1997, the hotel was also faced with a financial problem triggered by an increase of four-star hotel rooms in Kingston by 42 per cent and a decrease of tourist arrivals to Kingston. The occupancy level was around 60 per cent for a few years, but owing to the increase in room capacity in the city, a price war had started. This resulted in the average room rate falling from US$100 to around US$83.

Giving in to union demands and agreeing to above-inflation salary increases in the past had resulted in payroll cost (as a percentage of revenue) increasing from 22 per cent in 1995 to 32 per cent in 1997. The bottom line impact of these challenges was that the profitability of the hotel gradually dropped from 22 per cent in 1993 to an alarming 8 per cent in 1997.

As a survival strategy the management was compelled to restructure the operations. While there is nothing new to the downsizing phenomenon, the incidence of organization downsizing has increased considerably in recent years. Commentators warn of the potentially damaging effects of downsizing and redundancy programmes on the survivors and the culture of downsized organizations. The management decided to make 18 per cent of the permanent staff redundant. A bold counterproposal of an unprecedented wage freeze was sent to the union who were demanding a 40 per cent wage increase. The climate was not appropriate for introducing a quality management system that required high labour moral, motivation and commitment. However, the rebranding to Le Meridien and upgrading of the hotel had been committed with the owners. An official launching of "Le Meridien" (by the prime minister of Jamaica) for the end of 1997 had been confirmed.

In this context, the management decided to go ahead with the following during the 1997/1998 financial year:

- Redundancy of fifty-one employees
- Not changing the wage freeze stand in union negotiations
- Frequent frank dialogue with the employees with regards to the financial problems faced by the company and working together in "quality circles" to solve operational problems
- Internal marketing and public relations to convince the employees that quality assurance is the key to solving the financial problems
- Implementing the planned product upgrade
- Completion of the rebranding process by the end of 1997
- Introducing the ISO 9002 Quality Management system as a foundation for the future
- Reviewing the possibility of obtaining four-diamond grading by the American Automobile Association (AAA) and the Green Globe Award within three years

VISION FOR THE FUTURE

The management decided to pay special attention to training and development of a quality culture at the Pegasus. The vision was that this culture would be the backbone of the future quality standards achievements. It was considered important for this backbone to be strengthened with strategic inputs and quality inputs of the desired standards. At the same time this backbone (quality culture) should be strong enough to hold the present (organizational culture) and the future (vision) together.

QUALITY POLICY

The labour dispute at that time arose as a result of the union's refusal to accept a proposal for a moratorium by the management. In spite of the labour dispute, the management won the support of the employees for the quality vision and 300 employees signed a quality policy, which has been displayed in the lobby of the Pegasus for the last four years. The policy, which was developed with input from the 300 employees, states: Le Meridien Jamaica Pegasus is committed to being the best up market business hotel in the Caribbean; by consistently delivering Le Meridien quality product and service standards, satisfying guest expectations, whilst building employee morale and achieving profit objectives. The agreed slogan is, "The Best Is Getting Better".

QUALITY ACTION

The following ten "commandments" related to the quality policy were developed with input from the 300 employees:

1. Make decisions based on findings from internal quality audits, guest surveys, employee surveys and Le Meridien quality audits.
2. Communicate the company policies and business objectives to all employees.
3. Employ skilled, committed and service oriented people with warm and friendly attitudes.
4. Train, develop, empower, reward and facilitate employees to achieve quality objectives.
5. Analyse productivity of the departments and take timely action to improve efficiency and profitability.
6. Satisfy shareholders by increasing the stock value.
7. Implement good public relations with all segments of the community.
8. Hold regular employee meetings to encourage innovative and creative thinking that will challenge conventional thoughts and practices.
9. Ensure that international standards with a European flavour, blended with the local culture, are implemented.
10. Implement ISO 9002 standards, receive and retain certification over the years.

The framed quality policy and quality actions are displayed in each department, section and office of the Pegasus.

COMMUNICATION

Communication is the key to success in any process of change. For twelve months, quality and ISO 9002 became items on the agenda of many regular meetings, such as:

- Morning briefing (20 minutes – standing) – five times a week with all departmental managers
- Le Meridien/quality meeting (60 minutes) – once a week with departmental managers

- Purchasing/project meeting (40 minutes) – once a week with five executives
- All managers meeting (60 minutes) – once a month
- Managers and union delegates meeting (60 minutes) – once a month

The Le Meridien/quality meeting was a new meeting created to coordinate rebranding and implementing ISO 9002 during the 1997/1998 financial year.

QUALITY ANALYSIS

Qualitative analysis of all corrective action forms (for every guest complaint) has to be done once a month as part of the ISO 9002 system. Corrective action forms are discussed at the morning briefings and with the use of a log, follow-up action is monitored by the general manager. The commitment from the general manager is essential for the system to work effectively and productively. Guest questionnaires, too, are analysed and distributed to all managers and departments once a month.

FOUNDATION FOR THE FUTURE

The key hotel activities and external factors that had an impact on the hotel's performance from April 1997 to March 1998 are summarized below.

PEOPLE

- A Le Meridien trainer from Paris trained thirty employees as on-the-job trainers and a series of training programmes for other employees was conducted by the trainers and management using Le Meridien manuals as guidelines.
- Twenty-three employees were trained as quality auditors to audit the quality of the operations of other departments.
- Good relationships were maintained with the union and employees in spite of prolonged wage negotiations and resulting industrial actions.
- Seven managers underwent brief training/exposure at Le Meridien New Orleans in the United States.
- Employees of the year were sent to Paris and London to join other employees of the year from seventy-three Le Meridien hotels on an award tour of exposure.
- The executive chef won an award "For Excellence in Food Preparation, Delivery and Presentation" during 1997, from the Jamaica Observer newspaper.

PRODUCT

- Le Meridien image, service and product standards were introduced and the hotel was rebranded as Le Meridien Jamaica Pegasus on

October 9, 1997 with the prime minister of Jamaica as the guest of honour.

- Various projects were undertaken to implement the essential upgrading. These included complete refurbishment of two bedroom floors, installation of a new chiller, installation of a new fire alarm system, painting the building exterior, upgrading of tennis courts, upgrading of gardens and public areas, etc.
- Food and beverage concepts were changed. The coffee shop was upgraded and a section was air-conditioned, the gourmet restaurant concept was fine-tuned to blend with the historic significance of Port Royal and the wine club was transformed into a pizza cellar. All menus were changed.
- The ISO 9002 Quality Management system was introduced. The hotel developed a quality policy with input from most of its employees.
- The hotel continued to be the focal point of social activities in Kingston, often being chosen as the location for major banquets. The hotel continued organizing food festivals and other major events, including 101 holiday events during the last 38 days in 1997.
- The hotel won the Jamaica Observer newspaper's first ever "Table talk" food award for the "Food Event of the Year".
- The Le Meridien mystery guest programme, with a 1,000 point checklist, was introduced by internally arranged monthly mystery guests.

PROMOTIONS

- Room reservations, banquet bookings, sales, public relations and advertising were combined and a new marketing department was created with the objective of being more aggressive in marketing.
- The start of the twenty-fifth year of operations of the hotel was celebrated with the governor general of Jamaica as the guest of honour.
- Management sales calls to local clients were accelerated.
- The hotel continued to be the focal point during the Jamaica Carnival. A "wet-feete" was held at the hotel as part of the carnival celebrations.
- A major wedding expo was held.
- Le Meridien promoted the hotel in its regional and worldwide publications, sales and advertising campaigns.
- The hotel continued to be in the limelight through planned public relations and publicity.
- Familiarization tours were arranged for Le Meridien vice president–sales, sales director, and reservation agents, to Washington, D.C., New York and London.

- Frequent participation in Le Meridien sales conferences and planned sales trips to North America, South America and Europe.
- Participation in Le Meridien sales promotion activities.

PROFIT

- Towards the end of the financial year, British Airways reduced the allotment of thirty-four rooms per day to six rooms per day as most crew members were provided accommodation in Montego Bay instead of Kingston.
- The number of rooms in Kingston was increased by 32 per cent and the four-star category rooms were increased by 42 per cent within a year. At the same period, the arrivals to Kingston were reduced by 2 per cent. With the supply of rooms in Kingston greatly exceeding the demand, the hotel experienced revenue problems. The hotel undertook major restructuring and re-engineering, affecting fifty-one job positions (18 per cent of the total permanent workforce), which were made redundant. The hotel spent J$11 million as redundancy payments, but was able to recover this within eight months from the savings on labour cost.
- For seven months, the hotel held its position of a wage freeze against the union demand for a 40 per cent wage increase for year one and a 35 per cent increase for year two, for line employees. After two "sit ins" and a strike, the matter was referred to the Industrial Disputes Tribunal and a 7.5 per cent wage increase for year one and a 7.5 per cent increase for year two were awarded. This is a "landmark" award in the Jamaican hotel industry as salary increases in hotels had been in the range of 30 per cent to 60 per cent for many years prior to this award. As a result of this award, a single-digit wage increase has become the norm in the Jamaican hotel industry today.

FOREIGN EXCHANGE

Authorised dealers may remit foreign exchange upto a reasonable limit, at the request of a traveller towards his hotel accommodation, tour arrangements, etc., in the countries proposed to be visited by him, provided it is out of the foreign exchange purchased by the traveller from an authorised person (including exchange drawn for private travel abroad) in accordance with the Rules, Regulations and Directions in force.

Authorised dealers may effect remittances at the request of agents in India who have tie up arrangements with hotels/agents, etc., abroad for providing hotel accommodations or making other tour arrangements for travellers from India provided the authorised dealer is satisfied that the remittance is being made out of the foreign exchange purchased by the concerned traveller from an authorised person (including exchange drawn for private travel abroad) in accordance with the Rules, Regulations and Directions in force. Authorised dealer may open foreign currency accounts in the name of agents in India who have tie up arrangements with hotels/agents, etc., abroad for providing hotel accommodations or making other tour arrangements for travellers from India provided:

- The credits to the account are by way of depositing
- Collections made in foreign exchange from travellers, and
- Refunds received from outside India on account of cancellation of bookings/tour arrangements, etc., and
- the debits in foreign exchange are for making payments towards hotel accommodation, tour arrangements, etc., outside India, in accordance with (ii) above.

An Act to consolidate and amend the law relating to foreign exchange with the objective of facilitating external trade and payments and for promoting the orderly development and maintenance of foreign exchange market in India.

SHORT TITLE, EXTENT, APPLICATION AND COMMENCEMENT

- This Act may be called the Foreign Exchange Management Act, 1999.
- It extends to the whole of India.
- It shall also apply to all branches, offices and agencies outside India owned or controlled by a person resident in India and also to any contravention thereunder committed outside India by any person to whom this Act applies.
- It shall come into force on such date as the Central Government may, by notification in the Official Gazette, appoint: Provided that different dates may be appointed for different provisions of this Act and any reference in any such provision to the commencement of this Act shall be construed as a reference to the coming into force of that provision.

  In this Act, unless the context otherwise requires:
  - "Adjudicating Authority" means an officer authorised under sub-section (1) of section 16;
  - "Appellate Tribunal" means the Appellate Tribunal for Foreign Exchange established under section 18;
  - "Authorised person" means an authorised dealer, money changer, off-shore banking unit or any other person for the time being authorised under sub-section (1) of section 10 to deal in foreign exchange or foreign securities;
  - "Bench" means a Bench of the Appellate Tribunal;
  - "capital account transaction" means a transaction which alters the

assets or liabilities, including contingent liabilities, outside India of persons resident in India or assets or liabilities in India of persons resident outside India, and includes transactions referred to in sub-section (3) of section 6;

- "Chairperson" means the Chairperson of the Appellate Tribunal;
- "Chartered accountant" shall have the meaning assigned to it in clause (b) of sub-section (1) of section 2 of the Chartered Accountants Act, 1949 (38 of 1949);
- "Currency" includes all currency notes, postal notes, postal orders, money orders, cheques, drafts, travellers cheques, letters of credit, bills of exchange and promissory notes, credit cards or such other similar instruments, as may be notified by the Reserve Bank;
- "Currency notes" means and includes cash in the form of coins and bank notes;
- "Current account transaction" means a transaction other than a capital account transaction and without prejudice to the generality of the foregoing such transaction includes:
  i. Payments due in connection with foreign trade, other current business, services, and short-term banking and credit facilities in the ordinary course of business,
  ii. Payments due as interest on loans and as net income from investments,
  iii. Remittances for living expenses of parents, spouse and children residing abroad, and
  iv. Expenses in connection with foreign travel, education and medical care of parents, spouse and children;
- "Director of Enforcement" means the Director of Enforcement appointed under sub-section (1) of section 36;
- "Export", with its grammatical variations and cognate expressions, means—
  i. The taking out of India to a place outside India any goods,
  ii. Provision of services from India to any person outside India;
- "Foreign currency" means any currency other than Indian currency;
- "Foreign exchange" means foreign currency and includes—
  i. Deposits, credits and balances payable in any foreign currency,
  ii. Drafts, travellers cheques, letters of credit or bills of exchange, expressed or drawn in Indian currency but payable in any foreign currency,
  iii. Drafts, travellers cheques, letters of credit or bills of exchange drawn by banks, institutions or persons outside India, but payable in Indian currency;

- "Foreign security" means any security, in the form of shares, stocks, bonds, debentures or any other instrument denominated or expressed in foreign currency and includes securities expressed in foreign currency, but where redemption or any form of return such as interest or dividends is payable in Indian currency;
- "Import", with its grammatical variations and cognate expressions, means bringing into India any goods or services;
- "Indian currency" means currency which is expressed or drawn in Indian rupees but does not include special bank notes and special one rupee notes issued under section 28A of the Reserve Bank of India Act, 1934 (2 of 1934);
- "Legal practitioner" shall have the meaning assigned to it in clause,
  i. Sub-section (1) of section 2 of the Advocates Act, 1961 (25 of 1961);
- "Member" means a Member of the Appellate Tribunal and includes the Chairperson thereof;
- "Notify" means to notify in the Official Gazette and the expression "notification" shall be construed accordingly;
- *"Person" includes*:
  i. An individual,
  ii. A Hindu undivided family,
  iii. A company,
  iv. A firm,
  v. An association of persons or a body of individuals, whether incorporated or not,
  vi. Every artificial juridical person, not falling within any of the preceding sub-clauses, and
  vii. Any agency, office or branch owned or controlled by such person;

• *"Person resident in India" means*:
  - A person residing in India for more than one hundred and eighty-two days during the course of the preceding financial year but does not include—
    i. A person who has gone out of India or who stays outside India, in either case—
      a. For or on taking up employment outside India, or
      b. For carrying on outside India a business or vocation outside India, or
      c. For any other purpose, in such circumstances as would indicate his intention to stay outside India for an uncertain period;

ii. A person who has come to or stays in India, in either case, otherwise than—
   a. For or on taking up employment in India, or
   b. For carrying on in India a business or vocation in India, or
   c. For any other purpose, in such circumstances as would indicate his intention to stay in India for an uncertain period;

iii. Any person or body corporate registered or incorporated in India,

iv. An office, branch or agency in India owned or controlled by a person resident outside India,

v. An office, branch or agency outside India owned or controlled by a person resident in India;

- "Person resident outside India" means a person who is not resident in India;
- "Prescribed" means prescribed by rules made under this Act;
- "Repatriate to India" means bringing into India the realised foreign exchange and—
  i. The selling of such foreign exchange to an authorised person in India in exchange for rupees, or
  ii. The holding of realised amount in an account with an authorised person in India to the extent notified by the Reserve Bank, and includes use of the realised amount for discharge of a debt or liability denominated in foreign exchange and the expression "repatriation" shall be construed accordingly;
- "Reserve Bank" means the Reserve Bank of India constituted under sub-section (1) of section 3 of the Reserve Bank of India Act, 1934 (2 of 1934);
  i. "Security" means shares, stocks, bonds and debentures, Government securities as defined in the Public Debt Act, 1944 (18 of 1944), savings certificates to which the Government Savings Certificates Act, 1959 (46 of 1959) applies, deposit receipts in respect of deposits of securities and units of the Unit Trust of India established under sub-section (1) of section 3 of the Unit Trust of India Act, 1963 (52 of 1963) or of any mutual fund and includes certificates of title to securities, but does not include bills of exchange or promissory notes other than Government promissory notes or any other instruments which may be notified by the Reserve Bank as security for the purposes of this Act;

(zb) "service" means service of any description which is made available to potential users and includes the provision of facilities in connection with banking, financing, insurance, medical assistance, legal assistance, chit fund, real estate, transport, processing, supply of electrical or other energy, boarding or lodging or both, entertainment, amusement or the purveying of news or other information, but does not include the rendering of any service free of charge or under a contract of personal service; (zc) "Special Director (Appeals)" means an officer appointed under section 18; (zd) "specify" means to specify by regulations made under this Act and the expression "specified" shall be construed accordingly; (ze) "transfer" includes sale, purchase, exchange, mortgage, pledge, gift, loan or any other form of transfer of right, title, possession or lien.

REGULATION AND MANAGEMENT OF FOREIGN EXCHANGE

Save as otherwise provided in this Act, rules or regulations made thereunder, or with the general or special permission of the Reserve Bank, no person shall:

- Deal in or transfer any foreign exchange or foreign security to any person not being an authorised person;
- Make any payment to or for the credit of any person resident outside India in any manner;
- Receive otherwise through an authorised person, any payment by order or on behalf of any person resident outside India in any manner;
  Explanation: For the purpose of this clause, where any person in, or resident in, India receives any payment by order or on behalf of any person resident outside India through any other person (including an authorised person) without a corresponding inward remittance from any place outside India, then, such person shall be deemed to have received such payment otherwise than through an authorised person;
- Enter into any financial transaction in India as consideration for or in association with acquisition or creation or transfer of a right to acquire, any asset outside India by any person.
  Explanation: For the purpose of this clause, "financial transaction" means making any payment to, or for the credit of any person, or receiving any payment for, by order or on behalf of any person, or drawing, issuing or negotiating any bill of exchange or promissory note, or transferring any security or acknowledging any debt.

HOLDING OF FOREIGN EXCHANGE

Save as otherwise provided in this Act, no person resident in India shall acquire, hold, own, possess or transfer any foreign exchange, foreign security or any immovable property situated outside India.

CURRENT ACCOUNT TRANSACTIONS

Any person may sell or draw foreign exchange to or from an authorised person if such sale or drawal is a current account transaction: Provided that the Central Government may, in public interest and in consultation with the Reserve Bank, impose such reasonable restrictions for current account transactions as may be prescribed.

CAPITAL ACCOUNT TRANSACTIONS

- Subject to the provisions of sub-section
- Any person may sell or draw foreign exchange to or from an authorised person for a capital account transaction.
- *The Reserve Bank may, in consultation with the Central Government, specify*:
  - Any class or classes of capital account transactions which are permissible;
  - The limit up to which foreign exchange shall be admissible for such transactions:

    Provided that the Reserve Bank shall not impose any restriction on the drawal of foreign exchange for payments due on account of amortization of loans or for depreciation of direct investments in the ordinary course of business.
- Without prejudice to the generality of the provisions of sub-section (2), the Reserve Bank may, by regulations, prohibit, restrict or regulate the following:
  - Transfer or issue of any foreign security by a person resident in India;
  - Transfer or issue of any security by a person resident outside India;
  - Transfer or issue of any security or foreign security by any branch, office or agency in India of a person resident outside India;
  - Any borrowing or lending in foreign exchange in whatever form or by whatever name called;
  - Any borrowing or lending in rupees in whatever form or by whatever name called between a person resident in India and a person resident outside India;
  - Deposits between persons resident in India and persons resident outside India;

- Export, import or holding of currency or currency notes;
- Transfer of immovable property outside India, other than a lease not exceeding five years, by a person resident in India;
- Acquisition or transfer of immovable property in India, other than a lease not exceeding five years, by a person resident outside India;
- Giving of a guarantee or surety in respect of any debt, obligation or other liability incurred:
  i. By a person resident in India and owed to a person resident outside India; or
  ii. By a person resident outside India.

- A person resident in India may hold, own, transfer or invest in foreign currency, foreign security or any immovable property situated outside India if such currency, security or property was acquired, held or owned by such person when he was resident outside India or inherited from a person who was resident outside India.
- A person resident outside India may hold, own, transfer or invest in Indian currency, security or any immovable property situated in India if such currency, security or property was acquired, held or owned by such person when he was resident in India or inherited from a person who was resident in India.
- Without prejudice to the provisions of this section, the Reserve Bank may, by regulation, prohibit, restrict, or regulate establishment in India of a branch, office or other place of business by a person resident outside India, for carrying on any activity relating to such branch, office or other place of business.

EXPORT OF GOODS AND SERVICES

- *Every exporter of goods shall*:
  - Furnish to the Reserve Bank or to such other authority a declaration in such form and in such manner as may be specified, containing true and correct material particulars, including the amount representing the full export value or, if the full export value of the goods is not ascertainable at the time of export, the value which the exporter, having regard to the prevailing market conditions, expects to receive on the sale of the goods in a market outside India;
  - Furnish to the Reserve Bank such other information as may be required by the Reserve Bank for the purpose of ensuring the realisation of the export proceeds by such exporter.
- The Reserve Bank may, for the purpose of ensuring that the full export value of the goods or such reduced value of the goods as the

Reserve Bank determines, having regard to the prevailing market conditions, is received without any delay, direct any exporter to comply with such requirements as it deems fit.

- Every exporter of services shall furnish to the Reserve Bank or to such other authorities a declaration in such form and in such manner as may be specified, containing the true and correct material particulars in relation to payment for such services.

REALISATION AND REPATRIATION OF FOREIGN EXCHANGE

Save as otherwise provided in this Act, where any amount of foreign exchange is due or has accrued to any person resident in India, such person shall take all reasonable steps to realise and repatriate to India such foreign exchange within such period and in such manner as may be specified by the Reserve Bank.

EXEMPTION FROM REALISATION AND REPATRIATION IN CERTAIN CASES

The provisions of sections 4 and 8 shall not apply to the following, namely:

- Possession of foreign currency or foreign coins by any person up to such limit as the Reserve Bank may specify;
- Foreign currency account held or operated by such person or class of persons and the limit up to which the Reserve Bank may specify;
- Foreign exchange acquired or received before the 8th day of July, 1947 or any income arising or accruing thereon which is held outside India by any person in pursuance of a general or special permission granted by the Reserve Bank;
- Foreign exchange held by a person resident in India up to such limit as the Reserve Bank may specify, if such foreign exchange was acquired by way of gift or inheritance from a person referred to in clause *(c)*, including any income arising therefrom;
- Foreign exchange acquired from employment, business, trade, vocation, services, honourarium, gifts, inheritance or any other legitimate means up to such limit as the Reserve Bank may specify; and
- Such other receipts in foreign exchange as the Reserve Bank may specify.

Authorised Person

- The Reserve Bank may, on an application made to it in this behalf, authorise any person to be known as authorised person to deal in foreign exchange or in foreign securities, as an authorised dealer, money changer or off-shore banking unit or in any other manner as it deems fit.

- An authorisation under this section shall be in writing and shall be subject to the conditions laid down therein.
- An authorisation granted under sub-section (1) may be revoked by the Reserve Bank at any time if the Reserve Bank is satisfied that:
  - It is in public interest so to do; or
  - The authorised person has failed to comply with the condition subject to which the authorisation was granted or has contravened any of the provisions of the Act or any rule, regulation, notification, direction or order made thereunder:

    Provided that no such authorisation shall be revoked on any ground referred to in clause (b) unless the authorised person has been given a reasonable opportunity of making a representation in the matter.
- An authorised person shall, in all his dealings in foreign exchange or foreign security, comply with such general or special directions or orders as the Reserve Bank may, from time to time, think fit to give, and, except with the previous permission of the Reserve Bank, an authorised person shall not engage in any transaction involving any foreign exchange or foreign security which is not in conformity with the terms of his authorisation under this section.
- An authorised person shall, before undertaking any transaction in foreign exchange on behalf of any person, require that person to make such declaration and to give such information as will reasonably satisfy him that the transaction will not involve, and is not designed for the purpose of any contravention or evasion of the provisions of this Act or of any rule, regulation, notification, direction or order made thereunder, and where the said person refuses to comply with any such requirement or makes only unsatisfactory compliance therewith, the authorised person shall refuse in writing to undertake the transaction and shall, if he has reason to believe that any such contravention or evasion as aforesaid is contemplated by the person, report the matter to the Reserve Bank.
- Any person, other than an authorised person, who has acquired or purchased foreign exchange for any purpose mentioned in the declaration made by him to authorised person under sub-section (5) does not use it for such purpose or does not surrender it to authorised person within the specified period or uses the foreign exchange so acquired or purchased for any other purpose for which purchase or acquisition of foreign exchange is not permissible under the provisions of the Act or the rules or regulations or direction or order made

thereunder shall be deemed to have committed contravention of the provisions of the Act for the purpose of this section.

RESERVE BANK'S POWERS TO ISSUE DIRECTIONS TO AUTHORISED PERSON

- The Reserve Bank may, for the purpose of securing compliance with the provisions of this Act and of any rules, regulations, notifications or directions made thereunder, give to the authorised persons any direction in regard to making of payment or the doing or desist from doing any act relating to foreign exchange or foreign security.
- The Reserve Bank may, for the purposc of ensuring the compliance with the provisions of this Act or of any rule, regulation, notification, direction or order made thereunder, direct any authorised person to furnish such information, in such manner, as it deems fit.
- Where any authorised person contravenes any direction given by the Reserve Bank under this Act or fails to file any return as directed by the Reserve Bank, the Reserve Bank may, after giving reasonable opportunity of being heard, impose on the authorised person a penalty which may extend to ten thousand rupees and in the case of continuing contravention with an additional penalty which may extend to two thousand rupees for every day during which such contravention continues.

POWER OF RESERVE BANK TO INSPECT AUTHORISED PERSON

- The Reserve Bank may, at any time, cause an inspection to be made, by any officer of the Reserve Bank specially authorised in writing by the Reserve Bank in this behalf, of the business of any authorised person as may appear to it to be necessary or expedient for the purpose of:
  - Verifying the correctness of any statement, information or particulars furnished to the Reserve Bank;
  - Obtaining any information or particulars which such authorised person has failed to furnish on being called upon to do so;
  - Securing compliance with the provisions of this Act or of any rules, regulations, directions or orders made thereunder.
- It shall be the duty of every authorised person, and where such person is a company or a firm, every director, partner or other officer of such company or firm, as the case may be, to produce to any officer making an inspection under sub-section (1), such books, accounts and other documents in his custody or power and to furnish any statement or information relating to the affairs of such person, company or firm

as the said officer may require within such time and in such manner as the said officer may direct.

CONTRAVENTION AND PENALTIES

- If any person contravenes any provision of this Act, or contravenes any rule, regulation, notification, direction or order issued in exercise of the powers under this Act, or contravenes any condition subject to which an authorisation is issued by the Reserve Bank, he shall, upon adjudication, be liable to a penalty up to thrice the sum involved in such contravention where such amount is quantifiable, or up to two lakh rupees where the amount is not quantifiable, and where such contravention is a continuing one, further penalty which may extend to five thousand rupees for every day after the first day during which the contravention continues.
- Any Adjudicating Authority adjudging any contravention under sub-section (1), may, if he thinks fit in addition to any penalty which he may impose for such contravention direct that any currency, security or any other money or property in respect of which the contravention has taken place shall be confiscated to the Central Government and further direct that the foreign exchange holdings, if any of the persons committing the contraventions or any part thereof, shall be brought back into India or shall be retained outside India in accordance with the directions made in this behalf.

  Explanation: For the purposes of this sub-section, "property" in respect of which contravention has taken place, shall include:
  - Deposits in a bank, where the said property is converted into such deposits;
  - Indian currency, where the said property is converted into that currency; and
  - Any other property which has resulted out of the conversion of that property.

  Enforcement of the orders of Adjudicating Authority.
- Subject to the provisions of sub-section (2) of section 19, if any person fails to make full payment of the penalty imposed on him under section 13 within a period of ninety days from the date on which the notice for payment of such penalty is served on him, he shall be liable to civil imprisonment under this section.
- No order for the arrest and detention in civil prison of a defaulter shall be made unless the Adjudicating Authority has issued and served a notice upon the defaulter calling upon him to appear before him on the date specified in the notice and to show cause why he should not be committed to the civil prison, and unless the Adjudicating

Authority, for reasons in writing, is satisfied:

- That the defaulter, with the object or effect of obstructing the recovery of penalty, has after the issue of notice by the Adjudicating Authority, dishonestly transferred concealed, or removed any part of his property, or
- That the defaulter has, or has had since the issuing of notice by the Adjudicating Authority, the means to pay the arrears or some substantial part thereof and refuses or neglects or has refused or neglected to pay the same.

- Notwithstanding anything contained in sub-section (1), a warrant for the arrest of the defaulter may be issued by the Adjudicating Authority if the Adjudicating Authority is satisfied, by affidavit or otherwise, that with the object or effect of delaying the execution of the certificate the defaulter is likely to abscond or leave the local limits of the jurisdiction of the Adjudicating Authority.
- Where appearance is not made pursuant to a notice issued and served under sub-section (1), the Adjudicating Authority may issue a warrant for the arrest of the defaulter.
- A warrant of arrest issued by the Adjudicating Authority under sub-section (3) or sub-section
- May also be executed by any other Adjudicating Authority within whose jurisdiction the defaulter may for the time being be found.
- Every person arrested in pursuance of a warrant of arrest under this section shall be brought before the Adjudicating Authority issuing the warrant as soon as practicable and in any event within twenty-four hours of his arrest (exclusive of the time required for the journey): Provided that, if the defaulter pays the amount entered in the warrant of arrest as due and the costs of the arrest to the officer arresting him, such officer shall at once release him.

  Explanation: For the purposes of this sub-section, where the defaulter is a Hindu undivided family, the *karta* thereof shall be deemed to be the defaulter.
- When a defaulter appears before the Adjudicating Authority pursuant to a notice to show cause or is brought before the Adjudicating Authority under this section, the Adjudicating Authority shall give the defaulter an opportunity showing cause why he should not be committed to the civil prison.
- Pending the conclusion of the enquiry, the Adjudicating Authority may, in his discretion, order the defaulter to be detained in the custody of such officer as the Adjudicating Authority may think fit or release him on his furnishing the security to the satisfaction of the Adjudicating Authority for his appearance as and when required.

- Upon the conclusion of the enquiry, the Adjudicating Authority may make an order for the detention of the defaulter in the civil prison and shall in that event cause him to be arrested if he is not already under arrest: Provided that in order to give a defaulter an opportunity of satisfying the arrears, the Adjudicating Authority may, before making the order of detention, leave the defaulter in the custody of the officer arresting him or of any other officer for a specified period not exceeding fifteen days, or release him on his furnishing security to the satisfaction of the Adjudicating Authority for his appearance at the expiration of the specified period if the arrears are not satisfied.
- When the Adjudicating Authority does not make an order of detention under sub-section (9), he shall, if the defaulter is under arrest, direct his release.
- Every person detained in the civil prison in execution of the certificate may be so detained,—
  - Where the certificate is for a demand of an amount exceeding rupees one crore, up to three years, and
  - *In any other case, up to six months*: Provided that he shall be released from such detention on the amount mentioned in the warrant for his detention being paid to the officer-in-charge of the civil prison.
- A defaulter released from detention under this section shall not, merely by reason of his release, be discharged from his liability for the arrears, but he shall not be liable to be arrested under the certificate in execution of which he was detained in the civil prison.
- A detention order may be executed at any place in India in the manner provided for the execution of warrant of arrest under the Code of Criminal Procedure, 1973 (2 of 1974).

POWER TO COMPOUND CONTRAVENTION

- Any contravention under section 13 may, on an application made by theperson committing such contravention, be compounded within one hundred and eighty days from the date of receipt of application by the Director of Enforcement or such other officers of the Directorate of Enforcement and Officers of the Reserve Bank as may be authorised in this behalf by the Central Government in such manner as may be prescribed.
- Where a contravention has been compounded under sub-section (1), no proceeding or further proceeding, as the case may be, shall be initiated or continued, as the case may be, against the person committing such contravention under that section, in respect of the contravention so compounded.

APPOINTMENT OF ADJUDICATING AUTHORITY

- For the purpose of adjudication under section 13, the Central Government may, by an order published in the Official Gazette, appoint as many officers of the Central Government as it may think fit, as the Adjudicating Authorities for holding an enquiry in the manner prescribed after giving the person alleged to have committed contravention under section 13, against whom a complaint has been made under sub-section
- Hereinafter in this section referred to as the said person a reasonable opportunity of being heard for the purpose of imposing any penalty: Provided that where the Adjudicating Authority is of opinion that the said person is likely to abscond or is likely to evade in any manner, the payment of penalty, if levied, it may direct the said person to furnish a bond or guarantee for such amount and subject to such conditions as it may deem fit.
- The Central Government shall, while appointing the Adjudicating Authorities under sub-section (1), also specify in the order published in the Official Gazette, their respective jurisdictions.
- No Adjudicating Authority shall hold an enquiry under sub-section (1) except upon a complaint in writing made by any officer authorised by a general or special order by the Central Government.
- The said person may appear either in person or take the assistance of a legal practitioner or a chartered accountant of his choice for presenting his case before the Adjudicating Authority.
- Every Adjudicating Authority shall have the same powers of a civil court which are conferred on the Appellate Tribunal under sub-section (2) of section 28 and:
  - All proceedings before it shall be deemed to be judicial proceedings within the meaning of sections 193 and 228 of the Indian Penal Code (45 of 1860);
  - Shall be deemed to be a civil court for the purposes of sections 345 and 346 of the Code of Criminal Procedure, 1973 (2 of 1974).
- Every Adjudicating Authority shall deal with the complaint under sub-section (2) as expeditiously as possible and endeavour shall be made to dispose of the complaint finally within one year from the date of receipt of the complaint: Provided that where the complaint cannot be disposed off within the said period, the Adjudicating Authority shall record periodically the reasons in writing for not disposing off the complaint within the said period.

APPEAL TO SPECIAL DIRECTOR (APPEALS)

- The Central Government shall, by notification, appoint one or more

Special Directors (Appeals) to hear appeals against the orders of the Adjudicating Authorities under this section and shall also specify in the said notification the matter and places in relation to which the Special Director (Appeals) may exercise jurisdiction.

- Any person aggrieved by an order made by the Adjudicating Authority, being an Assistant Director of Enforcement or a Deputy Director of Enforcement, may prefer an appeal to the Special Director (Appeals).
- Every appeal under sub-section (1) shall be filed within forty-five days from the date on which the copy of the order made by the Adjudicating Authority is received by the aggrieved person and it shall be in such form, verified in such manner and be accompanied by such fee as may be prescribed: Provided that the Special Director (Appeals) may entertain an appeal after the expiry of the said period of forty-five days, if he is satisfied that there was sufficient cause for not filing it within that period.
- On receipt of an appeal under sub-section (1), the Special Director (Appeals) may after giving the parties to the appeal an opportunity of being heard, pass such order thereon as he thinks fit confirming, modifying or setting aside the order appealed against.
- The Special Director (Appeals) shall send a copy of every order made by him to the parties to appeal and to the concerned Adjudicating Authority.
- The Special Director (Appeals) shall have the same powers of a civil court which are conferred on the Appellate Tribunal under sub-section (2) of section 28 and:
  - All proceedings before him shall be deemed to be judicial proceedings within the meaning of sections 193 and 228 of the Indian Penal Code (45 of 1860);
  - Shall be deemed to be a civil court for the purposes of sections 345 and 346 of the Code of Criminal Procedure, 1973 (2 of 1974).

ESTABLISHMENT OF APPELLATE TRIBUNAL

The Central Government shall, by notification, establish an Appellate Tribunal to be known as the Appellate Tribunal for Foreign Exchange to hear appeals against the orders of the Adjudicating Authorities and the Special Director (Appeals) under this Act.

APPEAL TO APPELLATE TRIBUNAL

- Save as provided in sub-section (2), the Central Government or any person aggrieved by an order made by an Adjudicating Authority, other than those referred to sub-section (1) of section 17, or the Special Director (Appeals), may prefer an appeal to the Appellate

Tribunal: Provided that any person appealing against the order of the Adjudicating Authority or the Special Director (Appeals) levying any penalty, shall while filing the appeal, deposit the amount of such penalty with such authority as may be notified by the Central Government: Provided further that where in any particular case, the Appellate Tribunal is of the opinion that the deposit of such penalty would cause undue hardship to such person, the Appellate Tribunal may dispense with such deposit subject to such conditions as it may deem fit to impose so as to safeguard the realisation of penalty.

- Every appeal under sub-section (1) shall be filed within a period of forty-five days from the date on which a copy of the order made by the Adjudicating Authority or the Special Director (Appeals) is received by the aggrieved person or by the Central Government and it shall be in such form, verified in such manner and be accompanied by such fee as may be prescribed: Provided that the Appellate Tribunal may entertain an appeal after the expiry of the said period of forty-five days if it is satisfied that there was sufficient cause for not filing it within that period.
- On receipt of an appeal under sub-section (1), the Appellate Tribunal may, after giving the parties to the appeal an opportunity of being heard, pass such orders thereon as it thinks fit, confirming, modifying or setting aside the order appealed against.
- The Appellate Tribunal shall send a copy of every order made by it to the parties to the appeal and to the concerned Adjudicating Authority or the Special Director (Appeals), as the case may be.
- The appeal filed before the Appellate Tribunal under sub-section (1) shall be dealt with by it as expeditiously as possible and endeavour shall be made by it to dispose of the appeal finally within one hundred and eighty days from the date of receipt of the appeal: Provided that where any appeal could not be disposed of within the said period of one hundred and eighty days, the Appellate Tribunal shall record its reasons in writing for not disposing of the appeal within the said period.
- The Appellate Tribunal may, for the purpose of examining the legality, propriety or correctness of any order made by the Adjudicating Authority under section 16 in relation to any proceeding, on its own motion or otherwise, call for the records of such proceedings and make such order in the case as it thinks fit.

COMPOSITION OF APPELLATE TRIBUNAL

- The Appellate Tribunal shall consist of a Chairperson and such number of Members as the Central Government may deem fit.

- *Subject to the provisions of this Act,*:
  - The jurisdiction of the Appellate Tribunal may be exercised by Benches thereof;
  - A Bench may be constituted by the Chairperson with one or more Members as the Chairperson may deem fit;
  - The Benches of the Appellate Tribunal shall ordinarily sit at New Delhi and at such other places as the Central Government may, in consultation with the Chairperson, notify;
  - The Central Government shall notify the areas in relation to which each Bench of the Appellate Tribunal may exercise jurisdiction.
- Notwithstanding anything contained in sub-section (2), the Chairperson may transfer a Member from one Bench to another Bench.
- If at any stage of the hearing of any case or matter it appears to the Chairperson or a Member that the case or matter is of such a nature that it ought to be heard by a Bench consisting of two Members, the case or matter may be transferred by the Chairperson or, as the case may be, referred to him for transfer, to such Bench as the Chairperson may deem fit.

QUALIFICATIONS FOR APPOINTMENT

- *A person shall not be qualified for appointment as the Chairperson or a Member unless he*:
  - In the case of Chairperson, is or has been, or is qualified to be, a Judge of a High Court; and
  - In the case of a Member, is or has been, or is qualified to be, a District Judge.
- *A person shall not be qualified for appointment as a Special Director (Appeals) unless he*:
  - Has been a member of the Indian Legal Service and has held a post in Grade I of that Service; or
  - Has been a member of the Indian Revenue Service and has held a post equivalent to a Joint Secretary to the Government of India.

TERM OF OFFICE

The Chairperson and every other Member shall hold office as such for a term of five years from the date on which he enters upon his office: Provided that no Chairperson or other Member shall hold office as such after he has attained,:

- In the case of the Chairperson, the age of sixty-five years;
- In the case of any other Member, the age of sixty-two years.

TERMS AND CONDITIONS OF SERVICE

The salary and allowances payable to and the other terms and conditions of service of the Chairperson, other Members and the Special Director (Appeals) shall be such as may be prescribed: Provided that neither the salary and allowances nor the other terms and conditions of service of the Chairperson or a Member shall be varied to his disadvantage after appointment.

VACANCIES

If, for reason other than temporary absence, any vacancy occurs in the office of the Chairperson or a Member, the Central Government shall appoint another person in accordance with the provisions of this Act to fill the vacancy and the proceedings may be continued before the Appellate Tribunal from the stage at which the vacancy is filled.

RESIGNATION AND REMOVAL

- The Chairperson or a Member may, by notice in writing under his hand addressed to the Central Government, resign his office: Provided that the Chairperson or a Member shall, unless he is permitted by the Central Government to relinquish his office sooner, continue to hold office until the expiry of three months from the date of receipt of such notice or until a person duly appointed as his successor enters upon his office or until the expiry of term of office, whichever is the earliest.
- The Chairperson or a Member shall not be removed from his office except by an order by the Central Government on the ground of proved misbehaviour or incapacity after an enquiry made by such person as the President may appoint for this purpose in which the Chairperson or a Member concerned has been informed of the charges against him and given a reasonable opportunity of being heard in respect of such charges.

MEMBER TO ACT AS CHAIRPERSON IN CERTAIN CIRCUMSTANCES

- In the event of the occurrence of any vacancy in the office of the Chairperson by reason of his death, resignation or otherwise, the senior-most Member shall act as the Chairperson until the date on which a new Chairperson, appointed in accordance with the provisions of this Act to fill such vacancy, enters upon his office.
- When the Chairperson is unable to discharge his functions owing to absence, illness or any other cause, the senior most Member shall

discharge the functions of the Chairperson until the date on which the Chairperson resumes his duties.

STAFF OF APPELLATE TRIBUNAL AND SPECIAL DIRECTOR (APPEALS)

- The Central Government shall provide the Appellate Tribunal and the Special Director (Appeals) with such officers and employees as it may deem fit.
- The officers and employees of the Appellate Tribunal and office of the Special Director (Appeals) shall discharge their functions under the general superintendence of the Chairperson and the Special Director (Appeals), as the case may be.
- The salaries and allowances and other conditions of service of the officers and employees of the Appellate Tribunal and office of the Special Director (Appeals) shall be such as may be prescribed.

PROCEDURE AND POWERS OF APPELLATE TRIBUNAL AND SPECIAL DIRECTOR

- The Appellate Tribunal and the Special Director (Appeals) shall not be bound by the procedure laid down by the Code of Civil Procedure, 1908 (5 of 1908) but shall be guided by the principles of natural justice and, subject to the other provisions of this Act, the Appellate Tribunal and the Special Director (Appeals) shall have powers to regulate its own procedure.
- The Appellate Tribunal and the Special Director (Appeals) shall have, for the purposes of discharging its functions under this Act, the same powers as are vested in a civil court under the Code of Civil Procedure, 1908 (5 of 1908); while trying a suit, in respect of the following matters, namely:
  - Summoning and enforcing the attendance of any person and examining him on oath;
  - Requiring the discovery and production of documents;
  - Receiving evidence on affidavits;
  - Subject to the provisions of sections 123 and 124 of the Indian Evidence Act, 1872 (1 of 1872) requisitioning any public record or document or copy of such record or document from any office;
  - Issuing commissions for the examination of witnesses or documents;
  - Reviewing its decisions;
  - Dismissing a representation of default or deciding it *ex parte;*
  - Setting aside any order of dismissal of any representation for default or any order passed by it *ex parte;* and

  - Any other matter which may be prescribed by the Central Government.
- An order made by the Appellate Tribunal or the Special Director (Appeals) under this Act shall be executable by the Appellate Tribunal or the Special Director (Appeals) as a decree of civil court and, for this purpose, the Appellate Tribunal and the Special Director (Appeals) shall have all the powers of a civil court.
- Notwithstanding anything contained in sub-section (3), the Appellate Tribunal or the Special Director (Appeals) may transmit any order made by it to a civil court having local jurisdiction and such civil court shall execute the order as if it were a decree made by that court.
- All proceedings before the Appellate Tribunal and the Special Director (Appeals) shall be deemed to be judicial proceedings within the meaning of sections 193 and 228 of the Indian Penal Code (45 of 1860) and the Appellate Tribunal shall be deemed to be a civil court for the purposes of sections 345 and 346 of the Code of Criminal Procedure, 1973 (2 of 1974)

DISTRIBUTION OF BUSINESS AMONGST BENCHES

Where Benches are constituted, the Chairperson may, from time to time, by notification, make provisions as to the distribution of the business of the Appellate Tribunal amongst the Benches and also provide for the matters which may be dealt with by each Bench.

POWER OF CHAIRPERSON TO TRANSFER CASES

On the application of any of the parties and after notice to the parties, and after hearing such of them as he may desire to be heard, or on his own motion without such notice, the Chairperson may transfer any case pending before one Bench, for disposal, to any other Bench.

DECISION TO BE BY MAJORITY

If the Members of a Bench consisting of two Members differ in opinion on any point, they shall state the point or points on which they differ, and make a reference to the Chairperson who shall either hear the point or points himself or refer the case for hearing on such point or points by one or more of the other Members of the Appellate Tribunal and such point or points shall be decided according to the opinion of the majority of the Members of the Appellate Tribunal who have heard the case, including those who first heard it.

Right of appellant to take assistance of legal practitioner or chartered accountant and of Government, to appoint presenting officers.

- A person preferring an appeal to the Appellate Tribunal or the Special Director (Appeals) under this Act may either appear in person or take the assistance of a legal practitioner or a chartered accountant of his choice to present his case before the Appellate Tribunal or the Special Director (Appeals), as the case may be.
- The Central Government may authorise one or more legal practitioners or chartered accountants or any of its officers to act as presenting officers and every person so authorised may present the case with respect to any appeal before the Appellate Tribunal or the Special Director (Appeals), as the case may be.

MEMBERS, ETC. TO BE PUBLIC SERVANTS

The Chairperson, Members and other officers and employees of the Appellate Tribunal, the Special Director (Appeals) and the Adjudicating Authority shall be deemed to be public servants within the meaning of section 21 of the Indian Penal Code (45 of 1860).

CIVIL COURT NOT TO HAVE JURISDICTION

No civil court shall have jurisdiction to entertain any suit or proceeding in respect of any matter which an Adjudicating Authority or the Appellate Tribunal or the Special Director (Appeals) is empowered by or under this Act to determine and no injunction shall be granted by any court or other authority in respect of any action taken or to be taken in pursuance of any power conferred by or under this Act.

APPEAL TO HIGH COURT

Any person aggrieved by any decision or order of the Appellate Tribunal may file an appeal to the High Court within sixty days from the date of communication of the decision or order of the Appellate Tribunal on any question of law arising out of such order: Provided that the High Court may, if it is satisfied that the appellant was prevented by sufficient cause from filing the appeal within the said period, allow it to be filed within a further period not exceeding sixty days.

- *Explanation*: In this section "High Court" means,
  - The High Court within the jurisdiction of which the aggrieved party ordinarily resides or carries on business or personally works for gain; and
  - Where the Central Government is the aggrieved party, the High Court within the jurisdiction of which the respondent, or in a case where there are more than one respondent, any of the respondents, ordinarily resides or carries on business or personally works for gain.

DIRECTORATE OF ENFORCEMENT

- The Central Government shall establish a Directorate of Enforcement with a Director and such other officers or class of officers as it thinks fit, who shall be called officers of Enforcement, for the purposes of this Act.
- Without prejudice to provisions of sub-section (1), the Central Government may authorise the Director of Enforcement or an Additional Director of Enforcement or a Special Director of Enforcement or a Deputy Director of Enforcement to appoint officers of Enforcement below the rank of an Assistant Director of Enforcement.
- Subject to such conditions and limitations as the Central Government may impose, an officer of Enforcement may exercise the powers and discharge the duties conferred or imposed on him under this Act.

POWER OF SEARCH, SEIZURE, ETC

- The Director of Enforcement and other officers of Enforcement, not below the rank of an Assistant Director, shall take up for investigation the contravention referred to in section 13.
- Without prejudice to the provisions of sub-section (1), the Central Government may also, by notification, authorise any officer or class of officers in the Central Government, State Government or the Reserve Bank, not below the rank of an Under Secretary to the Government of India to investigate any contravention referred to in section 13.
- The officers referred to in sub-section (1) shall exercise the like powers which are conferred on income-tax authorities under the Income-tax Act, 1961 (43 of 1961) and shall exercise such powers, subject to such limitations laid down under that Act.

EMPOWERING OTHER OFFICERS

- The Central Government may, by order and subject to such conditions and limitations as it thinks fit to impose, authorise any officer of customs or any central excise officer or any police officer or any other officer of the Central Government or a State Government to exercise such of the powers and discharge such of the duties of the Director of Enforcement or any other officer of Enforcement under this Act as may be stated in the order.
- The officers referred to in sub-section (1) shall exercise the like powers which are conferred on the income-tax authorities under the Income-tax Act, 1961 (43 of 1961), subject to such conditions and limitations as the Central Government may impose.

PRESUMPTION AS TO DOCUMENTS IN CERTAIN CASES

Where any document:

- Is produced or furnished by any person or has been seized from the custody or control of any person, in either case, under this Act or under any other law; or
- Has been received from any place outside India (duly authenticated by such authority or person and in such manner as may be prescribed) in the course of investigation of any contravention under this Act alleged to have been committed by any person, and such document is tendered in any proceeding under this Act in evidence against him, or against him and any other person who is proceeded against jointly with him, the court or the Adjudicating Authority, as the case may be, shall—
  - Presume, unless the contrary is proved, that the signature and every other part of such document which purports to be in the handwriting of any particular person or which the court may reasonably assume to have been signed by, or to be in the handwriting of, any particular person, is in that person's handwriting, and in the case of a document executed or attested, that it was executed or attested by the person by whom it purports to have been so executed or attested;
  - Admit the document in evidence notwithstanding that it is not duly stamped, if such document is otherwise admissible in evidence;
  - In a case falling under clause *(i)*, also presume, unless the contrary is proved, the truth of the contents of such document.

SUSPENSION OF OPERATION OF THIS ACT

- If the Central Government is satisfied that circumstances have arisen rendering it necessary that any permission granted or restriction imposed by this Act should cease to be granted or imposed, or if it considers necessary or expedient so to do in public interest, the Central Government may, by notification, suspend or relax to such extent either indefinitely or for such period as may be notified, the operation of all or any of the provisions of this Act.
- Where the operation of any provision of this Act has under sub-section (1) been suspended or relaxed indefinitely, such suspension or relaxation may, at any time while this Act remains in force, be removed by the Central Government by notification.
- Every notification issued under this section shall be laid, as soon as may be after it is issued, before each House of Parliament, while it is

in session, for a total period of thirty days which may be comprised in one session or in two or more successive sessions, and if, before the expiry of the session immediately following the session or the successive sessions aforesaid, both Houses agree in making any modification in the notification or both Houses agree that the notification should not be issued, the notification shall thereafter have effect only in such modified form or be of no effect, as the case may be; so, however, that any such modification or annulment shall be without prejudice to the validity of anything previously done under that notification.

POWER OF CENTRAL GOVERNMENT TO GIVE DIRECTIONS

For the purposes of this Act, the Central Government may, from time to time, give to the Reserve Bank such general or special directions as it thinks fit, and the Reserve Bank shall, in the discharge of its functions under this Act, comply with any such directions.

CONTRAVENTION BY COMPANIES

- Where a person committing a contravention of any of the provisions of this Act or of any rule, direction or order made thereunder is a company, every person who, at the time the contravention was committed, was in charge of, and was responsible to, the company for the conduct of the business of the company as well as the company, shall be deemed to be guilty of the contravention and shall be liable to be proceeded against and punished accordingly: Provided that nothing contained in this sub-section shall render any such person liable to punishment if he proves that the contravention took place without his knowledge or that he exercised due diligence to prevent such contravention.
- Notwithstanding anything contained in sub-section (1), where a contravention of any of the provisions of this Act or of any rule, direction or order made thereunder has been committed by a company and it is proved that the contravention has taken place with the consent or connivance of, or is attributable to any neglect on the part of, any director, manager, secretary or other officer of the company, such director, manager, secretary or other officer shall also be deemed to be guilty of the contravention and shall be liable to be proceeded against and punished accordingly.

  Explanation: For the purposes of this section,
  - "Company" means any body corporate and includes a firm or other association of individuals; and
  - "Director", in relation to a firm, means a partner in the firm.

Death or Insolvency in Certain Cases

Any right, obligation, liability, proceeding or appeal arising in relation to the provisions of section 13 shall not abate by reason of death or insolvency of the person liable under that section and upon such death or insolvency such rights and obligations shall devolve on the legal representative of such person or the official receiver or the official assignee, as the case may be: Provided that a legal representative of the deceased shall be liable only to the extent of the inheritance or estate of the deceased.

BAR OF LEGAL PROCEEDINGS

No suit, prosecution or other legal proceeding shall lie against the Central Government or the Reserve Bank or any officer of that Government or of the Reserve Bank or any other person exercising any power or discharging any functions or performing any duties under this Act, for anything in good faith done or intended to be done under this Act or any rule, regulation, notification, direction or order made thereunder.

REMOVAL OF DIFFICULTIES

- If any difficulty arises in giving effect to the provisions of this Act, the Central Government may, by order, do anything not inconsistent with the provisions of this Act for the purpose of removing the difficulty: Provided that no such order shall be made under this section after the expiry of two years from the commencement of this Act.
- Every order made under this section shall be laid, as soon as may be after it is made, before each House of Parliament.

POWER TO MAKE RULES

- The Central Government may, by notification, make rules to carry out the provisions of this Act.
- Without prejudice to the generality of the foregoing power, such rules may provide for,:
  - The imposition of reasonable restrictions on current account transactions under section 5;
  - The manner in which the contravention may be compounded under sub-section (1) of section 15;
  - The manner of holding an enquiry by the Adjudicating Authority under sub-section (1) of section 16;
  - The form of appeal and fee for filing such appeal under sections 17 and 19;
  - The salary and allowances payable to and the other terms and conditions of service of the Chairperson and other Members of

the Appellate Tribunal and the Special Director (Appeals) under section 23;

- The salaries and allowances and other conditions of service of the officers and employees of the Appellate Tribunal and the office of the Special Director (Appeals) under sub-section (3) of section 27;
- The additional matters in respect of which the Appellate Tribunal and the Special Director (Appeals) may exercise the powers of civil court under clause *(i)* of sub-section (2) of section 28;
- The authority or person and the manner in which any document may be authenticated under clause *(ii)* of section 39; and
- Any other matter which is required to be, or may be, prescribed.

POWER TO MAKE REGULATIONS

- The Reserve Bank may, by notification, make regulations to carry out the provisions of this Act and the rules made thereunder.
- Without prejudice to the generality of the foregoing power, such regulations may provide for,:
  - The permissible classes of capital account transactions, the limits of admissibility of foreign exchange for such transactions, and the prohibition, restriction or regulation of certain capital account transactions under section 6;
  - The manner and the form in which the declaration is to be furnished under clause *(a)* of sub-section (1) of section 7;
  - The period within which and the manner of repatriation of foreign exchange under section 8;
  - The limit up to which any person may possess foreign currency or foreign coins under clause *(*a) of section 9;
  - The class of persons and the limit up to which foreign currency account may be held or operated under clause *(b)* of section 9;
  - The limit up to which foreign exchange acquired may be exempted under clause *(*d) of section 9;
  - The limit up to which foreign exchange acquired may be retained under clause *(*e) of section 9;
  - Any other matter which is required to be, or may be, specified.

RULES AND REGULATIONS TO BE LAID BEFORE PARLIAMENT

Every rule and regulation made under this Act shall be laid, as soon as may be after it is made, before each House of Parliament, while it is in session for a total period of thirty days which may be comprised in one session or in two or more successive sessions, and if, before the expiry of the session immediately following the session or the successive sessions aforesaid, both Houses agree in making any modification in the rule or regulation, or both Houses agree that the rule or regulation should not be made, the rule or regulation shall thereafter have effect only in such modified form or be of no effect, as the case may be; so, however, that any such modification or annulment shall be without prejudice to the validity of anything previously done under that rule or regulation.

REPEAL AND SAVING

- The Foreign Exchange Regulation Act, 1973 (46 of 1973) is hereby repealed and the Appellate Board constituted under sub-section (1) of section 52 of the said Act (hereinafter referred to as the repealed Act) shall stand dissolved.
- On the dissolution of the said Appellate Board, the person appointed as Chairman of the Appellate Board and every other person appointed as Member and holding office as such immediately before such date shall vacate their respective offices and no such Chairman or other person shall be entitled to claim any compensation for the premature termination of the term of his office or of any contract of service.
- Notwithstanding anything contained in any other law for the time being in force, no court shall take cognizance of an offence under the repealed Act and no adjudicating officer shall take notice of any contravention under section 51 of the repealed Act after the expiry of a period of two years from the date of the commencement of this Act.
- Subject to the provisions of sub-section (3) all offences committed under the repealed Act shall continue to be governed by the provisions of the repealed Act as if that Act had not been repealed.
- *Notwithstanding such repeal,*:
  - Anything done or any action taken or purported to have been done or taken including any rule, notification, inspection, order or notice made or issued or any appointment, confirmation or declaration made or any licence, permission, authorization or exemption granted or any document or instrument executed or any direction given under the Act hereby repealed shall, in so far as it is not inconsistent with the provisions of this Act, be deemed to have been done or taken under the corresponding provisions of this Act;
  - Any appeal preferred to the Appellate Board under sub-section (2) of section 52 of the repealed Act but not disposed of before the commencement of this Act shall stand transferred to and shall be disposed of by the Appellate Tribunal constituted under this Act;
  - Every appeal from any decision or order of the Appellate Board

under sub-section (3) or sub-section (4) of section 52 of the repealed Act shall, if not filed before the commencement of this Act, be filed before the High Court within a period of sixty days of such commencement: Provided that the High Court may entertain such appeal after the expiry of the said period of sixty days if it is satisfied that the appellant was prevented by sufficient cause from filing the appeal within the said period.

- Save as otherwise provided in sub-section (3), the mention of particular matters in sub-sections (2), (4) and (5) shall not be held to prejudice or affect the general application of section 6 of the General Clauses Act, 1897 (10 of 1897) with regard to the effect of repeal.

THE CONSERVATION OF FOREIGN EXCHANGE

- Short title, extent and commencement—(1) This Act may be called the Conservation of Foreign Exchange and Prevention of Smuggling Activities Act, 1974.
  - It extends to the whole of India.
  - It shall come into force on such date as the Central Government may, by notification in the Official Gazette, appoint.
- *Definitions-In this Act, unless the context otherwise requires,*:
  - "Appropriate Government" means, as respects a detention order made by the Central Government or by an officer of the Central Government or a person detained under such order, the Central Government, and as respects a detention order made by a State Government or by an officer of a State Government or a person detained under such order, the State Government;
  - "Detention order" means an order made under section 3;
  - "Foreigner" has the same meaning as in the Foreigners Act, 1946 (31 of 1946);
  - "Indian customs waters" has the same meaning as in clause (28) of the Customs Act, 1962 (52 of 1962);
  - "Smuggling" has the same meanings as in clause (39) of section 2 of the Customs Act, 1962, and all its grammatical variations and cognate expressions shall be construed accordingly;
  - "State Government", in relation to a Union territory, means the Administrator thereof;
  - Any reference in this Act to a law which is not in force in the State of Jammu and Kashmir shall, in relation to that State, be construed as a reference to the corresponding law, if any, in force in that State.
- *Power to make orders detaining certain persons*:
  - The Central Government or the State Government or any officer

of the Central Government, not below the rank of a Joint Secretary to that Government, specially empowered for the purposes of this section by that Government, or any officer of the State Government, not below the rank of a Secretary to that Government, specially empowered for the purposes of this section by that Government, may, if satisfied, with respect to any person (including a foreigner), that, with a view to preventing him from acting in any manner prejudicial to the conservation or augmentation of foreign exchange or with a view to preventing him from

i. Smuggling goods, or
ii. Abetting the smuggling of goods, or
iii. Engaging in transporting or concealing or keeping smuggled goods, or
iv. Dealing in smuggled goods otherwise than by engaging in transporting or concealing or keeping smuggled goods, or
v. Harbouring persons engaged in smuggling goods or in abetting the smuggling of goods, it is necessary so to do, make an order directing that such person be detained:

Provided that no order of detention shall be made on any of the grounds specified in this sub-section on which an order of detention may be made under section 3 of the Prevention of Illicit Traffic in Narcotic Drugs and Psychotropic Substances Act, 1988 or under section 3 of the Jammu and Kashmir Prevention of Illicit Traffic in Narcotic Drugs and Psychotropic Substances ordinance, 1988..

- When any order of detention is made by a State Government or by an officer empowered by a State Government, the State Government shall, within ten days, forward to the Central Government a report in respect of the order.
- For the purposes of clause (5) of article 22 of the Constitution, the communication to a person detained in pursuance of a detention order of the grounds on which the order has been made shall be made as soon as may be after the detention, but ordinarily not later than five days, and in exceptional circumstances and for reasons to be recorded in writing, not later than fifteen days, from the date of detention.

- Execution of detention orders-A detention order may be executed at any place in India in the manner provided for the execution of warrants of arrest under the Code of Criminal Procedure, 1973 (2 of 1974).
- Power to regulate place and conditions of detention-Every person in respect of whom a detention order has been made shall be liable:

- To be detained in such place and under such conditions including conditions as to maintenance, interviews or communication with others, discipline and punishment for breaches of discipline, as the appropriate Government may, by general or special order, specify; and
- To be removed from one place of detention to another place of detention, whether within the same State or in another State by order of the appropriate Government;
  Provided that no order shall be made by a State Government under clause (b) for the removal of a person from one State to another State except with the consent of the Government of that other State.
- *Grounds of detention severable*: Where a person has been detained in pursuance of an order of detention under sub-section (1) which has been made on two or more grounds, such order of detention shall be deemed to have been made separately on each of such grounds and accordingly:
  a. Such order shall not be deemed to be invalid or inoperative merely because one or some of the grounds is or are:
     i. Vague,
     ii. Non-existent,
     iii. Not relevant,
     iv. Not connected or not proximately connected with such person, or
     v. Invalid for any other reason whatsoever, and it is not, therefore, possible to hold that the Government or officer making such order would have been satisfied as provided in sub-section (1) of section 3 with reference to the remaining ground or grounds and made the order of detention;
- The Government or officer making the order of detention shall be deemed to have made the order of detention under the said sub-section (1) after being satisfied as provided in that sub-section with reference to the remaining ground or grounds.]

• Detention order not to be invalid or inoperative on certain grounds- No detention order shall be invalid or inoperative merely by reason:
  - That the person to be detained thereunder is outside the limited of the territorial jurisdiction of the Government or the officer making the order of detention, or
  - That the place of detention of such person is outside the said limits.

• Powers in relation to absconding persons (1) If the appropriate

Government has reason to believe that a person in respect of whom a detention order has been made has absconded or is concealing himself so that the order cannot be executed, the Government may:

- Make a report in writing of the fact to a Metropolitan Magistrate or a Magistrate of the first class having jurisdiction in the place where the said person ordinarily resides; and thereupon the provisions of sections 82, 83, 84 and 85 of the Code of Criminal Procedure, 1973 (2 of 1974), shall apply in respect of the said person and his property as if the order directing that he be detained were a warrant issued by the Magistrate;
- By order notified in the Official Gazette direct the said person to appear before such officer, at such place and within such period as may be specified in the order; and if the said person fails to comply with such direction, he shall, unless he proves that it was not possible for him to comply therewith and that he had, within the period specified in the order, informed the officer mentioned in the order of the reason which rendered compliance therewith impossible and of his whereabouts, be punishable therewith impossible and of his whereabouts, be punishable with imprisonment for a term which may extend to one year or with fine or with both. (2) Nothwithstanding anything contained in the Code of Criminal Procedure, 1973 (2 of 1974), every offence under clause (b) of sub-section (1) shall be cognizable.

• Advisory Board-For the purposes of sub-clause (a) of clause (c) of clause (7) of article 22 of the Constitution,:
  - The Central Government and each State Government shall, wherever necessary, constitute one or more Advisory Boards each of which shall consist of a Chairman and two other persons possessing the qualifications specified in sub-clause (a) of clause (4) of article 22 of the Constitution;
  - Save as otherwise provided in section 9, the appropriate Government shall, within five weeks from the date of detention of a person under a detention order make a reference in respect thereof to the Advisory Board constituted under clause (a) to enable the Advisory Board to make the report under sub-clause (a) of clause (4) of article 22 of the Constitution;
  - The Advisory Board to which a reference is made under clause (b) shall after considering the reference and the materials placed before it and after calling for such further information as it may deed necessary from the appropriate Government or from any person called for the purpose through the appropriate Government, from the person concerned, and if, in any particular

case, it considers it essential so to do or if the person concerned desires to be heard in person, after hearing him person, prepare its report specifying in a separate paragraph thereof its opinion as to whether or not there is sufficient cause for the detention of the person concerned and submit the same within eleven weeks from the date of detention of the person concerned;

- When there is a difference of opinion among the members forming the Advisory Board the opinion of the majority of such members shall be deemed to be the opinion of the Board;
- A person against whom an order of detention has been made under this Act shall not be entitled to appear by any legal practitioner in any matter connected with the reference to the Advisory Board, and the proceedings of the Advisory Board and its report, excepting that part of the report in which the opinion of the Advisory Board is specified, shall be confidential;
- In every case where the Advisory Board has reported that there is in its opinion sufficient cause for the detention of a person, the appropriate Government may confirm the detention order and continue the detention of the person concerned for such period as it thinks fit and in every case where the Advisory Board has reported that there is in its opinion no sufficient cause for the detention of the person concerned, the appropriate Government shall revoke the detention order and cause the person to be released forthwith.

• Cases in which and circumstances under which persons may be detained for period longer than three months without obtaining the opinion of Advisory Board-(1) Notwithstanding anything contained in this Act, any person (including a foreigner) in respect of whom an order of detention is made under this Act at any time before the 31st July, 1996, may be detained without obtaining, in accordance with the provisions of sub-clause (a) of clause (4) of article 22 of the Constitution, the opinion of an Advisory Board for a period longer than three months but not exceeding six months from the date of his detention, where the order of detention has been made against such person with a view to preventing him from smuggling goods or abetting the smuggling of goods or engaging in transporting or concealing or keeping smuggled goods and the Central Government or any Officer of the Central Government, not below the rank of an Additional Secretary to that Government, specially empowered for the purpose of this section by that Government, is satisfied that such person—

  - Smuggles or is likely to smuggle goods into, out of or through any area highly vulnerable to smuggling; or

- Abets or is likely to abet the smuggling of goods into, out of or through any area highly vulnerable to smuggling; or
- Engages or is likely to engage in transporting or concealing or keeping smuggled goods in any area highly vulnerable to smuggling, and makes a declaration to that effect within five weeks of the detention of such person.

  Explanation 1: In this sub-section, "area highly vulnerable to smuggling" means,:

  i. The Indian customs waters, contiguous to the State of Goa, Gujarat, Karnataka, Kerala, Maharashtra, Tamil Nadu and the Union territories of Daman and Diu and Pondicherry;
  ii. The Inland area fifty kilometres in width from the coast of India falling within the territories of the States of Goa, Gujarat, Karnataka, Kerala, Maharashtra, Tamil Nadu and the Union territories of Daman and Diu and Pondicherry;
  iii. The inland area fifty kilometres in width from the India-Pakistan border in the State of Gujarat, Jammu and Kashmir, Punjab and Rajasthan;
  iv. The customs air port of Delhi; and
  v. Such further or other Indian customs waters, or inland area not exceeding one hundred kilometres in width from any other coast or border of India, or such other customs station, as the Central Government may, having regard to the vulnerability of such waters, area or customs station, as the case may be, to smuggling, by notification in the Official Gazette, specify in this behalf.

     Explanation 2:

     1. For the purposes of Explanation 1, "customs airport" and "customs station" shall have the same meaning as in clauses (10) and (13) of section 2 of the Customs Act, 1962 (52 of 1962), respectively.
     2. In the case of any person detained under a detention order to which the provisions of sub-section (1) apply, section 8 shall have effect subject to the following modifications, namely:
        i. In clause (b), for the words "shall, within five weeks", the words "shall, within four months and two weeks" shall be substituted;
        ii. In clause (c),:
            1. For the words "the detention of the person concerned", the words "the continued detention of the person concerned" shall be substituted;

2. For the words "eleven weeks", the words "five months and three weeks" shall be substituted;

iii. In clause (f), for the words "for the detention", at both the places where they occur, the words "for the continued detention" shall be substituted.

- *Maximum period of detention*: The maximum period for which any person may be detained in pursuance of any detention order to which the provisions of section 9 do not apply and which has been confirmed under clause (f) of section 8 shall be a period of one year from the date of detention or the specified period, whichever period expires late and the maximum period for which any person may be detained in pursuance of any detention order to which the provisions of section 9 apply and which has been confirmed under clause (f) of section 8 read with sub-section (2) of section 9 shall be a period of two years from the date of detention or the specified period, whichever period expires later;

  Provided that nothing contained in this section shall affect the power of the appropriate Government in neither case to revoke or modify the detention order at any earlier time. Explanation In this section and section 10A-"specified period" means the period during which the Proclamation of Emergency issued under clause (1) of article 352 of the Constitution on the 3rd day of December, 1971 and the Proclamation of Emergency issued under that clause on the 25th day of June, 1975, are both in operation.

  – *Extension of period of detention*:

    i. Notwithstanding anything contained in any other provision of this Act, the detention of every person detained under a detention order which has been confirmed under clause (f) of section 8 before the commencement of the Conservation of Foreign Exchange and Prevention of Smuggling Activities (Amendment) Act, 1976, and which is in force immediately before such commencement shall, unless his detention has been continued by the appropriate Government under the said clause for a period shorter than one year from the date of his detention, continue until the expiry of a period of one year from the date of his detention under such order or until the expiry of the specified period, whichever period expires later: Provided that nothing contained in this sub-section shall affect the power of the appropriate Government to revoke or modify such detention order at any earlier time.

    ii. Notwithstanding anything contained in any other provision of this Act, the detention of every person detained under a detention order which has been confirmed under clause (f) of section 8 read with sub-section (2) of section 9 before the commencement of the Conservation of Foreign Exchange and Prevention of Smuggling Activities (Amendment) Act, 1976, and which is in force immediately before such commencement, shall, unless his detention has been continued by the appropriate Government under the said clause (f) read with the said sub-section (2) for a period shorter than two years from the date of his detention, continue until the expiry of a period of two years from the date of his detention under such order or until the expiry of the specified period, whichever period expires later: Provided that nothing contained in this sub-section shall affect the power of the appropriate Government to revoke or modify such detention order at any earlier time.

- *Revocation of detention orders*:
  - Without prejudice to provisions of section 21 of the General Clauses Act, 1897 (10 of 1897), a detention order may, at any time, be revoked or modified:
    i. Notwithstanding that the order has been made by an officer of a State Government, by that State Government or by the Central Government;
    ii. Notwithstanding that the order has been made by an officer of the Central Government or by a State Government, by the Central Government.
  - The revocation of a detention order shall not bar the making of another detention order under section (3) against the same person.
- *Temporary release of persons detained*:
  - The Central Government may, at any time, direct that any person detained in pursuance of a detention order made by that Government or an officer subordinate to that Government or by a State Government or by an officer subordinate to a State Government, may be released for any specified period either without conditions or upon such conditions specified in the directions as that person accepts, and may, at any time, cancel his release.
    i. A State Government may, at any time, direct that any person detained in pursuance of a detention order made by that Government or by an officer subordinate to that Government may be released for any specified period either without conditions or upon such conditions specified in the direction

as that person accepts, and may, at any time, cancel his release.

- In directing the release of any person under sub-section (1) or sub-section (1A) the Government directing the release may require him to enter into a bond with sureties for the due observance of the conditions specified in the direction.
- Any person released under sub-section (1) or sub-section (1A) shall surrender himself at the time and place, and to the authority, specified in the order directing his release or cancelling his release, as the case may be.
- If any person fails without sufficient cause to surrender himself in the manner specified in sub-section(3) he shall be punishable with imprisonment for a term which may extend to two years, or with fine, or with both.
- If any person released under sub-section(1) or sub-section(1A) fails to fulfill any of the conditions imposed upon him under the said sub-section or in the bond entered into by him, the bond shall be declared to be forfeited and any person bound thereby shall be liable to pay the penalty thereof.
- Notwithstanding anything contained in any other law and save as otherwise provided in this section, no person against whom a detention order made under this Act is in force shall be released whether on bail or bail bond or otherwise.

- Special provisions for dealing with emergency-(1) Notwithstanding anything contained in this Act or any rules of natural justice, the provisions of this section shall have effect during the period of operation of the Proclamation of Emergency issued under clause
  - Article 352 of the Constitution on the 3rd day of December, 1971, or the Proclamation of Emergency issued under that clause on the 25th day of June, 1975, or a period of twenty four months from the 25th day of June, 1975, whichever period is the shortest.
  - When making an order of detention under this Act against any person after the commencement of the Conservation of Foreign and Prevention of Smuggling Activities (Amendment) Act, 1975, the Central Government or the State Government or, as the case may be, the officer making the order of detention shall consider whether the detention of such person under this Act is necessary for dealing effectively with the emergency in respect of which the Proclamations referred to in sub-section (1) have been issued (hereafter in this section referred to as the emergency) and if, on such consideration, the Central Government or the State Government or, as the case may be, the officer is satisfied that

it is necessary to detain such person for effectively dealing with the emergency, that Government or officer may make a declaration to that effect and communicate a copy of the declaration to the person concerned: Provided that where such declaration is made by an officer, it shall be reviewed by the appropriate Government within fifteen days from the date of making of the declaration and such declaration shall cease to have effect unless it is confirmed by that Government, after such review, within the said period of fifteen days.

- The question whether the detention of any person in respect of whom a declaration has been made under sub-section (2) continues to be necessary for effectively dealing with the emergency shall be reconsidered by the appropriate Government within four months from the date of such declaration and thereafter at intervals not exceeding four months, and if, one such reconsideration, it appears to the appropriate Government that the detention of the person is no longer necessary for effectively dealing with the emergency, the Government may revoke the declaration.
- In making any consideration, review or reconsideration under sub-section (2) or (3) the appropriate Government or officer may, if such Government or officer considers it to be against the public interest to do otherwise, act on the basis of the information and materials in its or his possession without disclosing the facts or giving an opportunity of making a representation to the person concerned.
- It shall not be necessary to disclose to any person detained under a detention order to which the provisions of sub-section (2) apply, the grounds on which the order has been made during the period the declaration made in respect of such person under that sub-section is in force, and, accordingly, such period shall not be taken into account for the purpose of sub-section (3) of section 3
- In the case of every person detained under a detention order to which the provisions of sub-section (2) apply, being a person in respect of whom a declaration has been made thereunder, the period during which such declaration is in force shall not be taken into account for the purpose of computing:
  i. The periods specified in clauses (b) and (c) of section 8
  ii. The periods of "one year" and "five weeks" specified in sub-section (1), the period of "one year" specified in sub-section (2)(i), and the period of "six months" specified in sub-section (3), of section 9.

- Protection of action taken in good faith-No suit or other legal proceeding shall lie against the Central Government or a State Government, and no suit, prosecution or other legal proceedings shall lie against any person, for anything in good faith done or intended to be done in pursuance of this Act.
- *Repeal*: The Maintenance of Internal Security (Amendment) Ordinance, 1974 (11 of 1974), shall, on the commencement of this Act, stand repealed and accordingly the amendments made in the Maintenance of Internal Security Act, 1971 (26 of 1971), by the said Ordinance shall, on such commencement, cease to have effect.

CUSTOMS VALUATION

In exercise of the powers conferred by Section 156 of the Customs Act, 1962 (52 of 1962), read with Section 22 of the General Clauses Act, 1897 (10 of 1897), and in supersession of the Customs Valuation Rules, 1963 except as respect things done or omitted to be done before such super session, the Central Government hereby makes the following rules, namely:

- *Short title, commencement and application*:
  - These rules may be called the Customs Valuation (Determination of Price of Imported Goods) Rules, 1988.
  - They shall come into force on the 16th August, 1988.
  - They shall apply imported goods where a duty of customs is chargeable by reference to their value.
- *Definitions*: (1) In these rules, unless the context otherwise requires,-
  - "Computed value" means the value of imported goods determined in accordance with rule 7A of these rules; (aa) " deductive value" means the value determined in accordance with rule 7 of these rules;
  - "Goods of the same class or kind", means imported goods that are within a group of range of imported goods produced by a particular industry of industrial sector and includes identical goods of similar goods;
  - *"Identical goods" means imported goods*:
    i. Which are same in all respects, including physical characteristics, quality and reputation as the goods being valued except for minor differences in appearance that do not affect the value of the goods;
    ii. Produced in the country in which the goods being valued were produced; and
    iii. produced by the same person who produced the goods, or where no such goods are available, goods produced by a different person, but shall not include imported goods where

engineering, development work, art work, design work, plan or sketch undertaken in India were completed directly or indirectly by the buyer on these imported goods free of charge or at a reduced cost for use in connection with the production and sale for export of these imported goods;

- "Produced" includes grown, manufactured and mined;
- "Similar goods" means imported goods –
  i. Which although not alike in all respects, have like characteristics and like component materials which enable them to perform the same functions and to be commercially intercha-ngeable with the goods being valued having regard to the quality, reputation and the existence of trade mark;
  ii. Produced in the country in which the goods being valued were produced; and
  iii. Produced by the same person who produced the goods being valued, or where no such goods are available, goods produced by a different person, but shall not include imported goods where engineering, development work, art work, design work, plan or sketch undertaken in India were completed directly or indirectly by the buyer on these imported goods free of charge or at a reduced cost for use in connection with production and sale for export of these imported goods;
- "Transaction value" means the value determined in accordance with Rule 4 of these rules. (2) For the purpose of these rules, persons shall be deemed to be " related " only if –
  i. They are officers or directors of one another's businesses;
  ii. They are legally recognized partners in business;
  iii. They are employer and exployee;
  iv. Any person directly or indirectly owns, controls or holds 5 per cent or more of the outstanding voting stock or shares of both of them;
  v. One of them directly or indirectly controls the other;
  vi. Both of them are directly or indirectly controlled by a third person;
  vii. Together they directly or indirectly control a third person; or
  viii. They are members of the same family.
- *Explanation* I: The term " person" also includes legal persons.
- *Explanation* II: Persons who are associated in the business of one another in that one is the sole agent or sole distributor or sole concessionaire, however described, of the other shall be deemed to be related for the purpose of these rules, if they fall within the criteria of this sub-rule.

- *Determination of the method of valuation—For the purpose of these rules*:
  - i. The value of imported goods shall be the transaction value;
  - ii. If the value cannot be determined under the provisions of clause (i) above, the value shall be determined by proceeding sequentially through Rules 5 to 8 of these rules.
    1. *Transaction value*: (1) The transaction value of imported goods shall be the price actually paid or payable for the goods when sold for export to India, adjusted in accordance with the provisions of Rule 9 of these rules.
    2. The transaction value of imported goods under sub-rule (1) above shall be accepted provided that:
       - a. There are no restrictions as to the disposition or use of the goods by the buyer other than restrictions which are imposed or required by law or by the public authorities in India; or
- Limit the geographical area in which the goods may be resold; or
- Do not substantially affect the value of the goods;
  - The sale or price is not subject to same condition or consideration for which a value cannot be determined in respect of the goods being valued;
  - No part of the proceeds of any subsequent resale, disposal or use of the goods by the buyer will accrue directly or indirectly to the seller unless an appropriate adjustment can be made in accordance with the provisions of Rule 9 of these rules; and
  - the buyer and seller are not related, or where the buyer and seller are related, that transaction value is acceptable for customs purposes under the provisions of sub-rule below.
    - a. Where the buyer and seller are related, the transaction value shall be accepted provided that the examination of the circumstances of the sale of the imported goods indicate that the relationship did not influence the price.
    - b. In a sale between related persons, the transaction value shall be accepted, whenever the importer demonstrates that the declared value of the goods being valued, closely approximates to one of the following values ascertained at or about the same time:
      - i. The transaction value of identical goods, or of similar goods, in sales to unrelated buyers in India;
      - ii. The deductive value for identical goods or similar goods;
      - iii. The computed value for identical goods or similar goods.

      Provided that in applying the values used for comparison, due account shall be taken of demonstrated difference in commercial levels, quantity levels, adjustments in accordance with the provisions of Rule 9 of these rules and cost incurred by the seller in sales in which he and the buyer are not related;

c. Substitute values shall not be established under the provisions of clause (b) of this sub-rule.

– Transaction of value of identical goods.

i. Subject to the provisions of Rule 3 of these rules, the value of imported goods shall be the transaction value of identical goods sold for export to India and imported at or about the same time as the goods being valued.

ii. In applying this rule, the transaction value of identical goods in a sale at the same commercial level and in substantially the same quantity as the goods being valued shall be used to determine the value of imported goods.

iii. Where no sale referred to in clause (b) of sub-rule (1) of this rule, is found, the transaction value of identical goods sold at a different commercial level or in different quantities or both, adjusted to take account of the difference attributable to commercial level or to the quantity or both, shall be used, provided that such adjustments shall be made on the basis of the demonstrated evidence which clearly establishes the reasonableness and accuracy of the adjustments, whether such adjustment leads to an increase or decrease in the value. (2) Where the cost and charges referred to in sub-rule (2) of Rule 9 of these rules are included in the transaction value of identical goods, an adjustment shall be made, if there are significant differences in such costs and charges between the goods being valued and the identical goods in question arising from differences in distances and means of transport. (3) In applying this rule, if more than one transaction value of identical goods is found; the lowest such value shall be used to determine the value of imported goods.

- *Transaction value of similar goods*:

1. Subject to the provisions of Rule 3 of these rules, the value of imported goods shall be the transaction value of similar goods sold for export to India and imported at or about the same time as the goods being valued.
2. The provisions of clauses (b) and (c) of sub-rule (1), sub-rule (2) and sub-rule(3),of Rule 5 of these rules shall, mutatis mutandis, also apply in respect of similar goods.

Determination of value when transaction values is not available— If the value of imported goods cannot be determined under the provisions of rules 4, 5and 6, the value shall be determined under the provisions of rule 7 or, when the value cannot be determined under that rule, under rule 7A: Provided that at the request of the importer, and with the approval of the proper officer, the order of application of rules 7 and 7A shall be reversed.]

- Deductive value—
  - Subject to the provisions of Rule 3 of these rules, if the goods being valued or identical or similar imported goods are sold in India, in the condition as imported at or about the time at which the declaration for determination of value is presented, the value of imported goods shall be based on the unit price at which the imported goods or identical or similar imported goods are sold in the greatest aggregate quantity to persons who are not related to the sellers in India, subject to the following deductions:—
    i. Either the commission usually paid or agreed to be paid or the additions usually made for profits and general expenses in connection with sales in India of imported goods of the same class or kind;
    ii. The usual costs of transport and insurance and associated costs incurred within India;
    iii. The customs duties and other taxes payable in India by reason of importation or sale of the goods.
  - If neither the imported goods nor identical nor similar imported goods are sold at or about the same time of importation of the goods being valued, the value of imported goods shall, subject otherwise to the provisions of sub-rule (1) of this rule, be based on the unit price at which the imported goods or identical or similar imported goods are sold in India, at the earliest date after importation but before the expiry of ninety days after such importation.
    (a) If neither the imported goods not identical nor similar imported goods are sold in India in the conditions as imported, then, the value shall be based on the unit price at which the imported goods, after further processing, are sold in the greatest aggregate quantity to persons who are not related to the seller in India
    (b) In such determination, due allowance shall be made for the value added by processing and the deductions, provided for in items (i) to (iii) of sub-rule (1) of this rule.
  - *Computed value*: Subject to the provisions of rule 3, the value of imported goods shall be based on a computed value, which shall consist of the sum of:

a. The cost of value of materials and fabrication or other processing employed in producing the imported goods;
b. An amount for profit and general expenses equal to that usually reflected in sales of goods of the same class or kind as the goods being valued which are made by producers in the country of exportation for export to India;
c. Rhe cost or value of all other expenses under sub-rule (2) of rule 9 of these rules.

- Residual method—(1) Subject to the provisions of Rule 3 of these rules, where the value of imported goods cannot be determined under the provisions of any of the preceding rules, the value shall be determined using reasonable means consistent with the principles and general provisions of these rules and sub-section (1) of Section 14 of the Customs Act, 1962 (52 of 1962) and on the basis of data available in India. (2) No value shall be determined under the provisions of (5) this rule on the basis of-
  i. The selling price in India of the goods produced in India;
  ii. A system which provides for the acceptance for customs purposes \ of the highest of the two alternative values;
  iii. The price of the goods on the domestic market of country of exportation; [(iii a) the cost of production other than computed values which have been determined for identical or similar goods in accordance with the provisions of rule 7A.
  iv. The price of the goods for the export to a country other than India;
  v. Minimum customs values; or
  vi. Arbitrary or fictitious values.
- *Cost and services:*
  1. In determining the transaction value, there shall be added to the price actually paid or payable for the imported goods,-
     - The following cost and services, to the extent they are incurred by the buyer but are not included in the price actually paid or payable for the imported goods, namely:
     i. Commissions and brokerage, except buying commissions;
     ii. The cost of containers which are treated as being one for customs purposes with the goods in question;
     iii. The cost of packing whether for labour or materials;
     - The value, apportioned as appropriate, of the following goods and services where supplied directly or indirectly by the buyer free of charge or at reduced cost for use in connection with the production and sale for export of imported goods, to the extent that such value has not been included in the price actually paid of payable, namely:

i. Materials, components, parts and similar items incorporated in the imported goods;
ii. Tools, dies, moulds and similar items used in the production of the imported goods;
iii. Materials consumed in the production of the imported goods;
iv. Engineering, development, art work, design work, and and plans and sketches undertaken elsewhere than in India and necessary for the production of the imported goods;
   - Royalties and license fees related to the imported goods that the buyer is required to pay, directly or indirectly, as a condition of the sale of the goods being valued, to the extent that such royalties and fees are not included in the price actually paid or payable.
   - The value of any part of the proceeds of any subsequent resale, disposal or use of the imported goods that accrues, directly or indirectly, to the seller;
   - All other payments actually made or to be made as a condition of sale of the imported goods, by the buyer to the seller, or by the buyer to a third party to satisfy an obligation of the seller to the extent that such payments are not included in the price actually paid of payable.

2. For the purposes of sub-section (1) and sub section (1A) of section14 of the Customs Act, 1962 (52 of 1962) and these rules, the value of the imported goods shall be the value of such goods, for delivery at the time and place of importation and shall include:
   a. The cost of transport of the imported goods to the place of importation;
   b. Loading, unloading and handling charges associated with the delivery of the imported goods at the place of importation; and
   c. The cost of insurance:
      i. Where the coast of transport referred to in clause (a) is not ascertainable, such cost shall be twenty per cent of the free on board value of the goods;
      ii. The charges referred to in clause (b) shall be one per cent of the free on board value of the goods plus the coast of transport referred to in clause (a) plus the coast of insurance referred to in clause (c);
      iii. Where the coast referred to in clause (c) is not ascertainable, such cost shall be 1.125 per cent of free on board value of the goods;

Provided further that in the case of goods imported by air, where the cost referred to in clause (a) is ascertainable, such cost shall not exceed twenty per cent of free on board value of the goods: Provided also that where the free on board value of the goods is not ascertainable, the coasts referred to in clause (a) shall be twenty per cent of the free on board value of the goods plus cost of insurance for clause (i) above and the cost referred to in clause (c) shall be 1.125 per cent of the free on board value of the goods plus cost of transport for clause (iii) above.

3. Additions to the price actually paid or payable shall be made under this rule on the bases of objective and quantifiable data.
4. No addition shall be made to the price actually paid or payable in determining the value of the imported goods except as provided for in this rule.

- *Declaration by the importer*:
  1. *The importer or his agent shall furnish*:
     a. A declaration disclosing full and accurate details relating to the value of imported goods; and
     b. Any other statement, information or document including an invoice of the manufacturer or producer of the imported goods where the oops are imorted from or through a person other than the manufacturer or producer, as considered necessary by the proper officer for determination of the value of imported goods under these rule.
  2. Nothing contained in these rules shall be construed as restricting or calling into question the right of the proper officer of customs to satisfy himself as to the truth or accuracy of any statement, information, document or declaration presented for valuation purposes.
  3. The provisions of the Customs Act, 1962 (52 of 1962) relating to confiscation, penalty and prosecution shall apply to cases where wrong declaration, information, statement or documents are furnished under these rules.
- Rejection of declared value – (1) When the proper officer has reason to doubt the truth or accuracy of the value declared in relation to any imported goods, he may ask the importer of such goods to furnish further information including documents or other evidence and if, after receiving such further information, or in the absence of a response of such importer, the proper officer still has reasonable doubt about the truth or accuracy of the value so declared, it shall be deemed that the value of such imported goods cannot be determined under the provisions of sub-rule (1) of rule 4.(2) At the request of and importer, the proper officer, shall intimate the

importer in writing the grounds for doubting the truth or accuracy of the value declared in relation to goods imported by such importer and provide a reasonable opportunity of being heard, before taking a final decision under sub-rule (1).]

- *Settlement of dispute*: In case of dispute between the importer and the proper officer of customs valuing the goods, the same shall be resolved consistent with the provisions contained in sub-section (1) of Section 14 of the Customs Act, 1962 (52 of 1962).
- *Interpretative Notes*: The interpretative notes specified in the Schedule to these rules shall apply for the interpretation of these rules.
  - Substituted by M.F. (D.R) Notification No.26/95-Cus.(N.T.),dated 24-4-1995.
  - Inserted by M.F.(D.R.) Notification No.26/95-Cus,(N.T.), dated 24-4-1995.
  - Inserted by M.F.(D.R.) Notification No.26/95-Cus.(N.T.), dated 24-4-1995.
  - Inserted by M.F.(D.R.) Notification No.26/95-Cus.(N.T.),dated 24-4-1995
  - Substituted by M.F.(D.R.)F.No.528/167/88-Cus.,(TV)/ICD, dated 6-9-1988.
  - Inserted by M.F.(D.R.)Notification No.26/95-Cus.(N.T.),dated 24-4-95
  - Substituted by M.F.(D.R.)Notification No.39/90(N.T.)-Cus., dated 5-7-1990
  - Substituted (w.e.f.1-10-1991) by M.F.(D.R.) Notification No.67/91 Cus. (N.T.), dated 1-10-1991.
  - Inserted by M.F.(D.R.)Notification No.10/98-Cus.(N.T.),dated 19-2-1998.

THE SCHEDULE

General Note:

Use of generally accepted accounting principles:

- " Generally accepted accounting principles" refer to the recognized consensus or substantial authoritative support within a country at a particular time as to which economic resources and obligations shall be recorded as assets and liabilities, which changes in assets and liabilities should be recorded, how the assets and liabilities and changes in them should be measured, what information should be disclosed and how it should be disclosed and which financial statements should be prepared. These standards may be broad guidelines of general application as well as detailed practices and procedures.

Notes to Rules

In Rule 2(2) (v), for the purposes of these rules, one person shall be deemed to control another when the former is legally or operationally in a position to exercise restraint or direction over the latter.

Note to Rule 4

Price Actually Paid or Payable

The price actually paid or payable is the total payment made or to be made by the buyer to or for the benefit of the seller for the imported goods. The payment need not necessarily take the form of a transfer of money. Payment may be made way of letters of credit or negotiable instruments. Payment may be made directly or indirectly. An example of an indirect payment would be the settlement by the buyer, whether in whole or in part, of a debt owed by the seller.

Activities undertaken by the buyer on his own account, other that those for which an adjustment is provided in Rule 9, are not considered to be and indirect payment to the seller, even though they might be regarded as of benefit to the seller. The costs of such activities shall not, therefore, be added to the price actually paid or payable in determining the value of imported goods. The value of imported goods shall not include the following charges or costs provided that they are distinguished from the price actually paid or payable for the imported goods: Charges for construction, erection, assembly, maintenance or technical assistance, undertaken after importation on imported goods such as industrial plant, machinery or equipment;

- The cost of transport after importation;
- Duties and taxes in India.

The price actually paid or payable refers to the price for the imported goods. Thus the flow of dividends or other payments from the buyer to the seller that do not relate to the imported goods are not part of the customs value.

Rule 4(2)(a)(iii)

Among restrictions which would not render a price actually paid or payable unacceptable are restrictions which do not substantially affect the value of the goods. An example of such restrictions would be the case where a seller requires a buyer of automobiles no to sell or exhibit them prior to a fixed date which represents the beginning of a model year.

Rule 4(2)(b)

If the sale or price is subject to some condition or consideration for which a value cannot be determined with respect to the goods being valued, the transaction value shall not be acceptable for customs purposes.

Some examples of this include:

- The seller establishes the price of the imported goods on condition that the buyer will also buy other goods in specified quantities;
- The price of the imported goods is dependent upon the price or prices at which the buyer of the imported goods sells other goods to the seller of the imported goods;
- The price is established on the basis of a form of payments extraneous to the imported goods, such as where the imported goods are semi-finished goods which have been provided by the seller on condition that he will receive a specified quantity of the finished goods.

However, conditions or considerations relating to the production or marketing of the imported goods shall to result in rejection of the transaction value. For example, the fact that the buyer furnishes the seller with engineering and plans undertaken in India shall not result in rejection of the transaction value for the purposes of Rule 4. Likewise, if the buyer undertakes on his own account, even though by agreement with the seller, activities relating to the marketing or the imported goods, the value of these activities is not part of the value of imported goods nor shall such activities result in rejection of the transaction value.

Rule 4(3)

- Rule 4(3) (a) and Rule 4(3) (b) provide different means of establishing the acceptability of a transaction value.
- Rule 4(3) (a) provides that where the buyer and the seller are related, the circumstances surrounding the sale shall be examined and the transaction value shall be accepted as the value of imported goods provided that the relationship did not influence the price. It is not intended that there should be an examination of the circumstances in all cases where the buyer and the seller are related. Such examination will only be required where there are doubts about the acceptability of the price. Where the proper officer of customs has no doubts about the acceptability of the price, it should be accepted without requesting further information from the importer. For example, the proper officer of customs may have previously examined the relationship, or he may already have detailed information concerning the buyer and the seller, and may already be satisfied from such examination or information that the relationship did not influence the price.
- Where the proper officer of customs is unable to accept the transaction value without further enquiry, he should give the importer an opportunity to supply such further detailed information as may be necessary to enable him to examine the circumstances surrounding

the sale. In this context, the proper officer of customs should be prepared to examine relevant aspects of the transaction, including the way in which the buyer and seller organize their commercial relations and the way in which the price in question was arrived at, in order to determine whether the relationship influenced the price. Where it can be shown that the buyer and seller, although related under the provisions of Rule 2(2), buy from and sell to each other as if they were not related, this would demonstrate that the price had not been influenced by the relationship. As example of this, if the price had been settled in a manner consistent with the normal pricing practices of the industry in question or with the way the seller settles prices for sales to buyers who are not related to him, this would demonstrate that the price had not been influenced by the relationship. As a further example, where it is shown that the price is adequate to ensure recovery of all costs plus a profit which is representative of the firm's overall profit realised over a representative period of time (*e.g.* on an annual basis) in sales of goods of the same class or kind, this would demonstrate that the price had not been influenced.

- Rule 4(3)(b) provides an opportunity for the importer to demonstrate that the transaction value closely approximates to a "test" value previously accepted by the proper offer of customs and is therefore acceptable under the provisions of rule 4. Where a test under rule 4(3) (b) is met, it is not necessary to examine the question of influence under [Rule 4(3)(a)]. If the proper officer of customs has already sufficient information to be satisfied, without further detailed enquiries, that one the tests provided in rule 4(3)(b) has been met, there is no reason for him to require the importer to demonstrate that the test can be met. In rule 4(3)(b) the term " unrelated buyers" means buyers who are not related to the seller in any particular case.

Rule 4(3)(b)

A number of factors must be taken into consideration in determining whether one value " closely approximates" to another value. These factors include the nature of the imported goods, the nature of the industry itself, the season in which the goods are imported, and whether the difference in value is commercially significant.

Since these factors may vary from case to case, it would be impossible to apply a uniform standard such as a fixed percentage, in each case. For example, a small difference in value in a case involving one type of goods could be unacceptable while a large difference in a case involving another type of goods might be acceptable in determining whether the transaction value closely approximates to the "test" values set forth in rule 4(3)(b).

Notes to Rule 5

- In applying rule 5, the proper officer of customs shall, wherever possible, use a sale of identical goods at the same commercial level and in substantially the same quantities as the goods being valued. Where no such sale is found, a sale of identical goods that takes place under any one of the following three conditions may be used:
  - A sale at the same commercial level but in different quantities;
  - A sale at a different commercial level but in substantially the same quantities; or
  - A sale at a different commercial level and in different quantities.
- Having found a sale under any one of these three conditions adjustments will then be made, as the case may be, for:
  a. Quantity factors only;
  b. Commercial level factors only; or
  c. Both commercial level and quantity factors.
- For the purposes of rule 5, the transaction value of identical imported goods means a value, adjusted as provided for in rule 5(1)(b) and (c) and rule 5(2), which has already been accepted under rule 4.
- A condition for adjustment because of different commercial levels or different quantities is that such adjustment, whether it leads to an increase or a decrease in the value, be made only on the basis of demonstrated evidence that clearly establishes the reasonableness and accuracy of the adjustment, *e.g.* valid price lists containing prices referring to different levels or different quantities. As an example of this, if the imported goods being valued consist of a shipment of 10 units and the only identical imported goods for which a transaction value exists involved a sale of 500 units, and it is recognized that the seller grants quantity discounts, the required adjustment may be accomplished by resorting to the seller's price list and using that price applicable to a sale of 10 units. This does not require that a sale had to have been made in quantities of 10 as long as the price list has been established as being bona fide through sales at other quantities. In the absence of such an objective measure, however, the determination of a value under the provisions of rule 5 is not appropriate.

Note to Rule 6

- In applying rule 6, the proper officer of customs shall, wherever possible, use a sale of similar goods at the same commercial level and in substantially the same quantities as the goods being valued. For the purpose of rule 6, the transaction value of similar imported goods means the value of imported goods, adjusted as provided for in rule 6(2) which has already been accepted under rule 4.

- All other provisions contained in note to rule 5 shall mutatis mutandis also apply in respect of similar goods.

Note to Rule 7

- The term "unit/price at which.... Goods are sold in the greatest aggregate quantity" means the price at which the greatest number of units is sold in sales to persons who are not related to the persons from whom they buy such goods at the first commercial level after importation at which such sales take place.
- As an example of this, goods are sold from a price list which grants favourable unit prices for purchases made in larger quantities.

Sale quantity Unit price Number of sales Total quantity sold at each price1-10 units 100 10 sales of 5 units, 65.5 sales of 3 units 11-25 units 95 5 sales of 11 units. 55 over 25 units 90 1 sale of 30 units 80

1 Sale of 50 Units

The greatest number of units sold at a price is 80, therefore, the unit price in the greatest aggregate quantity is 90.

- As another example of this, two sales occur, in the first sale 500 units are sold at a price of 95 currency units each. In the second sale 400 units are sold at a price of 90 currency units each. In this example, the greatest number of units sold at a particular price is 500, therefore, the unit price n the greatest aggregate quantity is 95.
- A third example would be the following situation where various quantities are sold at various prices.
  - Sales sale quantity Unit price
    40 units 100 30 units 90
    15 units 100 50 units 95
    25 units 105 35 units 90
    5 units 100
  - Total quantity sold Unit price
    65 90 50 95
    60 100 25 105

In this example, the greatest number of units sold at a particular price is 65, therefore, the unit price in the greatest aggregate quantity is 90.

- Any sale in India, as described in paragraph 1 above to a person who supplies directly or indirectly free of charge or at reduced cost for use in connection with the production and sale for export of the imported goods any of the elements specified in rule 9(1) (b), should not be taken into account in establishing the unit price for the purposes of rule 7.

- It should be noted that "profit and general expenses" referred to in rule 7(1) should be taken as a whole. The figure for the purposes of this deduction should be determined on the basis of information supplied by or on behalf of the importer unless his figures are inconsistent with those obtaining in sales in India, of imported goods of the same class or kind. Where the importers figures are inconsistent with such figures, the amount for profit and general expenses may be based upon relevant information other than that supplied by or on behalf of the importer.
- The "general expenses" include the direct and indirect costs of marketing the goods in question.
- Local taxes payable by reason of the sale of the goods for which deduction is not made under the provisions of rule 7(1)(iii) shall be deducted under the provisions of rule 7(1)(i).
- In determining either the commissions or the usual profits and general expenses under the provisions of rule 7(1), the question whether certain goods are "of the same class or kind" as other goods must be determined on a case-by-case basis by reference to the circumstances involved. Sales in India, of the narrowest group or range of imported goods of the same class or kind, which includes the goods being valued, for which the necessary information can be provided, should be examined. For the purposes of rule 7 "goods of the same class or kind" includes goods imported from the same country as the goods being valued as well as goods imported from other countries.
- For the purposes of rule 7(2) the "earliest date" shall be the date by which sales of the imported goods or of identical or similar imported, goods are made in sufficient quantity to establish the unit price.
- Where the method in rule 7(3) is used, deductions made for the value added by further processing shall be based on objective and quantifiable data relating to the cost of such work. Accepted industry formulas, recipes, methods or construction, and other industry practices would form the basis of the calculations.
- It is recognized that the method of valuation provided for in rule 7(3) would normally not be applicable when, as a result of the further processing, the imported goods lose their identity. However there can be instances where, although the identity of the imported goods is lose their identity. However there can be instances where, although the identity of the imported goods is lost, the value added by the processing can be determined accurately without unreasonable difficulty. On the other hand, there can also be instances where the

imported goods maintain their identity but form such a minor elements in the goods sold in the country of importation that the use of this valuation method would be unjustified. In view of the above, each situation of this type must be considered on a case-by-case basis.

Note to Rule 7A

- As a general rule, value of imported goods is determined under these rules on the basis of information readily available in India. In order to determine a computed value, however, it may be necessary to examine the costs of producing the goods being valued and other information which has to be obtained from outside India. Furthermore, in most cases, the producer of the goods will be outside the jurisdiction of the proper officer. The use of the computed value method will generally be limited to those cases where the buyer and seller are related, and the producer is prepared to supply to the proper officer the necessary costing and to provide facilities for any subsequent verification which may be necessary.
- The "cost or value" referred to in clause (a) of rule 7A is to be determined on the basis of information relating to the production of the goods being valued supplied by or on behalf of the producer. It is to be based upon the commercial accounts of the producer, provided that such accounts are consistent with the generally accepted accounting principles applied in the country where the goods are produced.
- The "cost or value" shall include the cost of elements specified in clauses (1)(a)(ii) and (1)(a)(iii) of rule 9. It shall also include the value, apportioned as appropriate under the provisions of the relevant note to rule 9, of any element specified in rule 9(1)(b) which has been supplied directly or indirectly by the buyer for use in connection with the production of the imported goods. The value of the elements specified in rule 9(1)(b)(iv) which are undertaken in India shall be included only to the extent that such elements are charged to the producer. It is to be understood that no cost or value of the elements referred to in this paragraph shall be counted twice in determining the computed value.
- The "amount for profit and general expenses" referred to in clause (b) of rule 7A is to be determined on the basis of information supplied by or on behalf of the producer unless the producer's figures are inconsistent with those usually reflected in sales of goods of the same class or kind as the goods being valued which are made by producers in the country of exportation for export to India.
- It should be noted in this context that the "amount for profit and

general expenses" has to be taken as a whole. It follows that if, in any particular case, the producer's profit figure is low and his general expenses are high, the producer's profit and general expenses taken together may nevertheless be consistent with that usually reflected in sales of goods of the same class or kind. Such a situation might occur, for example, if a product were being launched in India and the producer accepted a nil or low profit to offset high general expenses associated with the launch. Where the producer can demonstrate a low profit on his sales of the imported goods because of particular commercial circumstances, his actual profit figures should be taken into account provided that he has valid commercial reasons to justify them and his pricing policy reflects usual pricing policies in the branch of industry concerned. Such a situation might occur for example, where producers have been forced to lower prices temporarily because of an unforeseeable drop in demand, or where they sell goods to complement a range of goods being produced in India and accept a low profit to maintain competitivity. Where the producer's own figures for profit and general expenses are not consistent with those usually reflected in sales of goods of the same class or kind as the goods being valued which are made by producers in the country of exportation for export to India, the amount for profit and general expenses may be based upon relevant information other than that supplied by or on behalf of the producer of the goods.

- The "general expenses" referred to in clause(b) of rule 7A covers the direct and indirect costs of producing and selling the goods for export which are not included under clause (a)of rule 7A.
- Whether certain goods are "of the same class or kind" as other goods must be determined on a case-by-case basis with reference to the circumstances involved. In determining the usual profits and general expenses under the provisions of rule 7A, sales for export to India of the narrowest group or range of goods, which includes the goods being valued, for which the necessary information can be provided, should be examined. For the purposes of rule 7A "goods of the same class or kind" must be from the same country as the goods being valued.

Note to Rule 8

- Value of imported goods determined under the provisions of rule 8 should to the greatest extent possible, be based on previously determined customs values.
- The methods of valuation to be employed under rule 8 may be those laid down in (rules 4 to 7A), inclusive, but a reasonable flexibility in

the application of such methods would be in conformity with the aims and provision of rule 8.

- *Some examples of reasonable flexibility are as follows*:
  - *Identical goods*: The requirement that the identical goods should be imported at or about the same time as the goods being valued could be flexibly interpreted; identical imported goods produced in a country other than the country of exportation of the goods being valued could be the basis for customs valuation; customs values of identical imported goods already determined under the provisions of (rules 7 and 7A) could be used.
  - *Similar goods*: The requirement that the similar goods should be imported at or about the same time as the goods being valued could be flexibly interpreted; similar imported goods produced in a country other than the country of exportation of the goods being valued could be the basis for customs valuation; customs values of similar imported goods already determined under the provisions of (rules 7 and 7A) could be used.
  - *Deductive method*: The requirement that the goods shall have been sold in the "condition as imported" in rule 7(1) could be flexibly interpreted; the ninety days requirement could be administered flexibly.

Note to Rule 9

In rule 9(1)(a)(i), the term "buying commissions" means fees paid by an importer to his agent for the service of representing him abroad in the purchase of the goods being valued.

Rule 9(1)(b)(ii)

- There are two factors involved in the apportionment of the elements specified in rule 9(1)(b)(ii) to the imported goods – the value of the element itself and the way in which that value is to be apportioned to the imported goods. The apportionment of these elements should be made in a seasonable manner appropriate to the circumstances and in accordance with generally accepted accounting principles.
- Concerning the value of the element, if the importer acquires the element from a seller not related to him at a given cost, the value of the element is that cost. If the element was produced by the importer or by a person related to him, its value would be the cost of producing it. If the element had been previously used by the importer, regardless of whether it had been acquired or produced by such importer, the original cost of acquisition or production would have to be adjusted

downward to reflect its use in order to arrive at the value of the element.

- Once a value has been determined for the element it is necessary to apportion that value to the imported goods. Various possibilities exist. For example, the value might be apportioned to the first shipment if the importer wishes to pay duty on the entire value at one time. As another example, the importer may request that the value be apportioned over the number of units produced up to the time of the first shipment. As a further example, he may request that the value be apportioned over the entire anticipated production where contracts or firm commitments exists for that production. The method of apportionment used will depend upon the documentation provided by the importer.
- As an illustration of the above, an importer provides the producer with a mould to be used in the production of the imported goods and contracts with him to buy 10,000 units. By the time of arrival of the first shipment of 1,000 units the producer has already produced 4,000 units. The importer may request the proper officer of customs to apportion the value of the mould over 1,000 units, 4,000 units or 10,000 units.

Rule 9(1)(b)(iv)

- Additions for the elements specified in rule 9(1)(b)(iv) should be based on objective and quantifiable data. In order to minimize the burden for both the importer and proper officer of customs in determining the values to be added, data readily available in the buyer's commercial record system should be used in so far as possible.
- For those elements supplied by the buyer which were purchased or leased by the buyer, the addition would be the cost of the purchase or the lease. No addition shall be made for those elements available in the public domain, other than the cost of obtaining copies of them.
- The case with which it may be possible to calculate the values to be added will depend on a particular firm's structure and management practice, as well as its accounting methods.
- For example, it is possible that a firm which imports a variety of products from several countries maintains the records of its design centre outside the country of importation in such a way as to show accurately the costs attributable to a given product. In such cases, a direct adjustment may appropriately be made under the provisions of rule 9.
- In another case, a firm may carry the cost of the design centre outside the country of importation as a general overhead expense without

allocation to specific products. In this instance, an appropriate adjustment could be made under the provisions of rule 9 with respect to the imported goods by apportioning total design centre costs over total production benefiting from the design centre and adding such apportioned cost on a unit basis to imports.

- Variations in the above circumstances will, of course, require different factors to be considered in determining the proper method of allocation.
- In cases where the production of the element in question involves a number of countries and over a period of time, the adjustment should be limited to the value actually added to that element outside the country of importation.

Rule 9(1)(c)

- The royalties and license fees referred to in rule 9(1) (c) may include among other things, payments in respect to patents, trademarks and copyrights. However, the charges for the right to reproduce the imported goods in the country of importation shall not be added to the price actually paid or payable for the imported goods in determining the customs value.
- Payments made by the buyer for the right to distribute or resell the imported goods shall not be added to the price actually paid or payable for the imported goods if such payments are not a condition of the sale for export to the country of importation of the imported goods.

Rule 9(3)

Where objective and quantifiable data do not exist with regard to the additions required to be made under the provisions of rule 9, the transaction value cannot be determined under the provisions of rule 4. As an illustration of this, a royalty is paid on the basis of the price in a sale in the importing country of a litre of particular product that was imported by the kilogram and made up into a solution after importation. If the royalty is based partially on the imported goods and partially on other factors, which have nothing to do with the imported goods (such as when the imported goods are mixed with domestic ingredients and are no longer separately identifiable, or when the royalty cannot be distinguished from special financial arrangements between the buyer and the seller), it would be inappropriate to attempt to make an addition for the royalty. However, if the amount of this royalty is based only on the imported goods and can be readily quantified, an addition to the price actually paid or payable can be made.

- Substituted by M.F. (D.R.) Letter F.No 528/167/88-Cus.(TU/ICD), dated 28.10.1988.

- Inserted by M.F.(D.R.) Notification No.26/95-Cus.(N.T.),dated 24-4-1995.
- Subsitituted by M.F.(D.R.) Notification No.26/95-Cus.(N.T.),dated 24-4-1995.
- Subsitituted by M.F.(D.R.)Notification No.26/95-Cus.(N.T.),dated 24-4-1995.
- Substituted by M.F.(D.R.)Notification No.26/95-Cus.(N.T.),dated 24-4-95.

SMUGGLERS AND FOREIGN EXCHANGE MANIPULATORS

An Act to provide for the forfeiture of illegally acquired properties of smugglers and foreign exchange manipulators and for matters connected therewith or incidental thereto; Whereas for the effective prevention of smuggling activities and foreign exchange manipulations which are having a deleterious effect on the national economy it is necessary to deprive persons engaged in such activities and manipulations of their ill-gotten gains; And whereas such persons have been augmenting such gains by violations of wealth-tax, income-tax or other laws or by other means and have thereby been increasing their resources for operating in a clandestine manner; And whereas such persons have in many cases been holding the properties acquired by them through such gains in the names of their relatives, associates and confidants. Be it enacted by Parliament in the Twenty-sixth Year of the Republic of India as follows:

Short title, Extent and Commencement

- This act may be called the Smugglers and Foreign Exchange Manipulators (Forfeiture of Property) Act, 1976.
- It extends to the whole of India except the State of Jammu and Kashmir.
- It shall be deemed to have come into force on the 5th day of November, 1975.

Application

- The provisions of this Act shall apply only to the persons specified in sub-section (2).
- The persons referred to in sub-section (1) are the following, namely:
  - *Every person*:
    i. Who has been convicted under the Sea Customs Act, 1878 (8 of 1878), or the Customs Act, 1962 (52 of 1962), of an offence in relation to goods of a value exceeding one lakh of rupees; or

ii. Who having been convicted under the Sea Customs Act, 1878 (8 of 1878), or the Customs Act, 1962 (52 of 1962), has been convicted subsequently under either of those Acts; or
iii. Who having been convicted under the Foreign Exchange Regulation Act, 1947 (7 of 1947), or the Foreign Exchange Regulation Act, 1973 (46 of 1973), has been convicted subsequently under either or those Act;

- Every person in respect of whom an order of detention has been made under the Conservation of Foreign Exchange and Prevention of Smuggling Activities Act, 1974 (52 of 1974):Provided that-
  i. Such order of detention, being an order which the provisions of section 9 or section 12A of the said Act do not apply, has not been revoked on the report of the Advisory Board under section 8 of the said Act or before the receipt of the report of the Advisory Board or before making a reference to the Advisory Board; or
  ii. Such order of detention, being an order to which the provisions of section 9 of the said Act apply, has not been revoked before the expiry of the time for, or on the basis of, the review under sub-section (3) of section 9 or on the report of the Advisory board under section 8, read with sub-section (2) of section 9, of the said Act; or
  iii. Such order of detention, being an order to which the provisions of section 12A of the said Act apply, has not been revoked before the expiry of the time for, or on the basis of, the first review under sub-section (3) of that section, or on the basis of the report of the Advisory Board under section 8, read with sub-section (6) of section 12A, of that Act; or
  iv. Such order of detention has not been set aside by a Court of competent jurisdiction;
- Every person who is a relative of person referred to in clause (a) or clause (b);
- Every associate of a person referred to in clause (a) or clause (b);
- Any holder (hereafter in this clause referred to as the present holder) of any property which was at any time previously held by a person referred to in clause (a) or clause (b) unless the present holder or, as the case may be, any one who held such property after such person and before the present holder, is or was a transferee in good faith for adequate consideration.

  Explanation 1: For the purposes of sub-clause (i) of clause (a), the value of any goods in relation to which a person has been convicted of an offence shall be the wholesale price of the goods in the ordinary cause of trade in India as on the date of the commission of the offence.

Explanation 2: For the purposes of clause (c), "relative", in relation to a person, means:

i. Spouse of the person;
ii. Brother or sister of the person;
iii. Brother or sister of the spouse of the person;
iv. Any lineal ascendant or descendant of the person;
v. Any lineal ascendant or descendant of the spouse of the person;
vi. Spouse of a person referred to in clause (ii), clause (iii), clause (iv) or clause (v);
vii. Any lineal descendant of a person referred to in clause (ii) or clause (iii).

Explanation 3: For the purposes of clause (d), "associate", in relation to a person, means-

i. Any individual who, had been or is residing in the residential premises (including out-houses) of such person;
ii. Any individual who had been or is managing the affairs or keeping the accounts of such person;
iii. Any association of persons, body of individuals, partnership firm, or private company within the meaning of the Companies Act, 1956 (1 of 1956), of which such person had been or is a member, partner or director;
iv. Any individual who had been or is a member, partner or director of an association of persons, body of individuals, partnership firm or private company referred to in clause (iii) at any time when such person had been or is a member, partner or director of such association, body, partnership firm or private company;
v. Any person who had been or is managing the affairs, or keeping the accounts, of any association of persons, body of individuals, partnership firm or private company referred to in clause (iii);
vi. The trustee of any trust, where,-
    a. The trust has been created by such person; or
    b. The value of the assets contributed by such person (including the value of the assets, if any, contributed by him earlier) to the trust amounts, on the date on which the contribution is made, to not less than twenty

per cent of the value of the assets of the trust on that date;

vii. Where the competent authority, for reasons to be recorded in writing, considers that any properties of such person are held on his behalf by any other person, such other person.

Explanation 4: For the avoidance of doubt, it is hereby provided that the question whether any person is a person to whom the provisions of this Act apply may be determined with reference to any facts, circumstances or events (including any conviction or detention) which occurred or took place before the commencement of this Act

ACT NOT TO APPLY TO CERTAIN PERSONS

On and from the commencement of the provisions of the Narcotic Drugs and Psychotropic Substances Act, 1985 (61 of 1985), the provisions of this Act shall not apply to persons in relation to whom any order, or proceeding, may be made or taken under that Chapter.

Definitions

- In this Act, unless the context otherwise requires, "Appellate Tribunal" means the Appellate Tribunal for Forfeited Property constituted under section 12; "competent authority" means an officer of the Central Government authorised by it under sub-section (1) of section 5 to perform the functions of a competent authority under this Act; "illegally acquired property", in relation to any person to whom this Act applies, means-
  i. Any property acquired by such person, whether before or after the commencement of this act, wholly or partly out of or by means of any income, earnings or assets derived or obtained from or attributable to any activity prohibited by or under any law for the time being in force relating to any matter in respect of which Parliament has power to make laws; or
  ii. Any property acquired by such person, whether before or after the commencement of this Act, wholly or partly out of or by means of any income, earnings or assets in respect of which any such law has been contravened; or
  iii. Any property acquired by such person, whether before or after the commencement of this Act, wholly or partly out of or by means of any income, earnings or assets the source of which cannot be proved and which cannot be shown to be attributable to any act or thing done in respect of any matter in relation to which Parliament has no power to make laws; or

iv. Any property acquired by such person, whether before or after the commencement of this Act, for a consideration, or by any means, wholly or partly traceable to any property referred to in sub-clauses (i) to (iii) or the income or earnings from such property and includes-any property held by such person which would have been, in relation to any previous holder thereof, illegally acquired property under this clause if such previous holder had not ceased to hold it, unless such person or any other person who held the property at any time after such previous holder or, where there are two or more such previous holders, the last of such previous holders is or was a transferee in good faith for adequate consideration; any property acquired by such person, whether before or after the commencement of this Act, for a consideration, or by any means, wholly or partly traceable to any property falling under item (A), or the income or earnings therefrom; "prescribed" means prescribed by rules made under this Act; "property" includes any interest in property, movable or immovable; "trust" includes any other legal obligation. (2) Any reference in this Act to any law which is not in force in any area shall, in relation to that area, be construed as a reference to the corresponding law, if any, in force in that area. (3) Any reference in this Act to any officer or authority shall, in relation to any area in which there is no officer or authority with the same designation, be construed as a reference to such officer or authority as may be specified by the central Government by notification in the Official Gazette.

PROHIBITION OF HOLDING ILLEGALLY ACQUIRED PROPERTY

- As from the commencement of this Act, it shall not be lawful for any person to whom this Act applies to hold any illegally acquired property either by himself or through any other person on his behalf.
- Where any person holds any illegally acquired property in contravention of the provisions of sub-section (1), such property shall be liable to be forfeited to the Central Government in accordance with the provisions of this Act.

COMPETENT AUTHORITY

- The Central Government may, by order published in the Official Gazette, authorise as many officers of the Central Government (non below the rank of a Joint Secretary to the Government), as it thinks fit, to perform the functions of the competent authority under this Act.

- The competent authorities shall perform their functions in respect of such persons or classes or persons as the Central Government may, by order, direct.

NOTICE OF FORFEITURE

- If, having regard to the value of the properties held by any person to whom this Act applies, either by himself or through any other person on his behalf, his known sources, of income, earnings or assets, and any other information or material available to it as a result of action taken under section 18 or otherwise, the competent authority has reason to believe (the reasons for such belief to be recorded in writing) that all or any of such properties are illegally acquired properties, it may serve a notice upon such person (hereinafter referred to as the person affected) calling upon him within such time as may be specified in the notice, which shall not be ordinarily less than thirty days, to indicate the sources of his income, earnings or assets, out of which or by means of which he has acquired such property, the evidence on which he relies and other relevant information and particulars, and to show cause why all or any of such properties, as the case may be, should not be declared to be illegally acquired properties and forfeited to the Central Government under this Act.
- Where a notice under sub-section (1) to any person specifies any property as being held on behalf of such person by any other person, a copy of the notice shall also be served upon such other person.

FORFEITURE OF PROPERTY IN CERTAIN CASES:

- The competent authority may, after considering the explanation, if any, to the show-cause notice issued under section6, and the materials available before it and after giving to the person affected (and in a case where the person affected holds any property specified in the notice through any other person, to such other person also) a reasonable opportunity of being heard, by order, record a finding whether all or any of the properties in question are illegally acquired properties.
- Where the competent authority is satisfied that some of the properties referred to in the show-cause notice are illegally acquired properties but is not able to identify specifically such properties, then, it shall be lawful for the competent authority to specify the properties which,

to the best of its judgement, are illegally acquired properties and record a finding accordingly under sub-section (1).

- Where the competent authority records a finding under this section to the effect that any property is illegally acquired property, it shall declare that such property shall, subject to the provisions of this Act, stand forfeited to the central Government free from all encumbrances.
- Where any shares in a company stand forfeited to the Central Government under this Act, then, the company shall, notwithstanding any thing contained in the Companies Act, 1956 (1 of 1956), or the articles of association of the company, forthwith register the Central Government as the transferee of such shares.

RECTIFICATION OF MISTAKES

With a view to rectifying any mistakes apparent from the record, the competent authority or the Appellate Tribunal, as the case may be, may amend any order made by it within a period of one year from the date of the order: Provided that if any such amendment is likely to affect any person prejudicially, it shall not be made without giving to such person a reasonable opportunity of being heard.

FINDINGS UNDER OTHER LAWS NOT CONCLUSIVE FOR PROCEEDINGS UNDER THIS ACT

No finding of any officer of authority under any other law shall be conclusive for the purposes of any proceedings under this act.

SERVICE OF NOTICES AND ORDERS

Any notice or order issued or make under this Act shall be served:

- By tendering the notice or order or sending it by registered post to the person for whom it is intended or to his agent;
- If the notice or order cannot be served in the manner provided in clause (a), by affixing it on a conspicuous place in the property in relation to which the notice or order is issued or made, or on some conspicuous part of the premises in which the person for whom it is intended is known to have last resided or carried on business or personally worked for gain.

PROTECTION OF ACTION TAKEN IN GOOD FAITH

No suit, prosecution or other proceeding shall lie against the Central Government or any Officer of the Central or State Government for any thing which is done, or intended to be done, in good faith, in pursuance of this Act or the rules made thereunder.

ACT TO HAVE OVERRIDING EFFECT

The provisions of this Act shall have effect notwithstanding any thing inconsistent therewith contained in any other law for the time being in force.

PROVISIONS OF THE ACT NOT TO APPLY TO CERTAIN PROPERTIES HELP IN TRUST

Nothing contained in this Act shall apply in relation to any property held by a trust or an institution created or established wholly for public, religious or charitable purposes if:

- Such property has been so held by such trust or institution from a date prior to the commencement of this Act.
- Such property is wholly traceable to any property held by such trust or institution prior to the commencement of this Act.

POWER TO MAKE RULES

- The Central Government may, by notification in the Official Gazette, make rules to carry out the provisions of this Act.
- In particular and without prejudice to the generality of the foregoing power, such rules may provide for all or any of the following matters, namely:
  - The terms and conditions of service of the chairman and other members of the Appellate Tribunal under sub-section (3) of section 12;
    i. The fees which shall be paid for the inspection of the records and registers of the Appellate Tribunal or for obtaining a certified copy of any part thereof under sub-section (8) of section 12;
  - The powers of a civil court that may be exercised by the competent authority and the Appellate Tribunal under clause (f) of section 15;
  - Any other matter which has to be, or may be, prescribed.

BURDEN OF PROOF

In any proceedings under this Act, the burden of proving that any property specified in the notice served under section 6 in not illegally acquired property shall be on the person affected.

FINE IN LIEU OF FORFEITURE

- Where the competent authority makes declaration that any property stands forfeited to the Central Government under section 7 and it is a case where the source of only a part, being less than one-half, of the income, earnings or assets with which such property was acquired has not been proved to the satisfaction of the competent authority, it shall make an order giving an option to the person affected to pay, in lieu of forfeiture, a fine equal to one and one-fifth times the value of such part.

Explanation: For the purposes of this sub-section, the value of any part of income, earnings or assets, with which any property has been acquired, shall be,-

- In the case of any part of income of earnings, the amount of such part of income of earnings;
- In the case of any part of assets, the proportionate part of the full value of the consideration for the acquisition of such assets.

- Before making an order imposing a fine under sub-section (1), the person affected shall be given a reasonable opportunity of being head.
- Where the person affected pays the fine due under sub-section (1), within such time as may allowed in that behalf, the competent authority may, by order, revoke the declaration of forfeiture under section 7 and thereupon such property shall stand released.

PROCEDURE IN RELATION TO CERTAIN TRUST PROPERTIES

In the case of any person referred to in clause (vi) of Explanation 3 to sub-section (2) of section 2, if the competent authority, on the basis of the information and materials available to it, has reason to believe (the reasons for such belief to be recorded in writing) that any property held in trusts in illegally acquired property, it may serve a notice upon the author of the trust or, as the case may be, the contributor of the assets out of or by means of which such property was acquired by the trust and the trustees, calling upon them within such time as may be specified in the notice which shall not ordinarily be less than thirty days, to explain the source of the money or other assets out of or by means of which such property was acquired or, as the case may be, the source of the money or other assets which were contributed to the trust for acquiring such property and thereupon such notice shall be deemed to be a notice served under section 6 and all other provisions of this Act shall apply accordingly.

Explanation: For the purposes of this section "illegally acquired property", in relation to any property held in trust, includes:

- Any property which if it had continued to be held by the author of the trust of the contributor of such property to the trust would have been illegally acquired property in relation to such author or contributor;
- Any property acquired by the trust out of any contributions made by any person which would have been illegally acquired property in relation to such person had such person acquired such property out of such contributions.

CERTAIN TRANSFERS TO BE NULL AND VOID

Where after the issue of a notice under section 6 or under section 10, any property referred to in the said notice is transferred by any mode whatsoever such transfer shall, for the purposes of the proceedings under this Act, be ignored and if such property is subsequently forfeited to the Central Government under section 7, then, the transfer of such property shall be deemed to be null and void.

CONSTITUTION OF APPELLATE TRIBUNAL

- The Central Government may, be notification in the Official Gazette, constitute an Appellate Tribunal to be called the Appellate Tribunal for Forfeited Property consisting of a Chairman and such number of other members (being officers of the Central Government not below the rank of a Joint secretary to the Government) as the Central Government thinks fit, to be appointed by that Government for hearing appeals against the orders made under section 7, sub-section (1) of section 9 or section 10.
- The Chairman of the Appellate Tribunal shall be a person who is or has been or is qualified to be a judge of the Supreme Court or of a High Court.
- The terms and conditions of service of the Chairman and other members shall be such as may be prescribed.
- Any person aggrieved by an order of the competent authority made under section 7, sub-section (1) of section 9 or section 10, may, within forty-five days from the date on which the order is served on him, prefer an appeal to the Appellate Tribunal. Provided that the Appellate Tribunal may entertain any appeal after the said period of forty-five days, but not after sixty days, from the date aforesaid if it is satisfied that the appellant was prevented by sufficient cause from filling the appeal in time.
- On receipt of an appeal under sub-section (4), the Appellate Tribunal may, after giving an opportunity to the appellant to be heard, if he so desires, and after making such further enquiry as it deems fit, confirm, modify or set aside the order appealed against.
- The powers and functions of the Appellate tribunal may be exercised and discharged by Benches consisting of three members and constituted by the Chairman of the Appellate Tribunal.
  - Notwithstanding anything contained in sub-section (6), where the Chairman considers it necessary so to do for the expeditious disposal of appeals under this section, he may constitute a Bench of two members and a Bench so constituted may exercise and

discharge the powers and functions of the Appellate Tribunal: Provided that if the members of a Bench so constituted differ on any point or points, they shall state the point or points on which they differ and refer the same to a third members (to be specified by the chairman) for hearing on such point or points and such point or points shall be decided according to the opinion of that member.

- The Appellate Tribunal may regulate its own procedure.
- On application to the Appellate Tribunal and on payment of the prescribed fee, the Tribunal may allow a party to any appeal or any person authorised in this behalf by such party to inspect at any time during office hours, any relevant records and registers of the Tribunal and obtain a certified copy of any part thereof.

NOTICE OR ORDER NOT TO BE INVALID FOR ERROR IN DESCRIPTION

No notice issued or served, no declaration made, and no order passed, under this Act shall be deemed to be invalid by reason of any error in the description of the property or person mentioned therein if such property or person is identifiable from the description so mentioned.

BAR OF JURISDICTION

No order passed or declaration made under this Act shall be appealable except as provided therein and no civil court shall have jurisdiction in respect of any matter which the Appellate Tribunal or any competent authority is empowered by or under the Act to determine, and no injunction shall be granted by any Court or other authority in respect of any action taken or to be taken in pursuance of any power conferred by or under this Act.

COMPETENT AUTHORITY AND APPELLATE TRIBUNAL TO HAVE POWERS OF CIVIL COURT

The competent authority and the Appellate tribunal shall have all the powers of a civil court while trying a suit under the Code of Civil Procedure, 1908 (5 of 1908), in respect of the following maters, namely:

- Summoning and enforcing the attendance of any person and examining him on oath;
- Requiring the discovery and production of documents;
- Receiving evidence on affidavits;
- Requisitioning any public record or copy thereof from any court or office;
- Issuing commissions for examination of witnesses or documents;
- Any other matter which may be prescribed.

INFORMATION TO COMPETENT AUTHORITY

- Notwithstanding anything contained in any other law, the competent authority shall have power to require any officer or authority of the central Government or a State Government of a local authority to furnish information in relation to such persons, points or matters as in the opinion of the competent authority will be useful for, or relevant to, the purposes of this Act.
- Any officer of the Income-tax Department, the Customs Department or the Central Excise Department or any officer of Enforcement appointed under the Foreign Exchange Regulation Act, 1973 (46 of 1973), may furnish suo motu any information available with him to the competent authority if in the opinion of the officer such information will be useful to the competent authority for the purposes of this Act.

CERTAIN OFFICERS TO ASSIST COMPETENT AUTHORITY AND APPELLATE TRIBUNAL

For the purposes of any proceedings under this Act, the following officers are hereby empowered and required to assist the competent authority and the Appellate Tribunal, namely:

- Officers of the Customs Department;
- Officers of the Central Excise Department;
- Officers of the Income-tax Department;
- Officers of Enforcement appointed under the Foreign Exchange Regulation Act, 1973 (46 of 1973);
- Officers of Police;
- Such other officers of the Central of State Government as are specified by the Central Government in this behalf by notification in the Official Gazette.

POWER OF COMPETENT AUTHORITY TO REQUIRE CERTAIN OFFICERS TO EXERCISE CERTAIN POWERS

- For the purposes of any proceedings under this Act or the initiation of any such proceedings, the competent authority shall have power to cause to be conducted any enquiry, investigation or survey in respect of any person, place, property, assets, documents, books of account or any other relevant matters.
- For the purposes referred to in sub-section (1), the competent authority may, having regard to the nature of the enquiry, investigation or survey, require an officer of the Income-tax Department to conduct or cause to be conducted such enquiry, investigation or survey.

- Any officer of the Income-tax Department who is conducting or is causing to be conducted any enquiry, investigation or survey required to be conducted under sub-section (2), may, for the purpose of such enquiry, investigation or survey, exercise any power (including the power to authorise the exercise of any power) which may be exercised by him for any purpose under the Income-tax Act, 1961 (43 of 1961), and the provisions of the said Act shall, so far as may be, apply accordingly.

POWER TO TAKE POSSESSION

- Where any property has been declared to be forfeited to the Central Government under this Act, or where the person affected has failed to pay the fine due under sub-section (1) of section 9 within the time allowed therefore under sub-section (3) of the section, the competent authority may order the person affected as well as any other person who may be in possession of the property to surrender or deliver possession thereof to the competent authority or to any person duly authorised by it in this behalf within thirty days of the service of the order.
- If any person refuses or fails to comply with an order made under sub-section (1), the competent authority may take possession of the property and may for that purpose use such force as may be necessary.
- Notwithstanding anything contained in sub-section (2), the competent authority may, for the purpose of taking possession of any property referred to in sub-section (1), requisition the service of any police officer to assist the competent authority and it shall be the duty of such officer to comply with such requisition.

6

Fire Safety Engineering in a Hotel

OBSOLESCENCE

ILLUSTRATION OMITTED

To satisfy the mission, the objective is to develop and standardize an approach to assess the short- and long-term impacts of potential obsolescence. The approach will leverage from known system configuration and component availability information and will integrate additional programmatic information such as system reliability, supply support requirements, programme-level block changes, and technology roadmaps.

The OMT strives to assist the V-22 programme office's integrated product teams (IPTs) in reducing total ownership cost as a result of obsolescence issues by influencing pending aircraft design changes and maintenance concepts, and improving integrated logistics support products, based on current mission requirements and future mission needs.

Manufacturing Sources and Material Shortages

Loss of manufacturers or suppliers of critical items and raw materials resulting from discontinuance of production. DMSMS can be caused by rapid changes in item or material technology, uneconomical production requirements, foreign-source competition, federal environment or safety requirements, and limited ability or increasing cost of items and raw materials.

The DoD accounts for less than 1 per cent of the market share for integrated circuits, discrete, passive, and active devices used on legacy and new development systems. It is simply not cost effective for market suppliers to continue to produce those certain products needed to maintain the needs of the war fighters.

OBSOLESCENCE MANAGEMENT PROCESS FLOW

The V-22 programme office's OMT is guided by an obsolescence management plan that establishes a proactive process for predicting, identifying, and controlling obsolescence impacts that affect the programme from conceptual design through retirement. Processes defined within the plan provide the V-22 programme with a notice of obsolescence, the degree of impact of obsolescence, recommendations for mitigation, and an assessment of how soon the problem will impact the aircraft availability.

Those impacts are provided, in accordance with the V-22 change management process, as information to the IPTs charged with implementing a solution. All obsolescence notices are entered into a V-22 obsolescence verification and analysis system by means of case sheets. This allows tracking and status updates to be maintained and distributed. Case sheets are closed based on the resolution developed and approval by the appropriate IPTs. The information is then provided back to the maintenance plan to ensure currency of the data.

The first step in the V-22 obsolescence process is to assess and continuously monitor availability of the components used in the equipment for potential obsolescence risk. This is necessary so the programme can identify areas where it is vulnerable to potential obsolescence problems and plan for risk mitigation. In addition to continuous monitoring and contractor input, the V-22 OMT uses discontinuance notices delivered through GIDEP and the shared data warehouse or other available sources to provide an easy-to-use interface for part number enquiry listings. These processes enable the V-22 programme to take a focused, total-look approach.

Once a component has been identified as obsolete, an obsolescence risk assessment is performed. This verifies the current availability of a part, forecasts its future availability, identifies its sourcing depth, and identifies possible solution options if it is already obsolete. Once the initial assessment is complete, the team conveys the results to the appropriate points of contact for those systems, enabling them to take action. The parts are then monitored for availability status changes, and timely notifications are sent to the appropriate points of contact as changes are identified.

An obsolescence verification and analysis case sheet is assigned and completed on each unique part in order to verify current availability, forecast future availability, indicate sourcing depth, and identify possible solution options for those parts already obsolete.

The case sheet provides the basis for insight on the obsolescence impact at the next higher assembly or system level. The assessment results are intended as an aid to decision makers managing V-22 systems to help them improve afford-ability by minimizing costly redesigns.

Information from the development, production, and/or sustainment IPTs on the solution development and the approved implementation plan/funding is required for closure of the initial obsolescence notice entered into the reporting system.

Finally, after an obsolescence impact has been resolved, its solution is fed back into the process. It is important to maintain visibility of implemented solutions to ensure system changes are also managed for obsolescence. Resolution feedback will indicate when new parts are introduced into a system to replace or redesign obsolete parts, allowing the parts to be obtained and assessed for obsolescence and then monitored.

Resolution feedback can provide insight into when a system or component may no longer require monitoring (for example, if a system is replaced through attrition and will not be maintained by the government).

MONITORING TOOLS

The OMT employs a variety of obsolescence monitoring/prediction tools. No one tool can perform all of the necessary functions required to properly monitor each component. Each tool serves as a check and balance system to the others and provides notices, health analysis, prediction, and projection of component life span. The OMT uses, in comb-ination, AVCOM (Advanced Component Obsolescence Management); Total Parts Plus; QSTAR (Qinetic's Sustainment Technology Assessment Resource); TACTRAC (Transition Analysis of Component Tracking) andOMIS

RESULTS TO DATE

To date, the OMT has worked on over 400 obsolescence case sheets, resulting in the resolution and/or closure of over half in the past year. The OMT monitors over 50,000 components for the V-22. From fiscal year 1998 through fiscal 2004, the estimated cost avoidance for obsolescence management totaled over 39 million. Through the OMT's continuous efforts to streamline processes and become more efficient, the team has achieved an estimated cost avoidance of over 27 million for fiscal 2008 alone.

BENEFITS

- Minimize the impact of obsolescence to maximize your return on investment.
- Avoid costly re-designs due to component obsolescence.
- Minimize your obsolescence management overhead costs using.

Spectrum's Obsolescence
Management Service

- Reduce the effect that Moore's Law has on your product life cycle.
- Receive long-term professional Technical Support from Spectrum extending throughout the Obsolescence Management Plan period.

FEATURES

- Spectrum's Obsolescence Management Plans are based on the unique needs of each customer.

- Spectrum maintains a bonded inventory of customer-owned parts for future builds.
- Customers receive quarterly reports showing status of bonded inventory.
- Spectrum continuously monitors product billof- materials (BOMs) to identify additional component obsolescence that may require Obsolescence Management Plan updates.
- Technical Support service and repair facilities continue throughout the Obsolescence Management Plan period.

OBSOLESCENCE MANAGEMENT

Defence industry electronic equipment suppliers providing commercial off-the-shelf (COTS) solutions require Obsolescence Management to support the extended product life cycles typical of the industry. Moore's Law states that the transistor density on integrated circuits doubles every couple of years. This exponential growth and ever-shrinking transistor size results in increased performance and decreased cost. As a result, the direct impact for COTS vendors is near-term component obsolescence, leading to product end-of-life (EOL) or product re-design much earlier than desired in view of the product life cycle needs of the defence industry.

SERVICE OVERVIEW

Spectrum's Obsolescence Management Service is offered under our Product Life Cycle Management programme. It provides customer options beyond EOL notification and a single last time buy (LTB) opportunity for products going EOL. Upon product EOL, we work with our customer to prepare a unique Obsolescence Management

Plan that specifies the quantity of product required over a duration of time. LTB quantities of the component(s) going obsolete is placed into bonded inventory. The components placed into bonded inventory is customer-owned material. Spectrum monitors the product bill-of-materials (BOM) for further component obsolescence. Upon such occurance, Spectrum notifies the customer of the additional component(s) EOL and works with the customer to update the Obsolescence Management Plan.

COMPONENT MANAGEMENT SYSTEM

Spectrum product BOMs are continuously monitored for component obsolescence and/or other component changes using a state-of-the-art component database monitoring facility.

Upon receiving component change/obsolescence notification, we work with our customers to update their existing Obsolescence Management Plans to effectively reset the EOL clock. Proactive BOM monitoring provides Spectrum and our customers the ability to react quickly to critical information maximizing product life cycle and associated revenue.

BONDED INVENTORY

Based on the needs of the customer specific Obsolescence Management Plan, a LTB for components going obsolete will be purchased as customer-owned inventory and bonded. Customers are given credit for the components used from the bonded inventory upon shipment of the product.

QUARTERLY REPORTS

Spectrum reviews status of the customer-owned bonded inventory quarterly and sends a report to the customer with the following information about each component:

- Spectrum internal part number
- Manufacturer component part number
- Component description
- Quantity of each component

EXCESSIVE

Although their service is not often heralded, concierges can make a hotel stay an experience to remember, whether the guest is a celebrity or a mere mortal. It's the concierge's job to fulfill guests' requests, however outlandish. Take the Englishman staying at the Setai in Miami, who asked its concierge to figure out how to move his girlfriend's pet tiger to London. Not surprisingly, celebrities often demand the out-of-the-ordinary, like the well-known Australian rugby enthusiast who asked the Ritz-Carlton Georgetown to provide a special satellite dish so he could watch a 24-hour Australian rugby television channel.

Then there were the old stories about eccentrics like surrealist artist and animal-lover, Salvador Dali. He stayed regularly at the Meurice Hotel in Paris with his two pet ocelots, and asked the concierges to do things for him like catch flies in the Tuileries Garden.

Concierges working at Four Seasons hotels, for example, meet regularly for what Jon Winke, chef concierge since calls a "summit." Four Seasons concierges also often call upon concierges at other Four Seasons hotels for help; Winke, for example, said he recently was able to get accommodations at the Four Seasons Hotel for one of his regular guests, despite the fact the hotel was sold out. The guest, he said, "knows I can get things done for him he can't do on his own. The hotel did something nice for me, and now it's my turn to do something nice for them."

Another important resource used by concierges is the Clefs d'Or, an international professional group of concierges. Tommy Dean, who has been a concierge at the Four Seasons Hotel for almost 20 years, said the Clefs d'Or gives him access to concierges worldwide, and that networking through it has been invaluable. "It's an extended family that goes all over the world," he explained. Veteran concierges also say the Internet has radically changed the nature of their work and the demands guests make. All concierges use it. As Winke explained, "The Internet makes things a lot easier. It's a great resource and a godsend for me."

Frank Laino, executive head concierge of the Stafford in London, finds the Internet has changed guests' expectations. "A lot of clients are now better informed, they come to you with a mass of information they've pulled off the Internet. But a lot of time it serves to confuse people. We try to simplify things," he said. To that end, Laino writes a monthly newsletter, "Frankly Speaking," for the hotel's Web site that lists his top picks for what's on in London. Nor can all guests' wishes be fulfilled.

For example, the concierge at the Beverly Hills Hotel was once asked to find replacement parts for a guest, a request that was turned down. Wanting to surprise his wife on her 40th birthday, a guest at Parrot in the Turks and Caicos asked the hotel to arrange for some fake sharks to appear while he, she and their friends were snorkeling; the concierge declined to do this.

And a marriage proposal by a dinner guest at the hotel or orchestrated with the help of a concierge there, failed. Regardless, the best concierges continue to "try to make magic moments, something personalized," as Matthew, resort concierge at Topnotch Resort and Spa in Stowe, Vt., explains. "Sometimes we get people who want to have fun, and that's why we're here."

MAINTENANCE DECLINING EFFICIENCY

EFFICIENCY – STAFF PRODUCTIVITY

Basically, for the hotels engineering and maintenance staff, the day-to-day operation and maintenance of a large hotel is time-consuming.

Therefore, one of the striking advantages of Integrated Building Solutions (TBS) is the complete harmonization of the hotel's HVAC (heating, ventilation and air conditioning), fire, intrusion and CCTV (closed-circuit television) systems.

The integration of all of these disciplines means improved functionality for the hotel, and centralized display of all building information at the touch of a button. Furthermore, TBS also includes voice evacuation capabilities and controls for the hotel's phone system, guest services and background music. In total, the integrated TBS reduced significantly the workload of all involved maintenance staff.

At time when every penny counts, PMWorks, the preventive-maintenance solution from MTech, based here, is streamlining property efficiencies and protecting long-term capital investments for hotels. MTech is a leading provider of guest-response and preventive-maintenance solutions for the worldwide hotel industry.

The hotel management company is one such client. "We welcome Hospitality to our PMWorks family," said Luis Segredo, MTech president. "Management companies looking to grow, particularly with a diverse portfolio, need tools to help them manage the growth and justify it. With PMWorks, Winston Hospitality can show owners how they are protecting their properties and saving them costly repair dollars. As a subscription service that has been proven across many brands, PMWorks can meet Winston Hospitality's needs at the property level and provide the corporate office with operational and strategic reports.

"Co. continues to add management companies to its growing list of PMWorks users, even in this economic climate, because staffing cuts are requiring automation to help keep service and product levels high," he added. Michael president of Winston Hospitality, says that the proactive nature of PMWorks helps keep their hotels looking in great shape.

"We use PMWorks for everything from plumbing and paint touch-up to case goods and the HVAC system," Heeden said. "HVAC is really important because if it were to malfunction, it affects air quality and the noise is the number one complaint from guests."

Brand quality-assurance marks most often fall in the "outstanding" range for Hospitality properties. Heeden anticipates property mechanical systems will see fewer repairs and have a longer shelf life if each hotel follows the planned preventive-maintenance programme and PMWorks schedule.

WORKING

The Accounts Manager and liaison officer, explained that PM Works enables management companies to better manage the scheduling processes.

"The system provides a work load balanced schedule that lets you focus on the work that needs to be done," Edson said. "Time is no longer wasted preparing a complex schedule that must include critical reminders for Life, Health and Safety.

They are all there, in the system. It's a cost-effective solution for management companies that demand corporate-driven quality and consistency across a multi-branded portfolio."

Steps to Implementing Works at Hotel

- Enroll the property by faxing or e-mailing a signed agreement.
- Complete the Web data collection wizard. This is a simple and fast "prompted" collection of data. The hotelier is asked what the equipment is called (Ice machine One) and where it's located. A list of guestroom numbers completes the set up. On average a 100-room

property will take about two or three hours to set the entire programme up.

- Data is sent to a regional person, or back to the GM for a quick review to make sure the data is complete.
- The following Monday the hotel will receive its first work order packet VIA e-mail.

When the schedule is in place, hotels receive weekly service orders via e-mail. Each service includes step-by-step instructions on how to do the job right the first time.

As technicians complete tasks, they close orders from any touch-tone phone or Web browser. Every week new orders are sent to the property. Included are tasks not completed during previous weeks so nothing falls through the cracks? The management company receives an e-mail showing what properties are keeping up and which are falling behind.

"We receive status reports [green, yellow or red] to see which tasks are completed and which are not," Heeden said. "PMWorks customizes the process to fit the needs of each hotel. It generates the work orders once a week and let's us know where we are in the process. We use PMWorks in all of our hotels, have it ready to go at our properties under construction, and plan to use it in all of our new hotels.

"It takes a lot of the guess work out of the PM programme and keeps us on top of critical Life, Health and Safety PM's," he added.

The Hospitality offers services including management, development, rehabilitation, repositioning, and hotel ownership. Its senior management team brings years of experience and a wealth of knowledge to each of these areas and is committed to ensuring the satisfaction of guests and its partners. Its current portfolio includes four hotels, and at press time it was due to open one more.

REPLACEMENT POLICY OF HOTEL EQUIPMENT

PURPOSE

To establish a (PC) equipment replacement and upgrade policy for the Youngstown Metropolitan Housing Authority {CO.}rder to utilize the benefits of next-generation office environments, simplify technical support issues, and increase CO.ility to deploy new solutions to business problems.

STATEMENT

Guidelines and procedures are required to maintain a replacement cycle of personal Hotel equipment within the useful and expected lifetime of the equipment, while preventing a proliferation of aging, obsolete, out-of-warranty, unsupported, and incompatible systems.

CYCLE OF REPLACEMENT

It is Co. policy to cycle replaced computers through the major classifications of technology users PCs that have been replaced and are no longer appropriate for one classification of technology users should be used to upgrade and replace a PC with older technology within the agency.

In this manner, the PC with the oldest technology in the agency is phased out and the agency can continue to benefit from their investment in PCs.

REPLACEMENT RATIONALE

Hotel equipment, by their nature are relatively inexpensive Part and devices that have a limited life compared to other office equipment.

The rule of thumb for obsolescence of Hotel equipment *is 3-4 years.* However, changing business practices, new technology, and new software applications can impose increased demands on computing power that can force a more frequent replacement cycle for employees affected by the changing business practices or those using the new technology or software.

Replacement Versus Upgrade

It is Co. policy to replace PCs with the latest technology rather than to apply major upgrades to existing PCs. Current research indicates that:

- Upgrading is expensive because, more often than not, multiple system components must be upgraded in order to achieve the intended performance improvement.
- The purchase price of the various hardware components needed to accomplish an upgrade will exceed the purchase price of a new el equipment The cost of labour to install an upgrade to existing hardware will far exceed the cost of labour to install a new PC./ equipment
- Upgraded PCs have uncertain maintenance profiles and support costs.
- There is no increase in residual value of upgraded PCs.
- Upgrading PCs tend to increase the overall complexity in the installed hardware base.

CLASSIFICATIONS OF TECHNOLOGY USERS

There are three major classifications of technology users defined as:

Leading Edge Technology Users

Those individuals within the agency who need to be at the forefront of technology. Those individuals carry out but not limited to the following functions:

- Heavy usage of the CCS application (processing, programming, upgrading and maintenance)

- Heavy usage of database applications (Access)
- Heavy usage of the Internet (downloading virus fixes, programmes, HUD reports, uploading data to various HUD organizations, viewing HUD reports in PIC, research and analysis)

Power Users

Those individuals within the agency whose daily business operations require heavy utilization of information technology. They have a standardized suite of applications on their desktops; customized applications beyond the standardized suite; may use servers for database and decision-support; and often have access to department-specific applications, e-mail, Intranets and the Internet. Functions performed by these users are(but not limited to) the following:

- Moderate to heavy usage of the Microsoft Office suite (Excel, Word, Power Point, Publisher, Outlook, Access)
- Moderate to heavy usage of Adobe Acrobat and other applications used to complete grants, reports and forms for HUD
- Moderate to heavy usage of the Internet (uploading data to HUD, e-mailing, viewing HUD reports in PIC and other HUD areas, purchasing and reservations)
- Occasional to heavy usage of the CCS application

Mainstream Technology Users

Those individuals within the agency whose daily business operations require moderate utilization of technology for everyday office functions. They have a standardized suite of applications, access to file and print servers, and access to some host-based application using terminal emulation programmes. Functions performed by these users are(but not limited to) the following:

Conservative Technology Users

Those individuals within the agency whose daily business operations require the utilization of technology for everyday office functions only. They have a standardized suite of applications, access to file and print servers, and access to some host-based application using terminal emulation programmes.

Functions performed by these users (but are not limited to) are the following:

REPLACEMENT SCHEDULE

The following is a general guideline for replacing PCs. Departments should consult with "IS" for assistance in determining their specific replacement needs. Replacement schedules vary according to the four major classifications of technology users:

Leading Edge Technology Users

- Should maintain no more than two generations of technology.
- Should consider replacing PCs every second or third year, depending on applications in use.

Power Users

- Should maintain no more than two generations of technology
- Should consider replacing PCs every three to four years

Mainstream Technology Users

- Should maintain no more than two generations of technology.
- Should consider replacing PCs every four to five years.

Conservative Technology Users

- Should maintain no more than two generations of technology.
- Should consider replacing PCs every five years.
  - "IS" is not responsible for the installation and reconfiguration of "unsupported" software packages.
  - "IS" will NOT transfer the entire contents of a user's hard drive. Users who have not properly prepared their machine before their scheduled "upgrade installation date/time" will automatically be placed on the waiting list for future installations.
  - "IS" will NOT be responsible for the installation and reconfiguration of "unsupported" peripheral devices or devices that were installed by users. Equipment originally installed by users will be the user's responsibility to re-install on their new system.

ECONOMIC REPLACEMENT CYCLE

NOTIFICATION OF CLAIMS: WARRANTY SERVICE

If Purchaser discovers that any replacement part purchased through the Parts Operations ("Equipment S") has proven defective in material or workmanship, then written notice with an explanation of the claim shall be given promptly by Purchaser to Company but all claims for warranty service must be made within the warranty period.

Sony will charge the Purchaser for replacement parts and will credit the Purchaser if Company determines that the parts are covered by the warranty after the defective unit has been returned.

If after investigation Sony determines that the reported problem was not covered by the warranty, we reserve the right to charge the Purchaser for the cost of investigating the problem at its then prevailing time-and-materials rate. No replacement by Purchaser of any part thereof shall extend the warranty period as to the entire Product for which the Part is used. The specific warranty on the replacement part only shall be in effect for a period of ninety (90) days following its shipment, except where indicated above.

Exclusive Remedy: Acceptance

Purchaser's exclusive remedy and Company,s sole obligation is to supply a new or rebuilt replacement part, or issue a credit towards the purchase thereof, for any defective part covered by this warranty, failing which Company shall refund to Purchaser the purchase price for such part. Purchaser's failure to make a claim as provided in paragraph 1 above or continued use of the Part shall constitute an unqualified acceptance of such Part and a waiver by Purchaser of claims thereto.

Exceptions to Limited Warranty

Company shall have no liability or obligation to Purchaser with respect to any Part requiring service during the warranty period which is subjected to the following: abuse; improper use: negligence, accident, modification, failure of the end-user to follow the operating procedures outlined in the user's manual: failure of the end-user to follow the maintenance procedures in the service manual for the product in which the Part is used where a schedule is specified for regular replacement or maintenance or cleaning of certain parts (based on usage) and the end-user has failed to follow such schedule; attempted repair by non-qualified personnel; operation of unit outside of the published environment and electrical parameters, or if such Parts original identification (*e.g.*, trademark, serial number) markings have been defaced, altered or removed.

Sony excludes from warranty coverage Parts sold AS IS and/or WITH ALL FAULTS and excludes used Parts which have not been sold by Company to the Purchaser. Company also excludes from warranty coverage Parts located outside of the United States and Puerto Rico, and consumable items such as fuses and batteries.

Disclaimer of Warranty

Except for the foregoing warranties, company hereby disclaims and excludes all other warranties, express or implied including, but not limited to any and/or all implied warranties of merchantability, fitness for a particular purpose and/or any warranty with regard to any claim of infringement that may be provided in section of the uniform commercial code and/or in any other comparable state statue.

Limitation of Liability

The liability of company, if any, and purchaser's sole and exclusive remedy for damages for any claim of any kind whatsoever, regardless of the legal theory and whether arising in tort or contract, shall not be greater than the actual purchase price of the part with respect to which such claim is made. In no event shall sony be liable to purchaser for any special, indirect, incidental, or consequential damages of any kind including, but not limited to compensation, reimbursement or damages on account of the loss of present or prospective profits or for any other reason whatsoever.

TERMS AND CONDITION

Price and Payment Terms

The price and payment terms for the equipment are set forth in the sales covenants of the Quotation. In the event that the payment terms are not set forth in the Quotation or certain terms are not specified, the payment terms set forth in these terms and conditions shall apply. In addition, in the event that a specific schedule of payments is not set forth in the Quotation, Seller shall specify the required schedule of payments in its acknowledgement of order to Buyer.

All payment terms are subject to Seller's credit approval at the time of acknowledgment. Payments are due upon Buyer's receipt of an invoice or in the event that the payment terms are set forth in the Contract, as of the specific date listed on the applicable payment schedule of the Contract. If shipment or commissioning of the equipment is delayed by Buyer beyond the scheduled date, and the equipment is ready for delivery or the scheduled commissioning, final payment shall be due 10 days after such scheduled date.

Time is of the essence with respect to all payments. Payments that are outstanding more than ten (10) days from their respective due date shall bear an interest rate of one and one-half per cent (1 ½ per cent) per month (eighteen per cent (18 per cent) annually) until fully paid, including any interest payments thereon. If the rate of interest stated in the preceding sentence exceeds the maximum rate of interest that the applicable state law allows, then the rate of interest that will be assessed is the state maximum. In the event Buyer does not pay within the terms of this Contract, all collection costs incurred by Seller, including attorneys' fees will be paid by Buyer.

Payment for the sale of equipment furnished under this Contract shall not be subject to offset, deduction or back charges by Buyer, unless such offset, deduction or back charge is expressly accepted in writing by an authorized representative of Seller.

Any sums that have been deducted by Buyer in violation of this paragraph shall be considered overdue and are subject to the above interest charge. The price set forth in the Quotation and all payments due to Seller from Buyer shall be in the lawful currency of the United States of America unless otherwise specified in the Quotation. Unless otherwise set forth in the Quotation the terms of Payment for international transactions shall be as follows:

A deposit in an amount specified by Seller shall be paid via wire-transfer upon placement of order ("Initial Deposit") and the balance of the total purchase price shall be paid upon Seller's notification to Buyer that the equipment is being readied for international shipment.

If a Letter of Credit is to be used to cover any payments, Buyer shall open, in favour of Seller, an irrevocable, documentary Letter of Credit in the amount equal to those payments in the specific form and format described in Seller's letter of credit instructions available for review at The minimum requirements for any such letter of credit are that it must be payable "at sight" at the counters of Seller's bank in the USA, it must allow for confirmation by Seller's bank, it must allow partial shipments and partial draws from any point of origin and must allow trans-shipment and must specify that bank charges in addition to those charge by Seller's bank shall be payable by the Buyer.

The letter of credit shall specify the latest date of shipment for the Product to be at least sixty (60) days after the estimated Standard delivery time indicated in the Quotation and shall remain valid for at least thirty (30) days beyond the latest date of shipment. The letter of credit shall not require any documentation for collection other than those specified and agreed upon by the Seller. The Buyer agrees to have its issuing bank forward a draft version of the letter of credit to Seller for its review and approve prior to issuance of the final version.

Cancellation; Changes

If Buyer cancels the contract under for any reason, including any of the options below, Buyer will make payment of reasonable cancellation charges which shall include all incurred costs (direct material, labour, burden, and application engineering) on the completed work plus twenty-five per cent (25 per cent) of the contract price (ten per cent (10 per cent) of the Contract price if no engineering work has commenced).

Changes to the design, specifications, scope of supply, delivery schedule, product demonstration site, shipping instructions of the equipment or any material term of the Contract, may only be made upon execution by Buyer and Seller in writing ("Change Order"). Such Change Order shall state the parties' agreement on.

- Change in the specifications, designs, scope of work, delivery schedule or shipping instructions for the equipment,
- An adjustment to the purchase price, and
- An adjustment in the date of shipment of the equipment and/or the period of performance. Both parties agree and acknowledge that unless a Change Order is agreed upon in writing by both parties, the Contract shall not be modified in any manner. In addition, Seller has the right to suspend performance during the period while the change is being evaluated and negotiated.

In the event Buyer has communicated proposed changes to Seller, Seller, at its sole discretion, shall either

- Accept the Change Order;
- Reject the Change Order and continue performance under the existing Contract; or
- Cancel the Contract. In the event that Seller elects
- Above Buyer shall either
  - Agree to continue performance (of Seller) pursuant to the Contract
  - Cancel the contract.

Default

If Buyer fails to perform any of its obligations hereunder, including without limitation, failure to make payments as provided in Buyer fails to promptly give reasonable assurances of future performance when requested by Seller, then Seller may, upon five (5) days' written notice to Buyer, declare Buyer to be in default and Seller may suspend performance of its obligations hereunder without liability and retain all rights and remedies Seller may possess at law, in equity and/or as provided in this Contract.

Taxes, Permits, Fees, Laws

Unless expressly stated in Seller's invoice or the Quotation, the purchase price for the equipment furnished hereunder excludes all governmental or brokerage taxes, duties, fees, charges or assessments.

Seller may elect to add any such taxes, duties, fees, charges or assessments to the invoice amount payable to Seller by Buyer.

Buyer must provide Seller with documentation acceptable to Seller of any exemptions claimed from taxes, duties, permits, fees, charges or assessments in advance.

Except to the extent expressly assumed by Seller, Buyer shall secure and pay for all permits and fees necessary for the delivery and installation of the equipment.

It is Buyer's duty to ascertain that the equipment proposed by Seller and its subsequent installation and use is in accordance with applicable local laws, statues, ordinances and building codes ("laws").

Seller shall not be responsible for compliance of the equipment to such laws, but shall to the extent reasonably possible, promptly notify Buyer of any discrepancies that come to Seller's attention.

Delays, Force Majeure; Suspensions

If Seller is delayed at any time by the acts or omissions of Buyer, its agents, subcontractors or material suppliers, Change Orders, or by any Force Majeure defined below then the period of performance shall automatically be extended to accommodate Seller's revised engineering and production schedules, material purchases and/or labour remobilization.

- "Force Majeure" means circumstances beyond the respective party's reasonable control, including without limitation, acts of God, acts of public enemies, wars, other hostilities, blockades, insurrections, riots, epidemics, quarantine restrictions, floods, unavailability of components or supplies, lightning, fire, storms, earthquakes, washouts, arrests, restraints of rulers and people, civil disturbances, acts of any governmental or local authority, and any other acts and causes, not within the control of the party claiming excuse from performance, which by the exercise of due diligence and reasonable commercial effort, that party shall not have been able to foresee, avoid or overcome.
- During the period of any Force Majeure condition, the parties shall cooperate to perform under this Contract to the best of the parties' abilities.
- If either party in good faith is rendered wholly or partially unable by Force Majeure conditions to carry out its obligations under this Contract, or if Seller's supplier is unable to provide equipment or materials, and if that party gives prompt written notice and full particulars of such Force Majeure condition to the other party, that party shall be excused from performance of its obligations during the continuance of any such inability, but for no longer period. Such cause shall be remedied as far as possible with all reasonable speed, and with all reasonable commercial efforts, and notice shall be given when the cause is remedied.
- Notwithstanding the provisions of sub-part (c), if performance by a party is precluded or restrained by Force Majeure for more than one hundred-eighty (180) days, either party may terminate this Contract upon written notice to the other. In the event that Buyer terminates the Contract, Seller shall be entitled to recover from Buyer all incurred costs (direct material, labour, burden, and application engineering) on the completed work and work-in-process. In the event that Seller is delayed by the failure of Buyer to provide access to the site or furnished equipment, information or services in accordance with the schedule and requirements set forth in this Contract, Seller shall receive an equitable adjustment to the delivery schedule, and Contract price. Seller reserves the right to suspend, without any liability to or recourse from Buyer, all or part of the services to be performed hereunder (including the commissioning and shipment of equipment) during any period when, in the reasonable judgement of Seller, the health and/or safety of Seller and/or its subcontractors' personnel performing any such service could be jeopardized.

Source of Equipment

Seller reserves the right to manufacture the equipment at any one or more of its world-wide facilities and the price of the equipment shall not be affected by the source of the equipment. The Seller's factory at which the product demonstration will be conducted under Section 13 below will be communicated to Buyer in the Quotation or with Seller's acknowledgment.

Any request by Buyer for a change to that location of the product demonstration or other testing will require the issuance of a Change Order, including a change in Contract price, in accordance with, above. Buyer shall notify Seller as soon as pos5 sible, but not later than 14 days of the acknowledgements whether the source of the equipment may conflict with Buyer's requirements for country of origin labeling, content restrictions, or duty or freight, and Buyer and Seller shall consult with each other on the possible impact of such requirements on the Contract price.

Buyer's failure to notify Seller within the 14 day notice period shall create an irrefutable presumption that the source of the goods are acceptable to Buyer and that Buyer will bear the costs and consequences thereof.

Installation

Buyer is responsible for the installation of the equipment including, without limitation, all civil engineering work and foundations, unloading, unpacking and proper positioning of equipment, pre-aligning and anchoring of equipment, disposal of packing materials, filling of all fluid reservoirs and provision of and connecting all electrical wiring, electronic connections and utility services required for the equipment and the costs of the foregoing.

The equipment covered by this Contract may require special footings, foundations or floor surfaces depending upon the depth and condition of the existing concrete slab, foundation, or floor surface and other physical conditions all of which are the responsibility of Buyer.

Upon written request, Seller will furnish a layout or foundation drawing to assist Buyer in the installation, which drawing shall be approved in writing by Buyer. Such layout or foundation drawings are approximate and are submitted only to assist Buyer with respect to installation. Specifically, Buyer has the following responsibilities upon and/or before receipt of the equipment at Buyer's facility:

All site preparation, foundations, pits and government permits are the responsibility of the Buyer (Unless otherwise set forth in the quotation, the equipment covered by this quotation is designed for installation on normal plant or warehouse floors without additional foundations; however, special footings and foundations may be required for some machines depending upon the depth and condition of the existing concrete slab. In addition, some special lines require site preparation, concrete work or pits for proper installation, all of which is the responsibility of the Buyer to provide at Buyer's sole risk and expense. If required, this site preparation information is outlined on the approval drawing which must be signed by the Buyer before Seller begins design and engineering of the line.)

- Buyer is to remove the machinery from the containers and place it in approximate position for operation
- Buyer is to remove all packing materials and clean the machine
- Buyer is to provide any lifting equipment as required by the Seller's service representative
- Buyer is to provide and install all foundation anchors according to instructions provided by Seller
- Buyer is responsible for the filling of gear boxes and hydraulic reservoirs with required contents.
- Buyer to provide hydraulic oil for the machinery
- Buyer is to provide sufficient quantities of material for installation and testing of the machine
- Buyer to provide one maintenance person full time to work under the direction of the Seller's service representative during the installation and training
- Buyer to provide air lines to the machines per the approved layout drawing
- Buyer to connect 3 phase power to the machine control console
- Buyer is to provide an isolation transformer for the power supplied to the machine
- Buyer is responsible for maintenance and safe set up and operation of the machine
- Buyer is responsible for hotel meals and travel cost of Seller's service representative

Seller's service department can make a service representative available for consultation on site to assist with the Buyer's responsibilities listed above. This service will be priced at Seller's usual and customary daily service rates as announced from time to time plus reasonable expenses.

In addition to the foregoing, start up and commissioning of the equipment in Buyer's plant, including operator training, for a fixed number (depending upon the type of machinery) of eight (8) hour business days is included in the price, unless otherwise expressly stated in the Quotation, or acknowledgement.

Nonetheless, the Buyer is responsible for economy or equivalent class air travel, hotel and meals for serviceman's visit to commission the machine. Any additional installation or training time over the included fixed number of business days set forth in the Quotation or acknowledgement is available at Seller's usual and customary daily service rates as announced from time to time plus reasonable expenses.

Laws/Safety Standards

The equipment furnished hereunder conforms to the applicable ANSI B11 standards. However, the end user is the party responsible under the terms of all applicable Federal, state, local and regional laws applicable to such equipment including the Occupational Health and Safety Act of 1970, or the industrial safety laws applicable to the facility where the equipment is installed, to ensure the equipment meets such requirements, and Seller hereby disclaims any liability for any violations of the Act or other applicable or regulation law that may be imposed respecting the equipment furnished under this Contract.

Buyer shall train, require and cause its employees to (i) comply with directions set forth in documented inspections of the equipment and in maintenance, safety and operation instructions, manuals, drawings, safety notices and warnings and other instructions furnished by Seller; (ii) use, reasonable care and all safety equipment and applicable safety guards and safety systems in the set-up, adjustment, operation and maintenance and repair of the equipment; (iii) not remove, or permit anyone to remove any safety equipment, safety feature or warning signs from the equipment nor permanently remove or disable any guards or safety features; and (iv) assure that the equipment is used in accordance with all applicable laws, regulations, customs, permits and standards in force.

Product Demonstration and Acceptance

For certain equipment lines, systems and/or product applications, the Seller may determine that factory testing in the presence of Buyer ("Demonstration") is required.

If Seller does not require a Demonstration, Buyer may request a Demonstration however Buyer understands that unless Seller included a Demonstration in its Quotation, then request for the addition of a Demonstration shall be consider as a request for a change to the Contract (reference Section 5).

Buyer may also witness the standard final quality testing that Seller routinely performs prior to shipment from its factory at no additional charge. In the case of Demonstration, Seller will demonstrate the equipment at its facility only to the extent that the equipment purchased under this Contract can be appropriately demonstrated at such location.

If material is to be part of the testing process, Buyer is responsible to furnish, freight prepaid, the required amount of material necessary for this purpose. Such material must be of acceptable quality and conform to the material properties as specified in the Quotation.

The successful Demonstration of the equipment shall constitute acceptance by Buyer of the equipment and Buyer agrees to execute a certificate generated by Seller, in Seller's presence and prior to shipment of the equipment so stating.

Such certificate shall also constitute permission to ship the equipment after completion of any checklist, tear down and packaging.

In the absence of any Demonstration at Seller's facility, Buyer's receipt of the equipment delivered hereunder shall be an unqualified acceptance of and shall also constitute a waiver of any defect which reasonable inspection would have revealed unless Buyer gives Seller notice of rejection of the equipment within thirty (30) days after such receipt. In the event that Buyer gives such notice of rejection, Buyer shall afford Seller (1) reasonable opportunities to inspect any alleged non-conforming equipment and (2) a reasonable opportunity to make the equipment conforming, or provide substitute conforming equipment.

Buyer shall not return any equipment without Seller's prior written consent.

Dispute Resolution/Governing Law

All claims, disputes or controversies (whether in contract or tort, pursuant to statute or regulation, or otherwise, and whether pre-existing, present or future) arising out of or relating to: (a) these Terms and Conditions of Sale; (b) any advertisement, promotion, or proposal relating to these Terms and Conditions of Sale, or (c) the relationship which results from these Terms and Conditions of Sale (including relationships with third parties who are not party to these Terms and Conditions of Sale) (collectively "Claims") will be resolved, first, by a formal mediation conducted by an experienced mediator mutually agreed upon by Buyer and Seller, and, if mediation should fail to resolve the claim or dispute, secondly, by reference to and determination by binding arbitration governed by the Federal Arbitration Act and administered by the American Arbitration Association under its rules for the resolution of disputes, or under other mutually agreed procedures. Any such proceedings under mediation or arbitration shall be conducted in Hartford,

Connecticut in the United States of America, and the proceedings shall be conducted and all submissions of the parties and rulings of the arbitrator(s) shall be in the English language. Notwithstanding the rules of the arbitral body, the parties agree that (a) any arbitration proceeding shall be presided over by a neutral arbitrator selected by the parties who shall be admitted to the practice of law and be in good standing or in retirement status in the jurisdiction where the proceeding is held, (b) guidelines for "discovery" of facts through document production and deposition of witnesses by the parties shall be delineated by the arbitrator in writing, conducted in an orderly manner, conducted over a fixed period not to exceed 90 days — and failures to reasonably comply shall be subject to summary process in a court of law in the jurisdiction where the arbitration is being conducted, (c) the decision of the arbitrator shall be based on the relevant and credible facts as presented into evidence and (d) the arbitrator shall prepare a written memorandum of decision setting forth the findings of fact and conclusion of law. Because this method of dispute resolution is personal, individual and provides the exclusive method for resolving such disputes, Buyer further agrees, to the extent permitted by applicable laws, to waive any right to commence or participate in any class action or class-wide litigation or arbitration against Seller related to any Claim.

Both Parties Waive the Right to a Jury Trial

Buyer agrees that in the event of any breach of this Contract by Buyer that may cause irreparable harm to Seller for which an award of money damages is insufficient relief, Seller may, in addition to any remedies which Seller may have available to it, pursue injunctive or other equitable relief in a court of competent jurisdiction to prevent or curtail any breach by Buyer of its obligations to be performed under this Contract. All remedies provided to Seller under this Contract are cumulative, and may be exercised by Seller singularly or in conjunction with other available remedies, from time to time and at any time.

This provision shall survive the termination of the Contract governed by these Terms and Conditions of Sale. The Governing law shall be the laws of the Commonwealth of Massachusetts. With respect to international transactions, the UN Convention on the international sale of goods is hereby excluded from application to the contract.

Warranty

Seller warrants to the original purchaser that the equipment provided under this Contract shall be free from defects in material or workmanship for a period of one (1) year, measured from the date of shipment. The foregoing warranty will become void, and Seller will have no obligation whatsoever under this warranty, with respect to any of the following: equipment that is

(i) equipment that is not used or maintained in a normal and proper manner, in accordance with all manuals and instructions;

(ii) equipment that is modified, altered or repaired without the prior written approval of Seller;

(iii) Buyer fails to make any payments when due under

Section 4 or otherwise in this Contract or (iv) equipment that is that is assigned, sold or transferred to an entity other than the Buyer. Seller will repair or replace at its option components which upon inspection it finds to be defective, based on claims made in writing to Seller within a reasonable time after discovery and within the warranty period. Components alleged to be defective must be returned to Seller for repair or replacement, freight prepaid, within thirty (30) days of Buyer's receipt of the return authorization number, obtained from Seller, which must be clearly marked on the outside of the return container Replacement components may be shipped from Seller upon customer request and receipt of a valid purchase order number so the validity of the Warranty can be determined.

Unless otherwise specified, replacement components shall be Delivered to Buyer "FOB Seller's Factory" (UCC) for domestic shipments and "EX Works Seller's factory" (Incoterms) for international shipments. Any labour or equipment rental costs incurred in the dismantling and reassembly of the equipment shall be at Buyer's sole expense.

This warranty excludes equipment, materials and components furnished by the Seller but manufactured by another party, which may be incorporated in the equipment, line or system sold under this Contract. Such components and equipment shall bear no warranties other than the warranties extended by and enforceable against the manufacturer thereof at the time of delivery to Buyer (which warranties Seller will furnish on Buyer's written request), for the period stated in that warranty.

The warranty stated herein is personal to buyer and seller makes no other warranties or representations with respect to the equipment furnished hereunder and disclaims all other warranties, express or implied, including warranties of merchantability and fitness for a particular purpose. the above warranty shall constitute buyer's exclusive remedy with respect to the equipment furnished hereunder.

If Buyer removes or permits anyone to remove any safety equipment or warning signs or fails to observe any condition or if any injury or damage is caused, in whole or in part, by the end user's failure to comply with applicable federal, state or local safety requirements or Seller's instructions as provided in Section above, Seller shall have no obligation to Buyer, and Buyer shall indemnify and hold Seller harmless against any claims, loss or expense for injury or damage arising from the improper use of the equipment. Seller specifically disclaims any and all liability arising out of the operating of the equipment other than the warranty liabilities to the original Buyer.

Software

If any software programmes are deliverable, Buyer shall have a temporary license only, until full payment has been made whereupon Buyer shall receive a full license in accordance with its terms and conditions. Such temporary license can be suspended or terminated by Seller at any time by written notice to Buyer sent after the period for payment by Buyer has ended.

Upon SELLER'S receipt of full payment and subject to BUYER'S compliance with all material obligations under this Contract, SELLER hereby grants to BUYER a non-exclusive, perpetual, non-transferable right and license to use copies of software programmes embedded in, or used in connection with, equipment which BUYER has purchased hereunder, in Object Code only, for use by the Buyer only, in conjunction with the equipment, line and system.

No modification, download, transfer, or preparation of derivative works of such software whatsoever is permitted. Seller will not supply any Source Code under this Contract.

Miscellaneous

This Contract supersedes and replaces any and all prior or contemporaneous agreements, understandings, arrangements or representations, whether oral or written heretofore made between the parties and relating to the subject matter hereof, and constitutes the entire understanding of the parties with respect to the subject matter of this Contract.

If either Party, at its option, agrees to a waiver of any of the terms and conditions recited herein, such waiver shall not for any purpose be construed as a waiver of any succeeding breach of the same or any other terms and conditions; nor shall such a waiver be deemed as a course of conduct.

If any provision or clause, or portion thereof, of this Contract, or application thereof to any person or circumstances is held invalid or unconscionable, such invalidity or unconscionability shall not affect other provisions, or portions thereof, or applications of this Contract which can be given effect without the invalid or unconscionable provision, or portion thereof, or application, and to this end the provisions of these terms and conditions are declared to be severable.

Captions and heading in this Contract are strictly for the purpose of convenience and general reference only, and shall not affect the meaning or interpretation of any of the provisions of this Contract.

Except as required to obtain necessary licenses or governmental approvals, each party shall obtain the written approval (which approval shall not be unreasonably withheld) of the other in advance of the disclosure of any news releases, articles, brochures, advertisements, prepared speeches and other information releases, concerning this Contract or the work performed or to be performed hereunder.

LIMITATION OF LIABILITY

Buyer understands and acknowledges that seller shall not be liable for any special, direct, indirect, consequential, punitive or incidental damages of any kind, or labour, expenses, lost profits lost opportunities, or similar damages of any kind; and regardless of the legal theory or causes of action by which claims for any such damages as set forth in the entirety of the above section are advanced, whether or not seller has been advised of the possibility of any such damages.

For International Transactions

In addition to the foregoing, seller manufactures and sells its equipment in accordance with and not infringing on the customs, specifications, patents and standards of trade in force and in use and known to us in the united states of america. It is the responsibility of the buyer to assure that the equipment is used in accordance with and not infringing upon the customs, specifications, patents and standards of trade in force and in use in the country of installation.

Indemnity

Buyer agrees to indemnify and hold harmless Seller and its vendors from any and all claims or liabilities asserted against Seller or its vendors in connection with the manufacture, sale, delivery, re-sale, or repair or use of any equipment covered by or furnished under this Contract arising in whole or in part out of or by reason of the failure of Buyer, its agents, servants, employees or customers to follow directions, instructions, warnings or recommendations furnished by Seller or its vendors in connection with such equipment, or by reason of the failure of Buyer, its agents, servants, employees or customers to comply with all federal, state or local laws and regulations applicable to such equipment, including the Occupational Safety and Health Act or by reason of the negligence of Buyer, its agents, servants, employees or customers.

Patent Indemnity

In the event that the Buyer provides methods, directions, specifications or designs for equipment or tooling, Buyer shall indemnify and hold Seller harmless from and against any and all claims, demands, actions, lawsuits, proceedings, liabilities, losses, costs, expenses (including without limitation attorneys' fees) arising from or related to any actual or alleged infringement of any patents of any third party resulting from the methods, directions, specifications or design of the equipment or tooling supplied or required by Buyer for the equipment or the production of any parts or the processing of any material on the equipment.

If a permanent injunction shall prohibit the use, sale or distribution of the equipment or any part thereof by reason of any patent infringement covered by this indemnity, Buyer shall, at its own expense, either (a) procure for Seller a license for the right to continue using the equipment or the part thereof found to be infringing; (b) replace or modify the equipment or any part thereof found to be infringing so that the same becomes non-infringing, without any increase in the price of the equipment, or (c) reimburse Seller for the purchase price of the equipment.

The provisions of this section shall survive the performance or termination of this Contract.

7

Type of Fuels and their Characteristics

DESCRIPTION

Fuel is used to power anything, from cars to airplanes to toy motor boats. It is the lifeblood of our transp-ortation system. As our technology advances, society is able to use several natural and man-made sources to power our vehicles.

PETROLEUM

Petroleum is still the number one fuel source used to power industrial nations. Petroleum is also known as crude oil. It is found in large reservoirs throughout the Earth. Petrol is usually taken to a refinery that turns it into usable forms, such as gasoline. It is usually bought in barrel units. Petroleum prices rose from less than $20 a barrel in 1996 to more than $150 by June 2008.

Petroleum, in one form or another, is not a recent discovery but is now an important part of politics society and technology. The invention of the internal combustion engine was the major influence in the rise in the importance of petroleum. In the modern world petroleum has an influence across society, including geopolitics.

More than four thousand years ago, according to Herodotus and confirmed by Diodorus Siculus, asphalt was employed in the construction of the walls and towers of Babylon; there were oil pits near Ardericca (near Babylon), and a pitch spring on Zacynthus. Great quantities of it were found on the banks of the river Issus, one of the tributaries of the Euphrates. Ancient Persian tablets indicate the medicinal and lighting uses of petroleum in the upper levels of their society.

Today, about 90 per cent of vehicular fuel needs are met by oil. Petroleum also makes up 40 per cent of total energy consumption in the United States, but is responsible for only 2 per cent of electricity generation. Petroleum's worth as a portable, dense energy source powering the vast majority of vehicles and as the base of many industrial chemicals makes it one of the world's most important commodities.

The top three oil producing countries are Saudi Arabia, Russia, and the United States. About 80 per cent of the world's readily accessible reserves are located in the Middle East, with 62.5 per cent coming from the Arab 5: Saudi Arabia, UAE, Iraq, Qatar and Kuwait. A large portion of the world's total oil is found exists as unconventional sources, such as bitumen in Canada and Venezuela and oil shale. While significant volumes of oil are extracted from oil sands, particularly in Canada, logistical and technical hurdles remain, and Canada's oil sands are not expected to provide more than a few million barrels per day in the foreseeable future.

In its strictest sense, petroleum includes only crude oil, but in common usage it includes both crude oil and natural gas. Both crude oil and natural gas are predominantly a mixture of hydrocarbons. Under surface pressure and temperature conditions, the lighter hydrocarbons methane, ethane, propane and butane occur as gases, while the heavier ones from pentane and up are in the form of liquids or solids.

However, in the underground oil reservoir the proportion which is gas or liquid varies depending on the subsurface conditions, and on the phase diagram of the petroleum mixture.

An oil well produces predominantly crude oil, with some natural gas dissolved in it. Because the pressure is lower at the surface than underground, some of the gas will come out of solution and be recovered as associated gas or solution gas. A gas well produces predominately natural gas. However, because the underground temperature and pressure are higher than at the surface, the gas may contain heavier hydrocarbons such as pentane, hexane, and heptane in the gaseous state. Under surface conditions these will condense out of the gas and form natural gas condensate, often shortened to condensate. Condensate resembles gasoline in appearance and is similar in composition to some volatile light crude oils.

The proportion of hydrocarbons in the petroleum mixture is highly variable between different oil fields and ranges from as much as 97 per cent by weight in the lighter oils to as little as 50 per cent in the heavier oils and bitumens.

The hydrocarbons in crude oil are mostly alkanes, cycloalkanes and various aromatic hydrocarbons while the other organic compounds contain nitrogen, oxygen and sulfur, and trace amounts of metals such as iron, nickel, copper and vanadium. The exact molecular composition varies widely from formation to formation but the proportion of chemical elements vary over fairly narrow limits.

Crude oil varies greatly in appearance depending on its composition. It is usually black or dark brown (although it may be yellowish or even greenish). In the reservoir it is usually found in association with natural gas, which being lighter forms a gas cap over the petroleum, and saline water which, being heavier than most forms of crude oil, generally sinks beneath it.

Crude oil may also be found in semi-solid form mixed with sand and water, as in the Athabasca oil sands in Canada, where it is usually referred to as crude bitumen. In Canada, bitumen is considered a sticky, tar-like form of crude oil which is so thick and heavy that it must be heated or diluted before it will flow Venezuela also has large amounts of oil in the Orinoco oil sands, although the hydrocarbons trapped in them are more fluid than in Canada and are usually called extra heavy oil.

These oil sands resources are called unconventional oil to distinguish them from oil which can be extracted using traditional oil well methods. Between them, Canada and Venezuela contain an estimated 3.6 trillion barrels (570×109 m3) of bitumen and extra-heavy oil, about twice the volume of the world's reserves of conventional oil.

Petroleum is used mostly, by volume, for producing fuel oil and gasoline (petrol), both important "primary energy" sources. 84 per cent by volume of the hydrocarbons present in petroleum is converted into energy-rich fuels (petroleum-based fuels), including gasoline, diesel, jet, heating, and other fuel oils, and liquefied petroleum gas.

The lighter grades of crude oil produce the best yields of these products, but as the world's reserves of light and medium oil are depleted, oil refineries are increasingly having to process heavy oil and bitumen, and use more complex and expensive methods to produce the products required. Because heavier crude oils have too much carbon and not enough hydrogen, these processes generally involve removing carbon from or adding hydrogen to the molecules, and using fluid catalytic cracking to convert the longer, more complex molecules in the oil to the shorter, simpler ones in the fuels.

Due to its high energy density, easy transportability and relative abundance, oil has become the world's most important source of energy since the mid-1950s. Petroleum is also the raw material for many chemical products, including pharmaceuticals, solvents, fertilizers, pesticides, and plastics; the 16 per cent not used for energy production is converted into these other materials.

Petroleum is found in porous rock formations in the upper strata of some areas of the Earth's crust. There is also petroleum in oil sands (tar sands). Known reserves of petroleum are typically estimated at around 190 km3 (1.2 trillion (short scale) barrels) without oil sands, or 595 km3 (3.74 trillion barrels) with oil sands.

Consumption is currently around 84 million barrels (13.4×106 m3) per day, or 4.9 km3 per year. Because the energy return over energy invested (EROEI) ratio of oil is constantly falling (due to physical phenomena such as residual oil saturation, and the economic factor of rising marginal extraction costs), recoverable oil reserves are significantly less than total oil in place[citation needed]. At current consumption levels, and assuming that oil will be consumed only from reservoirs, known recoverable reserves would be gone around 2039[citation needed], potentially leading to a global energy crisis. However, to date discoveries of new oil reserves have more than matched increased usage. In addition, there are factors which may extend or reduce this estimate, including the increasing demand for petroleum in developing nations, particularly China and India; further new discoveries; increased economic viability of recoveries from more difficult to exploit sources; energy conservation and use of alternative energy sources; and new economically viable exploitation of unconventional oil sources.

NATURAL GAS

Natural Gas is a vital component of the world's supply of energy. It is one of the cleanest, safest, and most useful of all energy sources. Despite its importance, however, there are many misconceptions about natural gas. For instance, the word 'gas' itself has a variety of different uses, and meanings. When we fuel our car, we put 'gas' in it. However, the gasoline that goes into your vehicle, while a fossil fuel itself, is very different from natural gas. The 'gas' in the common barbecue is actually propane, which, while closely associated and commonly found in natural gas, is not really natural gas itself. While commonly grouped in with other fossil fuels and sources of energy, there are many characteristics of natural gas that make it unique. Below is a bit of background information about natural gas, what exactly it is, how it is formed, and how it is found in nature.

Natural gas refers to methane-based gas found in coal beds. It can also be found in landfills, bogs and marshes because of special organisms called methanogens. Before being used as a fuel, natural gas must go through extensive processing to remove all of the other associated chemicals until only the methane is left.

Natural gas is a gas consisting primarily of methane. It is found associated with fossil fuels, in coal beds, as methane clathrates, and is created by methanogenic organisms in marshes, bogs, and landfills. It is an important fuel source, a major feedstock for fertilizers, and a potent greenhouse gas.

Natural gas is considered 'dry' when it is almost pure methane, having had most of the other commonly associated hydrocarbons removed. When other hydrocarbons are present, the natural gas is 'wet'.

Natural gas has many uses, residentially, commercially, and industrially. Found in reservoirs underneath the earth, natural gas is commonly associated with oil deposits. Production companies search for evidence of these reservoirs by usingsophisticated technology that helps to find the location of the natural gas, and drill wells in the earth where it is likely to be found.

Once brought from underground, the natural gas is refined to remove impurities like water, other gases, sand, and other compounds. Some hydrocarbons are removed and sold separately, including propane and butane.

Other impurities are also removed, like hydrogen sulfide (the refining of which can produce sulfur, which is then also sold separately). After refining, the clean natural gas is transmitted through a network of pipelines, thousands of miles of which exist in the United States alone. From these pipelines, natural gas is delivered to its point of use.

Natural gas can be measured in a number of different ways. As a gas, it can be measured by the volume it takes up at normal temperatures and pressures, commonly expressed in cubic feet. Production and distribution companies commonly measure natural gas in thousands of cubic feet (Mcf), millions of cubic feet, billions of cubic feet (Bcf), or trillions of cubic feet.

While measuring by volume is useful, natural gas can also be measured as a source of energy. Like other forms of energy, natural gas is commonly measured and expressed in British thermal units (Btu). One Btu is the amount of natural gas that will produce enough energy to heat one pound of water by one degree at normal pressure. To give an idea, one cubic foot of natural gas contains about 1,027 Btus. When natural gas is delivered to a residence, it is measured by the gas utility in 'therms' for billing purposes. A therm is equivalent to 100,000 Btu's, or just over 97 cubic feet, of natural gas.

Natural gas is often informally referred to as simply gas, especially when compared to other energy sources such as electricity. Before natural gas can be used as a fuel, it must undergo extensive processing to remove almost all materials other than methane.

The by-products of that processing include ethane, propane, butanes, pentanes and higher molecular weight hydrocarbons, elemental sulfur, and sometimes helium and nitrogen.

Formation of Natural Gas

Natural gas is a fossil fuel like oil and coal. Fossil fuels are, essentially, the remains of plants and animals and microorganisms that lived millions and millions of years ago. So, how do these once living organisms become an inanimate mixture of gases?

There are many different theories as to the origins of fossil fuels. The most widely accepted theory says that fossil fuels are formed when organic matter (such as the remains of a plant or animal) is compressed under the earth, at very high pressure for a very long time.

This is referred to as thermogenic methane. Similar to the formation of oil, thermogenic methane is formed from organic particles that are covered in mud and other sediment. Over time, more and more sediment and mud and other debris are piled on top of the organic matter.

This sediment and debris puts a great deal of pressure on the organic matter, which compresses it. This compression, combined with high temperatures found deep underneath the earth, break down the carbon bonds in the organic matter. The deeper under the earth's crust, the higher the temperature.

At low temperatures (shallower deposits), more oil is produced relative to natural gas. At higher temperatures, however, more natural gas is created, as opposed to oil.

That is why natural gas is usually associated with oil in deposits that are 1 to 2 miles below the earth's crust. Deeper deposits, very far underground, usually contain primarily natural gas, and in many cases, pure methane. Natural gas can also be formed through the transformation of organic matter by tiny microorganisms.

This type of methane is referred to as biogenic methane. Methanogens, tiny methane producing microorganisms, chemically break down organic matter to produce methane. These microorganisms are commonly found in areas near the surface of the earth that are void of oxygen. These microorganisms also live in the intestines of most animals, including humans.

Formation of methane in this manner usually takes place close to the surface of the earth, and the methane produced is usually lost into the atmosphere. In certain circumstances, however, this methane can be trapped underground, recoverable as natural gas. An example of biogenic methane is landfill gas. Waste-containing landfills produce a relatively large amount of natural gas, from the decomposition of the waste materials that they contain. New technologies allow this gas to be harvested and added to the supply of natural gas.

A third way in which methane (and natural gas) is believed to be formed is through abiogenic processes. Extremely deep under the earth's crust, there exist hydrogen-rich gases and carbon molecules.

As these gases gradually rise towards the surface of the earth, they may interact with minerals that also exist underground, in the absence of oxygen. This interaction may result in a reaction, forming elements and compounds that are found in the atmosphere (including nitrogen, oxygen, carbon dioxide, argon, and water). If these gases are under very high pressure as they move towards the surface of the earth, they are likely to form methane deposits, similar to thermogenic methane.

Although there are several ways that methane, and thus natural gas, may be formed, it is usually found underneath the surface of the earth. As natural gas has a low density, once formed it will rise towards the surface of the earth through loose, shale type rock and other material. Most of this methane will simply rise to the surface and dissipate into the atmosphere.

However, a great deal of this methane will rise up into geological formations that 'trap' the gas under the ground. These formations are made up of layers of porous, sedimentary rock (similar to a sponge, that absorbs the gas), with a denser, impermeable layer of rock on top.

This impermeable rock traps the natural gas under the ground. If these formations are large enough, they can trap a great deal of natural gas underground, in what is known as a reservoir.

There are a number of different types of these formations, but the most common is created when the impermeable sedimentary rock forms a 'dome' shape, like an umbrella that catches all of the natural gas that is floating to the surface. There are a number of ways that this sort of 'dome' may be formed.

For instance, faults are a common location for oil and natural gas deposits to exist. A fault occurs when the normal sedimentary layers sort of 'split' vertically, so that impermeable rock shifts down to trap natural gas in the more permeable limestone or sandstone layers.

Essentially, the geological formation which layers impermeable rock over more porous, oil and gas rich sediment, has the potential to form a reservoir. The picture below shows how natural gas and oil can be trapped under impermeable sedimentary rock, in what is known as an anticlinal formation.

To successfully bring these fossil fuels to the surface, a hole must be drilled through the impermeable rock to release the fossil fuels under pressure. Note that in reservoirs that contain oil and gas, the gas, being the least dense, is found closest to the surface, with the oil beneath it, typically followed by a certain amount of water.

With natural gas trapped under the earth in this fashion, it can be recovered by drilling a hole through the impermeable rock. Gas in these reservoirs is typically under pressure, allowing it to escape from the reservoir on its own.

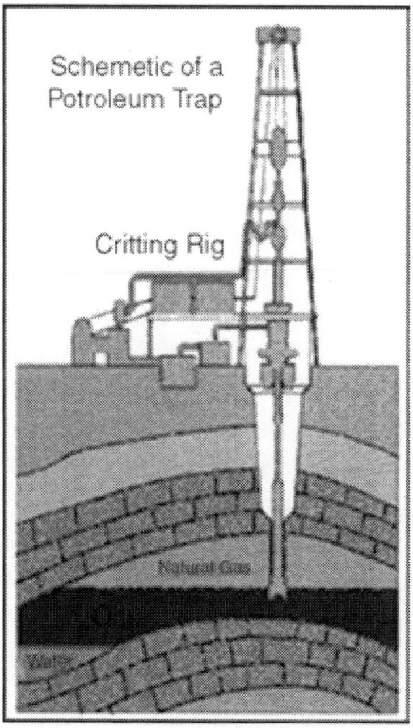

Fossil Natural Gas

In the past, natural gas was almost always a byproduct of producing oil, since the small, light gas carbon chains come out of solution as it undergoes pressure reduction from the reservoir to the surface, similar to uncapping a bottle of soda pop where the carbon dioxide effervesces. Unwanted natural gas can be a disposal problem at the well site.

If there is not a market for natural gas near the wellhead it is virtually valueless since it must be piped to the end user. Until recently, such unwanted gas was burned off at the wellsite, but due to environmental concerns this practice is becoming less common. Often, unwanted (or 'stranded' gas without a market) gas is pumped back into the reservoir with an 'injection' well for disposal or repressurizing the producing formation. Another solution is to export the natural gas as a liquid. [2]Gas-to-liquid, (GTL) is a developing technology that converts stranded natural gas into synthetic gasoline, diesel or jet fuel through the Fischer-Tropsch process developed in World War II Germany. Such fuels can be transported through conventional pipelines and tankers to users.

Proponents claim GTL fuels burn cleaner than comparable petroleum fuels. Most major international oil companies are in advanced development stages of GTL production, with a world-scale (140,000 bbl/day) GTL plant in Qatar scheduled to come online before 2010. In locations such as the United States with a high natural gas demand, pipelines are constructed to take the gas from the wellsite to the end consumer.

Fossil natural gas can be "associated" (found in oil fields) or "non-associated" (isolated in natural gas fields), and is also found in coal beds (as coalbed methane). It sometimes contains significant quantities of ethane, propane, butane, and pentane—heavier hydrocarbons removed prior to use as a consumer fuel—as well as carbon dioxide, nitrogen, helium and hydrogen sulfide.[1] Natural gas is commercially produced from oil fields and natural gas fields.

Gas produced from oil wells is called casinghead gas or associated gas. The natural gas industry is producing gas from increasingly more challenging resource types: sour gas, tight gas, shale gas and coalbed methane.

The world's largest proven gas reserves are located in Russia, with 4.757 × 1013 m^3 (1.6 × 1015 cu ft). Russia is also the world's largest natural gas producer, through the Gazprom company. Major proven resources (with year of estimate) (in billion cubic metres) are world 175,400, Russia 47,570 (2006), Iran 26,370, Qatar 25,790, Saudi Arabia 6,568 and United Arab Emirates 5,823.

The world's largest gas field is Qatar's offshore North Field, estimated to have 25 trillion cubic metres[2] (9.0 × 1014 cu ft) of gas in place—enough to last more than 200 years at optimum production levels. The second largest natural gas field is the South Pars Gas Field in Iranian waters in the Persian Gulf. Connected to Qatar's North Field, it has estimated reserves of 8 to 14 trillion cubic metres (2.8 × 1014 to 5.0 × 1014 cu ft) of gas. Because natural gas is not a pure product, when non-associated gas is extracted from a field under supercritical (pressure/temperature) conditions, it may partially condense upon isothermic depressurizing—an effect called retrograde condensation. The liquids thus formed may get trapped by depositing in the pores of the gas reservoir. One method to deal with this problem is to reinject dried gas free of condensate to maintain the underground pressure and to allow reevaporation and extraction of condensates.

The major difficulty in the use of natural gas is transportation and storage because of its low density. Natural gas pipelines are economical, but are impractical across oceans. Many existing pipelines in North America are close to reaching their capacity, prompting some politicians representing colder areas to speak publicly of potential shortages. In Europe gas pipeline network is already dense in the West[14]. New pipelines are planned or under construction in the Eastern Europe and between gas fields in Russia, Near East and Northern Africa and Western Europe. (See also: List of natural gas pipelines)

LNG carriers can be used to transport liquefied natural gas (LNG) across oceans, while tank trucks can carry liquefied or compressed natural gas (CNG) over shorter distances. Sea transport using CNG carrier ships that are now under development may be competitive with LNG transport in specific conditions.

For LNG transport a liquefaction plant is needed at the exporting end and regasification equipment at the receiving terminal. Shipborne regasification equipment is also practicable. LNG transportation is established as the preferred technology for long distance, high volume transportation of natural gas, whereas pipeline transport is preferred for transport for distances up to typically 4.000 km overland and approximately half that distance over seas.

For CNG transport high pressure, typically above 200 bars, is used. Compressors and decompression equipment are less capital intensive and may be economical in smaller unit sizes than liquefaction/regasification plants. For CNG mode the crucial problem is the investment and operating cost of carriers. Natural gas trucks and carriers may transport natural gas directly to end-users, or to distribution points such as pipelines for further transport.

In the past, the natural gas which was recovered in the course of recovering petroleum could not be profitably sold, and was simply burned at the oil field (known as flaring). This wasteful practice is now illegal in many countries[15].

Additionally, companies now recognize that value for the gas may be achieved with LNG, CNG, or other transportation methods to end-users in the future. The gas is now re-injected back into the formation for later recovery. This also assists oil pumping by keeping underground pressures higher. In Saudi Arabia, in the late 1970s, a "Master Gas System" was created, ending the need for flaring.

Satellite observation unfortunately shows that some large gas-producing countries still use flaring and venting routinely. The natural gas is used to generate electricity and heat for desalination. Similarly, some landfills that also discharge methane gases have been set up to capture the methane and generate electricity.

Natural gas is often stored underground inside depleted gas reservoirs from previous gas wells, salt domes, or in tanks as liquefied natural gas. The gas is injected during periods of low demand and extracted during periods of higher demand. Storage near the ultimate end-users helps to best meet volatile demands, but this may not always be practicable.

With 15 nations accounting for 84 per cent of the worldwide production, access to natural gas has become a significant factor in international economics and politics. In this respect, control over the pipelines is a major strategic factor.[18] In particular, in the 2000s, Gazprom, the Russian national energy company, has engaged in disputes with Ukraine and Belarus over the price of its natural gas, which have created worries that gas deliveries to parts of Europe could be cut off for political reasons.

Natural gas is often described as the cleanest fossil fuel, producing less carbon dioxide per joule delivered than either coal or oil.[10], and far fewer pollutants than other fossil fuels. However, in absolute terms it does contribute substantially to global carbon emissions, and this contribution is projected to grow. According to the IPCC Fourth Assessment Report in 2004 natural gas produced about 5,300 Mt/yr of CO2 emissions, while coal and oil produced 10,600 and 10,200 respectively; but by 2030, according to an updated version of the SRES B2 emissions scenario, natural gas would be the source of 11,000 Mt/yr, with coal and oil now 8,400 and 17,200 respectively. (Total global emissions for 2004 were estimated at over 27,200 Mt.)

In addition, natural gas itself is a greenhouse gas far more potent than carbon dioxide when released into the atmosphere but is not of large concern due to the small amounts in which this occurs. Natural gas is generally comprised of methane, which has a radiative forcing twenty times greater than carbon dioxide. This means a ton of methane in the atmosphere traps in as much radiation as 20 tons of carbon dioxide. Carbon dioxide still receives the lion's share of attention over greenhouse gases because it is in much higher concentrations. It is inevitable in using natural gas on a large scale that some of it will leak into the atmosphere.

When drilled in the US, the CO2 pumped out with the natural gas is released directly into the atmosphere. This amount of CO2 is not counted with the release of the CO2 when natural gas is burned

HYDROGEN FUEL

Hydrogen is the simplest element known to man. Each atom of hydrogen has only one proton. It is also the most plentiful gas in the universe. Stars are made primarily of hydrogen.

The sun is basically a giant ball of hydrogen and helium gases. In the sun's core, hydrogen atoms combine to form helium atoms. This process-called fusion-gives off radiant energy.

This radiant energy sustains life on earth. It gives us light and makes plants grow. It makes the wind blow and rain fall. It is stored as chemical energy in fossil fuels. Most of the energy we use today came from the sun's radiant energy.

Hydrogen gas is lighter than air and, as a result, it rises in the atmosphere. This is why hydrogen as a gas (H2) is not found by itself on earth. It is found only in compound form with other elements. Hydrogen combined with oxygen, is water (H2O). Hydrogen combined with carbon, forms different compounds such as methane (CH4), coal, and petroleum. Hydrogen is also found in all growing things-biomass. It is also an abundant element in the earth's crust.

Hydrogen has the highest energy content of any common fuel by weight(about three times more than gasoline), but the lowest energy content by volume (about four times less than gasoline). It is the lightest element, and it is a gas at normal temperature and pressure.

There are chemical reactions that can also produce energy that can be used as fuel. Hydrogen fuel is one example. Oxygen and hydrogen are combined in a proton exchange fuel cell. When the two are chemically combined, they can produce electricity that is used as fuel, creating water and vapors as a byproduct.

Today, there are an estimated 400 to 500 hydrogen-fueled vehicles in the U.S., mostly in California. Most of these vehicles are buses and automobiles powered by electric motors. They store hydrogen gas or liquid on board and convert the hydrogen into electricity for the motor using a fuel cell. Only a few of these vehicles burn the hydrogen directly (producing almost no pollution).

The present cost of fuel cell vehicles greatly exceeds that of conventional vehicles in large part due to the expense of producing fuel cells. Hydrogen vehicles are starting to move from the laboratory to the road.

One California family has recently leased a hydrogen car for personal use. The U.S. postal service, a package delivery company, a few Florida Park rangers, and a few private utility companies are also using hydrogen vehicles. It will probably be at least 10 years, though, before you can walk into your local car dealer and drive away in an affordable hydrogen-powered car. Even then, you will need a place to refuel your hydrogen car.

Currently, there are 63 hydrogen refueling stations nationwide, about half of which are located in California. This is the so-called "chicken and egg" problem that hydrogen developers are working hard to solve. Namely: who will buy hydrogen cars if there are no refueling stations?

And who will pay to build a refueling station if there are no cars and customers? One possible solution is to eliminate refueling stations entirely. Automobile manufacturers have already designed a refrigerator-sized hydrogen generator for your garage that works off electricity. Consumers would simply refill their cars with hydrogen each night while it is parked.

Pollution Problem

According to reports from the Environmental Protection Agency (EPA), Spokane's carbon monoxide levels are among the poorest in the nation, and it will only get worse if we keep contributing to it with our polluting cars. Our precious cars that we use so often give off "carbon monoxide, nitrogen oxides, hydrocarbons, and carbon dioxide," and contribute to "urban smog, rural air pollution, acid rain, and the buildup of greenhouse gases in the atmosphere". We need our cars, but we also need to reduce the pollution.

Carbon-based Fuel Alternatives

The best way to reduce the pollution while keeping our cars is to start buying emission-free vehicles. Some people will argue that we should just run our current cars on alternative carbon-based fuels, such as propane or natural gas. These fuels are cleaner than gasoline or diesel and would help clean the air of some pollutants, but the inescapable facts are that they are fossil fuels, their supplies are limited, and the greenhouse gas contributions are expected to be about the same as those of oil-based fuels.

In other words, they still pollute. In fact, combustion of any fuel produces some emissions. Combusted fuel and burning crank case oil produce hydrocarbons while heat from the engine produces nitrogen oxides. The only way to completely escape this pollution is by using electric motors (Begley and Hager 108). Vehicles using electric motors are completely emission-free and generally get their electricity from batteries, the sun, or hydrogen fuel cells.

Pollution-free Vehicles: Battery-powered Cars

Battery-powered electric cars have many advantages over internal combustion engines, such as being emission free, being more efficient, and having fewer moving parts that inevitably wear out and break.

The problems with batteries, however, are their range, recharge times, size, and weight. The short driving range, typically about 100 miles, makes it impractical for driving long distances because it takes so long to recharge: about 8 hours.

Furthermore, current lead-acid batteries consume over 17 times as much space and 45 times as much weight as gasoline tanks (45 cubic feet of space and 6,750 pounds for a driving range equivalent to 15 gallons of gasoline). Ford,

General Motors, and Chrysler are jointly working on "better batteries than those currently available" in order to solve these problems.

Solar-Powered Cars

"Solar cars, simply put, are electric cars that derive some fraction of their energy from the sun". Since the sun is not out at night or when it is very cloudy, solar cars are equipped with batteries. When the sun is out, the car can move, charge its batteries, or both. They have the advantage of not needing as much city power to charge them as battery-powered cars, and some solar cars have ranges of about 135 miles. The range is higher than that of battery-powered cars because they can charge themselves and run longer using the sun, but since they are dependent on batteries when the sun is not out, they have the drawbacks of their counterparts: namely, the size, weight, and range restrictions associated with batteries.

Alternative

The best pollution-free alternative to batteries while still using clean electric motors is the hydrogen fuel cell. Hydrogen-powered "fuel cells hold enormous promise as a power source for a future generation of cars". They do not have the restraints that batteries do, either.

Hydrogen is consumed by a pollution-free chemical reaction—not combustion—in a fuel cell. The fuel cell simply combines hydrogen and oxygen chemically to produce electricity, water, and waste heat.

Nothing else. And hydrogen is the most abundant element in the universe, constituting about 93 per cent of all atoms. "It is found in water (H20), fossil fuels (basically, compounds of hydrogen and carbon), and all plants and animals". "What better replacement for finite, non-renewable gasoline?". "Hydrogen has often been called the perfect fuel. Its major reserve on earth (water) is inexhaustible. The use of hydrogen is compatible with nature, rather than intrusive. We will never run out of hydrogen".

Hydrogen can be obtained from water by the process of electrolysis, or splitting water molecules using electricity. We cannot, however, forget the external effects of getting the electricity from power plants. Many power plants across the country, producing electricity to charge batteries or to produce hydrogen, run on carbon-based fuels, such as coal, and therefore produce emissions. Here in Spokane, however, where our electricity comes from the water-powered generators at Washington Water Power, this is not a problem, and hydrogen-fuel-cell-powered vehicles can be truly emission free.

The fuel cells are compatible with the cold winters we have in Spokane. There are several types of fuel cells, but the one most suited for cars is called the proton-exchange membrane (PEM) fuel cell. Some of its main features are its ability to start quickly and to run at moderate temperatures (150° instead of

1,900°, like some other versions), which will help because it does not need to heat up very much in order to run. The PEM fuel cell is compact and lightweight: a big advantage for cars. Furthermore, its maximum efficiency of 60 per cent (energy delivered from hydrogen to motor as electricity) is about 3 times greater than the efficiency of internal combustion engines (most of the energy from combustion is lost in heat and friction before it even pushes down on the pistons) The range of fuel-cell-powered vehicles is not limited by batteries, but by the amount of fuel in the storage tank.

Recent developments in hydrogen storage technology have come up with "carbon-adsorption" systems. These are refrigerated and pressurized tanks that can store massive amounts of hydrogen. Calculations estimate that over 7 gallons of hydrogen could be stored in a single gram of this new material.

This allows a range of nearly 5,000 miles from a single tank!. These tanks would weigh less than 200 pounds, occupy about half the amount of space used by current gasoline tanks and could be refueled in 4-5 minutes. The carbon-adsorption tanks would also work well in Spokane's cold winters, as the process improves greatly as the temperature decreases. This tank could easily become the storage method of choice if research, improvements, and advancements continue. Even if nothing came from these or future developments, the current "range for hydrogen fuel cell vehicles is comparable to that for gasoline internal combustion engine vehicles".

Hydrogen Safety

Many people are concerned with hydrogen's safety. And with good reason. Hydrogen is a fuel and is therefore combustible. Its combustion properties deserve the same caution any fuel should be given. Hydrogen has been suffering an image problem since the Hindenburg tragically caught fire and burned in New Jersey. (There were 62 survivors and 35 fatalities; 27 of the deaths resulted from jumping from the airship.

Some died from burns and injuries caused by the diesel fuel fire, not from the burning hydrogen "Fortunately... 'hydrogen is not a particularly dangerous fuel.'

If it leaks or spills, hydrogen disperses and evaporates much faster than gasoline, which minimizes the explosion hazard". "The hazards of hydrogen are different from but not greater than those of conventional fuels". Hydrogen can be and has been handled carefully and safely, just like any other inherently dangerous fuel such as gasoline. Hydrogen tanks have been put through series of demanding safety tests. They have been completely engulfed in flames at over 1,650°F for up to 70 minutes, perforated by solid objects (such as armor-piercing bullets), and squeezed until they break with safety valves completely blocked. Sometimes the gas leaked out, sometimes it burnt, but it never exploded.

On the Road

Many large and well-known corporations trust and realise the potential of hydrogen. Some companies that already have hydrogen fueled vehicles on the road are: (1) Mercedes-Benz, with about 20 cars and vans,(2) BMW, which is testing liquid hydrogen in two sedans and plans to have a fleet of 100 hydrogen vehicles on the road in the 1990s, (3) Mazda, which had 3 vehicles as of 1993, and (4) Ballard Power Systems, which is developing and selling fuel cells and hydrogen-fuel-cell-powered buses. Various individuals and universities are also researching and developing hydrogen vehicles.

STRAIGHT VEGETABLE OIL

A fast food restaurant leftover, straight vegetable oil (SVO) can also act as a fuel. Special fuel tanks reduce its high viscosity to make it flow better. This fuel cannot be run through standard engines. They must be converted to handle filtered vegetable oil. This includes modifying engines to run at 150 degrees F and 120 degree fuel temperatures.

You may have heard of compressed natural gas as alternative fuel before, and you might have even heard about biodiesel as fuel before as well, but have you ever considered using straight vegetable oil (SVO) as an alternative type of fuel for your vehicle?

If not, don't feel like you are out of the loop; a great majority of the world probably has no idea that straight vegetable oil can be used as fuel, and if you are one of those people then this is the perfect place for you to start. You don't have to convert it to biodiesel and you don't have to make any special modifications to the oil; if you want to you can just put it in your car and go, but there are some things that you should keep in mind before doing so.

Things to Keep in Mind about Straight Vegetable Oil as Fuel

Of course, with every miracle type of fuel that comes out that can help to reduce our dependence on foreign oil, there are some downsides. The upside to the use of SVO as fuel is that it is readily and widely available, and if you want to you can put it in and take off.

At the same time, it does have its downside. First off, the viscosity of straight vegetable oil is certainly much higher than that of gasoline or any type of fuel out there. This doesn't affect much but it can affect your engine because of the fact that it burns differently and can cause damage to your vehicle.

There are a couple of alternatives to this; you can either modify your engine to be able to use straight vegetable oil as is or you can mix it with kerosene or something similar and put it into your engine like that. It is not necessarily advisable to pour straight vegetable oil into your diesel fuel engine and go, but if you have an old car and a wish and a prayer, you might just be able to make it work!

Actually reformatting your vehicle to work with straight vegetable oil and use it as a type of fuel is one way to go about doing things, but that can be costly and expensive. It is well enough at this point that it is possible to use straight vegetable oil as fuel and that we are headed as a society in the right direction-away from the dependence on foreign oils for regular people like you and me. At this point, this type of fuel is far less advanced than biodiesel and compressed natural gas but it does have its upsides, and the kinks are being worked out. In the end a traditional gas station will (hopefully) be a thing of the past!

Vegetable fats and oils are lipid materials derived from plants. Physically, oils are liquid at room temperature, and fats are solid. Chemically, both fats and oils are composed of triglycerides, as contrasted with waxes which lack glycerin in their structure. Although many different parts of plants may yield oil, in commercial practice, oil is extracted primarily from seeds.

The melting temperature distinction between oils and fats is imprecise, since definitions of room temperature vary, and typically natural oils have a melting range instead of a single melting point.

Vegetable fats and oils may be edible or inedible. Examples of inedible vegetable fats and oils include processed linseed oil, tung oil, and castor oil used in lubricants, paints, cosmetics, pharmaceuticals, and other industrial purposes. Although thought of as esters of glycerin and a varying blend of fatty acids, fats and oils also typically contain free fatty acids, monoglycerides, and diglycerides.

Hydrogenated Oils

Unsaturated vegetable fats and oils can be transformed through partial or complete hydrogenation into fats and oils of higher melting point. The hydrogenation process involves "sparging" the oil at high temperature and pressure with hydrogen in the presence of a catalyst, typically a powdered nickel compound. As each double-bond is broken, two hydrogen atoms each form single bonds with the two carbon atoms. The elimination of double-bonds by adding hydrogen atoms is called saturation; as the degree of saturation increases, the oil progresses towards being fully hydrogenated. An oil may be hydrogenated to increase resistance to rancidity (oxidation) or to change its physical characteristics. As the degree of saturation increases, the oil's viscosity and melting point increase.

The use of hydrogenated oils in foods has never been completely satisfactory. Because the centre arm of the triglyceride is shielded somewhat by the end fatty acids, most of the hydrogenation occurs on the end fatty acids. This makes the resulting fat more brittle. A margarine made from naturally more saturated oils will be more plastic (more "spreadable") than a margarine made from, say, hydrogenated soy oil. In addition, partial hydrogenation results in the formation of large amounts of trans fats in the oil mixture, which, since the 1970s, have increasingly been viewed as unhealthy.

Crude oil, straight from the crushing operation, is not considered edible in the case of most oilseeds. The same is true for the remaining meal. For instance, animals fed raw soy meal will waste away, even though soy meal is high in protein. Researchers at Central Soya discovered that a trypsin inhibitor in soybeans could be deactivated by toasting the meal, and both licensed their invention, and sold soy meal augmented with vitamins and minerals as MasterMix, a product for farmers to mix with their own grain to produce a high quality feed.

The processing of soy oil is typical of that used with most vegetable oils. Crude soy oil is first mixed with caustic soda. Saponification turns triglycerides into soap. The soap is removed with a centrifuge.

Neutralized dry soap stock (NDSS) is typically used in animal feed, more to get rid of it than because it is particularly nourishing. The remaining oil is deodorized by heating under a near-perfect vacuum and sparged with water. The condensate is further processed to become vitamin E food supplement, while the oil can be sold to manufacturers and consumers at this point.

Some of the oil is further processed. By carefully filtering the oil at near-freezing temperatures, "winter oil" is produced. This oil is sold to manufacturers of salad dressings, so that the dressings do not turn cloudy when refrigerated.

The oil may be partially hydrogenated to produce various ingredient oils. Lightly hydrogenated oils have very similar physical characteristics to regular soy oil, but are more resistant to becoming rancid.

Margarine oils need to be mostly solid at 32 °C (90 °F) so that the margarine does not melt in warm rooms, yet it needs to be completely liquid at 37 °C (98 °F), so that it doesn't leave a "lardy" taste in the mouth.

Another major use of soy oil is for fry oils. These oils require substantial hydrogenation to keep the polyunsaturates of soy oil from becoming rancid.

Hardening vegetable oil is done by raising a blend of vegetable oil and a catalyst in near-vacuum to very high temperatures, and introducing hydrogen. This causes the carbon atoms of the oil to break double-bonds with other carbons, each carbon forming a new single-bond with a hydrogen atom. Adding these hydrogen atoms to the oil makes it more solid, raises the smoke point, and makes the oil more stable.

Hydrogenated vegetable oils differ in two major ways from other oils which are equally saturated. During hydrogenation, it is easier for hydrogen to come into contact with the fatty acids on the end of the triglyceride, and less easy for them to come into contact with the centre fatty acid. This makes the resulting fat more brittle than a tropical oil; soy margarines are less "spreadable". The other difference is that trans fatty acids (often called trans fat) are formed in the hydrogenation reactor, and may amount to as much as 40 per cent by weight of a partially hydrogenated oil. Trans acids are increasingly thought to be unhealthy.

ETHANOL

Ethanol is a naturally occurring gas that is usually found in small parts with other natural gases. However, ethanol can also be manually produced and used as fuel. Ethanol production includes the fermentation of corn stalks or sugar cane. Although ethanol burns cleaner than traditional gasoline, costs are equivalent to gasoline and fuel efficiency is more than a third less efficient.

In the world of biofuels, ethanol is king—the alcohol fuel is predicted to account for a full 9 per cent of total US fuel usage by 2018. If this trend pans out, not only will ethanol production have met and surpassed Bush's proposed goal of 14 billion gal/year of ethanol (enough to replace 75 per cent of oil imports from Middle East in 2025), it will have done so one decade ahead of plan. After the 9 per cent benchmark, however, the future becomes more uncertain. A likely discontinuation of government ethanol subsidies will mean that ethanol's price must drop to remain competitive against gasoline (which has about 40 per cent more energy content per gallon).

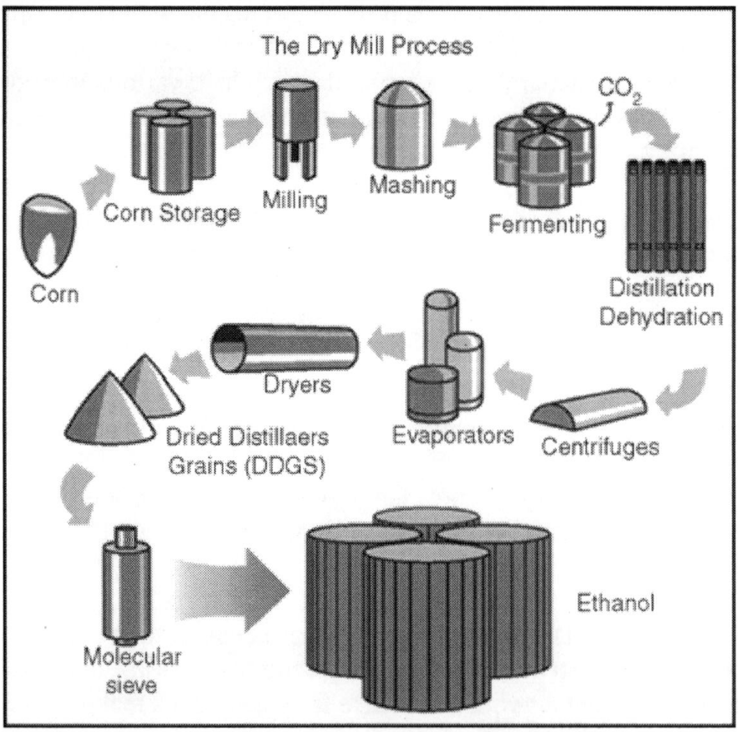

Although the alcohol fuel can be produced from a number of different biomass stocks (including wheat, sugar cane, and beets), in the United States, corn-based ethanol remains the most prominent possibility. (Brazil remains the world's largest producer of ethanol, distilling it from sugarcane for use within the country.) Strong corn-growing conditions in the US breadbasket and relative familiarity with the corn-ethanol production process mean that corn is probably the most efficient and feasible staple biomass stock for the fuel.

But corn ethanol is not without its challengers—recently, cellusolic ethanol has also been receiving increasing amounts of media attention (and research dollars).

Bio-butanol is another up-and-comer that threatens the corn-based camp's hold on American biofuel. Ethanol fuel is ethanol (ethyl alcohol), the same type of alcohol found in alcoholic beverages.

It can be used as a fuel, mainly as a biofuel alternative to gasoline, and is widely used by flex-fuel light vehicles in Brazil, and as an oxygenate to gasoline in the United States. Together, both countries were responsible for 89 per cent of the world's ethanol fuel production in 2008.[1] Because it is easy to manufacture and process and can be made from very common crops such as sugar cane, potato, manioc and corn, in several countries ethanol fuel is increasingly being blended as gasohol or used as an oxygenate in gasoline. Bioethanol, unlike petroleum, is a renewable resource that can be produced from agricultural feedstocks.

Anhydrous ethanol (ethanol with less than 1 per cent water) can be blended with gasoline in varying quantities up to pure ethanol and most modern gasoline engines will operate well with mixtures of 10 per cent ethanol. Most cars on the road today in the U.S. can run on blends of up to 10 per cent ethanol, and the use of 10 per cent ethanol gasoline is mandated in some cities.

Ethanol can be mass-produced by fermentation of sugar or by hydration of ethylene (ethene CH2=CH2) from petroleum and other sources. Current interest in ethanol mainly lies in bio-ethanol, produced from the starch or sugar in a wide variety of crops, but there has been considerable debate about how useful bio-ethanol will be in replacing fossil fuels in vehicles. Concerns relate to the large amount of arable land required for crops, as well as the energy and pollution balance of the whole cycle of ethanol production.[5][6] Recent developments with cellulosic ethanol production and commercialization may allay some of these concerns.

According to the International Energy Agency, cellulosic ethanol could allow ethanol fuels to play a much bigger role in the future than previously thought. Cellulosic ethanol offers promise as resistant cellulose fibres, a major and universal component in plant cells walls, can be used to generate ethanol.

Ethanol is a renewable energy source because the energy is generated by using a resource, sunlight, which is naturally replentished. Creation of ethanol starts with photosynthesis causing a feedstock, such as sugar cane or corn, to grow. These feedstocks are processed into ethanol.

About 5 per cent of the ethanol produced in the world in 2003 was actually a petroleum product. It is made by the catalytic hydration of ethylene with sulfuric acid as the catalyst. It can also be obtained via ethylene or acetylene, from calcium carbide, coal, oil gas, and other sources. Two million tons of petroleum-derived ethanol are produced annually. The principal suppliers are plants in the United States, Europe, and South Africa. Petroleum derived ethanol (synthetic ethanol) is chemically identical to bio-ethanol and can be differentiated only by radiocarbon dating.

Bio-ethanol is usually obtained from the conversion of carbon based feedstock. Agricultural feedstocks are considered renewable because they get energy from the sun using photosynthesis, provided that all minerals required for growth (such as nitrogen and phosphorus) are returned to the land. Ethanol can be produced from a variety of feedstocks such as sugar cane, bagasse, miscanthus, sugar beet, sorghum, grain sorghum, switchgrass, barley, hemp, kenaf, potatoes, sweet potatoes, cassava, sunflower, fruit, molasses, corn, stover, grain, wheat, straw, cotton, other biomass, as well as many types of cellulose waste and harvestings, whichever has the best well-to-wheel assessment.

An alternative process to produce bio-ethanol from algae is being developed by the company Algenol. Rather than grow algae and then harvest and ferment it the algae grow in sunlight and produce ethanol directly which is removed without killing the algae. It is claimed the process can produce 6000 gallons per acre per year compared with 400 gallons for corn production.

Currently, the first generation processes for the production of ethanol from corn use only a small part of the corn plant: the corn kernels are taken from the corn plant and only the starch, which represents about 50 per cent of the dry kernel mass, is transformed into ethanol. Two types of second generation processes are under development.

The first type uses enzymes and yeast to convert the plant cellulose into ethanol while the second type uses pyrolysis to convert the whole plant to either a liquid bio-oil or a syngas. Second generation processes can also be used with plants such as grasses, wood or agricultural waste material such as straw.

Dehydration

There are basically five dehydration processes to remove the water from an azeotropic ethanol/water mixture. The first process, used in many early fuel ethanol plants, is called azeotropic distillation and consists of adding benzene or cyclohexane to the mixture. When these components are added to the mixture, it forms an heterogeneous azeotropic mixture in vapour-liquid-liquid equilibrium, which when distilled produces anhydrous ethanol in the column bottom, and a vapour mixture of water and cyclohexane/benzene. When condensed, this becomes a two-phase liquid mixture. Another early method, called extractive distillation, consists of adding a ternary component which will increase ethanol relative volatility. When the ternary mixture is distilled, it will produce anhydrous ethanol on the top stream of the column.

With increasing attention being paid to saving energy, many methods have been proposed that avoid distillation all together for dehydration. Of these methods, a third method has emerged and has been adopted by the majority of modern ethanol plants.

This new process uses molecular sieves to remove water from fuel ethanol. In this process, ethanol vapour under pressure passes through a bed of molecular sieve beads. The bead's pores are sized to allow absorption of water while excluding ethanol. After a period of time, the bed is regenerated under vacuum to remove the absorbed water. Two beds are used so that one is available to absorb water while the other is being regenerated. This dehydration technology can account for energy saving of 3,000 btus/gallon (840 kJ/l) compared to earlier azeotropic distillation.

Fuel are classified primarily by the kind of electrolyte they employ. This classification determines the kind of chemical reactions that take place in the cell, the kind of catalysts required, the temperature range in which the cell operates, the fuel required, and other factors. These characteristics, in turn, affect the applications for which these cells are most suitable.

There are several types of fuel cells currently under development, each with its own advantages, limitations, and potential applications. Learn more about: Fuel cells are generally categorized by their electrolyte — the material sandwiched between the two electrodes.

This material's characteristics determine the optimal operating temperature and the fuel used to generate electricity. Each comes with its particular set of benefits and shortcomings.

Fuel Type	Electrolyte	Anode Gas	Cathode Gas	Temperature	Efficiency
Proton Exchange Membrane (PEM)	Solid polymer membrane	Hydrogen	Pure or atmospheric oxygen	75°C (180°F)	35–60%
Alkaline (AFC)	Potassium hydroxide	Hydrogen	Pure oxygen	Below 80°C	50–70%
Direct Methanol (DMFC)	Solid polymer membrane	Methanol solution in water	Atmospheric oxygen	75°C (180°F)	35–40%
Phosphoric Acid (PAFC)	Phosphorous	Hydrogen	Atmospheric oxygen	210°C (400°F)	35–50%
Molten Carbonate (MCFC)	Alkali-Carbonates	Hydrogen, methane	Atmospheric oxygen	650°C (1200°F)	40–55%
Solid Oxide (SOFC)	Ceramic Oxide	Hydrogen, methane	Atmospheric oxygen	800–1000°C (1500–1800°F)	45–60%

CALORIFIC VALUE OF FUEL

It can be defined as the amount of heat liberated in KJ or Kcal by the complete combustion of 1 Kg of fuel.

It is a well-established fact that when the same weight of the same substance burns to form the same products of combustion, the quantity of heat evolved is a constant, the value of which is independent of the rate of combustion. This quantity is known as the heat of chemical combination of the substance with oxygen. In relation to substances used as fuels, it is also known as the "calorific value." Thus 1 gram of carbon burning to carbon dioxide evolves 8,080 gram-calories of heat, and 1 gram of hydrogen burning to liquid water evolves 34,462 gram-calories. The calorific value of carbon is therefore said to be 8,080, and of hydrogen 34,462. The gram-calorie is defined as the quantity of heat required to raise the temperature of 1 gram of water by one degree Centigrade.

When alcohol is completely burned in air or oxygen, the products of combustion are water and carbon dioxide. The heat evolved, *i.e.*, the calorific value can be calculated theoretically from the data just given, as shown below.

The percentage composition in ethyl alcohol is: Carbon 52.13, hydrogen 1312, and oxygen 3475. Hence 1 gram of ethyl, alcohol contains: -

Carbon	0.5213	gram
Hydrogen	0.1312	"
Oxygen	0.3475	"

Deducting from the amount of hydrogen the quantity necessary to form water with the oxygen, *i.e.*,0.3475/8= 0 0434 gram, we have 01312 – 00434=00878.

Multiplying by the corresponding calorific values for the carbon and hydrogen and adding the products, we have: -

"Fuel," p. 158 (1914 edition).

Carbon	0.5213	×	8,080	=	4,212.1	Calories.
Hydrogen	0.0878	×	34,462	=	3,025.7	"
.-. Calorific value of ethyl alcohol				=	7,237.8	"

The calculation here shown at length may be summarized into the formula: Calorific value = 808 0 + 3446 (H – 0/8), where C, H, and 0 denote the percentages of carbon, hydrogen, and oxygen respectively.

A somewhat higher result is given if the values for carbon and hydrogen used in Berthelot's formula are taken - namely, 8,137 and 34.500, instead of those employed in the calculation shown. On the other hand, in summary calculations the round numbers 8,000 and 34,000 are often used.

In practice, of course, absolute alcohol is not employed as fuel; but the calculation shows the principle most simply, and the result is required in obtaining the theoretical calorific value of denatured alcohol, and of other alcohol mixtures, which are used as fuels. In a similar manner, the theoretical calorific value of absolute methyl alcohol, the percentage composition of which is C 37.47, H 1258, and 0 4995, is found to be 5,2125.

Acetone, C3H60, has the calculated value 7,4865: and benzene, C6H6, the value 10,111 4. Petrol is a variable mixture of hydrocarbons, but if taken as being substantially equivalent to octane, C8H18, its theoretical calorific value is 12,245 calories per gram.

"Gross" and "net" values. - The values here given are the " higher" or " gross" calorific values, corresponding with the formation of liquid water, as obtained in the calorimeter. If the water is vaporised, this operation absorbs some of the heat developed by the combustion.

	Moisture	**kWh / kg**	**kcal / kg**	**Weight kg / m3**	**kg = 1liter fuel**
Bark fir	50%	2,14	1,84	280	4,65
Briquettes	20%	4,9	4,214	660	2,03
Forest wood chip dry	40%	2,89	2,511	240	3,44
Forest wood chip fresh	55%	2	1,72	310	4,98
Miscanthus	10%	4,4	3,78	140	2,26
Rapeseed	9%	6,83	5,87	700	1,46
Sawdust	6%	4,2	3,629	160	2,36
Stover rapeseed	15%	4,17	3,58	115	2,43
Sunflower	9%	5,56	4,78	600	1,79
Wheat	15%	4,17	3,58	700	2,4
Wheat Straw	15%	4	3,44	100	2,49
Wood chip	20%	4,22	3,629	175	2,36
Wood granulate	8%	4,44	3,81	600	2,24
Woodlogs ash	45%	2,61	2,245	650	3,81
Woodlogs ash dry	20%	4,08	3,509	400	2,44
Coal	10%	7	6,02	750	1,36
Fuel gasoil		11,8	11,2	840	0,84
Natural gas		10,83	9,314	0	0

The quantity of water produced is governed by the amount of hydrogen burned. Thus in the case of ethyl alcohol the weight of hydrogen in 1 gram is 01312 gram, and this is equivalent to 1.808 grams of water.

Since the latent heat of vaporization of water is 537 calories per gram, the heat absorbed in vaporizing this water is 11808 × 537 = 634. Calories. This quantity, therefore, is to be deducted from the result obtained above for ethyl alcohol, whenever the " lower" or "net" value is required: 7,2378 – 6341 = 6,6037, the lower theoretical calorific value of absolute ethyl alcohol.

Further, if the alcohol in question is not absolute, but already contains water (as is always the case in practice), the vaporization of this water will also absorb heat, and the corresponding number of calories must be deducted.

Thus if the proportion of water be 10 per cent. by weight, 1 gram of the alcohol will contain 01 gram of water, and the further deduction will therefore be 01 × 537 = 53.7 calories.

Hence, finally, for 90 per cent. alcohol (by weight), when all the water already present and that produced in the combustion is vaporised, the calorific value is 6,6037 – 537 = 6,5500 gram-calories.

CONVENTIONAL FORMS OF FUEL

HYDROGEN

Hydrogen is the lightest of the elements with an atomic weight of 1.0. Liquid hydrogen has a density of 0.07 grams per cubic centimeter, whereas water has a density of 1.0 g/cc and gasoline about 0.75 g/cc. These facts give hydrogen both advantages and disadvantages. The advantage is that it stores approximately 2.6 times the energy per unit mass as gasoline, and the disadvantage is that it needs about 4 times the volume for a given amount of energy. A 15 gallon automobile gasoline tank contains 90 pounds of gasoline. The corresponding hydrogen tank would be 60 gallons, but the hydrogen would weigh only 34 pounds.

When hydrogen is burned in air the main product is water. Some nitrogen compounds may also be produced and may have to be controlled. Should greenhouse warming turn out to be an important problem, the key advantage of hydrogen is that carbon dioxide (CO_2) is not produced when hydrogen is burned.

Since hydrogen is not available in significant quantities in nature in pure form, the main present way of getting hydrogen is steam methane reforming, and this will probably remain the most economical way as long as methane (natural gas) is available cheaply and in large quantities, and hydrogen is required only in small quantities.

When the price of methane goes up to more than three times its present price because of scarcity, hydrogen will be obtained by splitting water H_2O into hydrogen H2 and oxygen O_2. The chemical reaction is written

$$2H_2O + \text{energy} \rightarrow 2H_2 + O_2.$$

The well developed way of splitting water is by electrolysis. If fossil fuels, *e.g.* coal, oil or natural gas, are used to generate the electricity, there is no advantage over using the fossil fuels directly.

Indeed you still get all the CO_2, and there is a considerable loss of energy. Therefore, the large scale use of hydrogen depends on using either nuclear or solar electricity. In both the nuclear and solar cases, there are possible but undeveloped technologies that don't use electricity as an intermediate form of energy. 2003 September: There is a thermochemical process for splitting water that is claimed to be twice as efficient as elactrolysis.

Here's an article on the sulfur-iodine cycle by Ken Schultz of General Atomic given at a Stanford University Global Climate and Energy sponsored meeting in 2003 April. To get good efficiency it requires reactors operating at a higher termperature (950 C) than present power reactors. Schultz's article also discusses solar thermal production of hydrogen. (There are also proposals to combine getting heat for houses and chemical processes and electrolysis with some saving of energy.)

In either case, the law of conservation of energy tells us that all the energy to be obtained by burning the hydrogen must be supplied by the primary source, *e.g.* nuclear or solar. Of course, since these processes aren't 100 per cent efficient, there is some loss of energy. Therefore, the use of hydrogen as an intermediate is justified only when there is some reason not to use the primary source directly. For vehicles the reason is that both nuclear nor solar power plants are too big to carry around, except that nuclear power is suitable for large ships.

If there is large scale use of solar energy, the energy is likely to be generated far from where it is used and at a different time. Hydrogen has been proposed as both a storage and transmission medium. It should work for these purposes. I don't know how hydrogen pipelines compare with high voltage electric transmission as means of long distance transmission of energy.

Hydrogen can be transported by pipelines similar to those used to transport natural gas. There are some addtional problems, because hydrogen tends to leak more and can embrittle some metals used for pipelines. The existence of a 240 km hydrogen pipeline in Germany operated by the company Air Liquide provides evidence that these difficulties can be overcome.

In a paper appearing in the July issue of Science magazine, Alex Farrell, assistant professor of energy and resources at UC Berkeley, and David Keith, associate professor of engineering and public policy at University, present various short- and long-term strategies that they say would achieve the same results as switching from gasoline-powered vehicles to hydrogen cars.

"Hydrogen cars are a poor short-term strategy, and it's not even ciear that they are a good idea in the long term," said Farrell. "Because the prospects for hydrogen cars are so uncertain, we need to think carefully before we invest all this money and all this public effort in one area."

Farrell and Keith compared the costs of developing fuel cell vehicles to the costs of other strategies for achieving the same environmental and economic goals. "There are three reasons you might think hydrogen would be a good thing to use as a transportation fuel - it can reduce air pollution, slow global climate change and reduce dependence on oil imports - but for each one there is something else you could do that would probably work better, work faster and be cheaper," Farrell said.

The biggest problem with hydrogen as a means to reduce pollution is that it has to be produced from another energy source. But the most cost competitive energy sources are all forms of fossil fuels. The production of the hydrogen is not 100 per cent efficient and producing it from fossil fuels produces pollution. The transportation and storage of the hydrogen also use substantial amounts of energy.

Hydrogen is also more difficult to store and transport and takes up much more space than liquid hydrocarbon fuels. It is not the only conceivable approach to pursue for reducing net pollution from vehicles for the purpose of reducing green house gasses.

Another approach to reduce the net production of green house gasses would be to develop a light-driven chemical process that would fix carbon out of atmospheric carbon dioxide to make hydrocarbon fuels. Or if cheap photovoltaic solar cells could be developed then another approach would be to use electricity from solar cells to drive the chemical process to fix carbon from carbon dioxide. Effectively gasoline would be generated from solar power. Then the gasoline could be burned in cars. This artificial carbon cycle would eliminate the net addition of carbon dioxide gas to the atmosphere.

ALTERNATIVE FUEL

Gas and diesel are the basic forms of fuel at the present time. If you are like anyone else in the world, you are realizing that the costs of fuel are rising, and it is getting to be more expensive every day to get to work, to take a vacation and for those who are farmers, to run equipment. Alternative forms of fuel must be found to reduce costs daily and weekly so that you can continue on with your life without spending a fortune on fuels. Gas and diesel are not the only forms of fuel that are needing to be addressed by everyone in the world, but also one must look at fuels that are used for heating the home. Home heating costs are rising just as fast as the cost to run your car, truck or tractor.

Various countries, including the US are looking to create and begin using other forms of fuel, which is known as alternative fuels. The use of biodiesel, electricity, ethanol, hydrogen, natural gas and propane are some of the forms of alternative fuels, but there are many more out there. While you are sitting there thinking about alternative fuels, you need to think about your car, the home, the manufacturer down the street, and how all this is going to link into a better cleaner future, that will leave everyone less dependent on oils and oil products.

Biodiesel is one form of alternative fuels, and is considered by the EPA as one of the best because it is not a straight gas, or a diesel, but it contains a mixture that uses much less of the oils as we know it other wise. If you are running any fleet of cars or trucks, or even tractors at the moment, you known just how high the prices of fuel can eat away at your pocket. When you hear someone on the news talking about bio diesel, it is a mixture of blends, that will consist of using twenty per cent or more of another product along with diesel to make diesel run cleaner, longer and will conserve on the diesel that is being used overall.

Alternative fuels include the use of methanol, ethanol and other types of alcohol for the use in machinery and in vehicles. Alternative fuels are just on the horizon, and working out well saving money for many people and for many businesses who are involved in finding and using alternative sources of energy.

When learning more about alternatives, you will find some methods of using methanol, ethanol or other alcohols are added to the gasoline as we know it, and they are adding up to 85 per cent of the overall liquid to create a new blend that works well in many types of machinery and in vehicles alike. To make the most of a situation, farmers are finding many of the crops they are already producing will give them the bi product, the alcohol needed to run vehicles and machinery enabling them to save money all at the same time.

Alternative fuels are being found not only in alcohol but in gasses, liquefied petroleum gasses, coal derived forms, and in hydrogen, electricity, and with the use of wind.

HEAT OUTPUT

The temperature and heat output of hydrothermal systems at oceanic spreading centers place strong constraints on the mechanism of heat transfer in oceanic crust. In this paper, we investigate time-dependent heat transfer from a vigorously convecting, crystallizing, and replenished magmatic sill beneath an ocean ridge axis, linked to an overlying hydrothermal system.

We first consider two different crystallization scenarios, "crystals suspended" and "crystals settling," coupled with crystallinity-dependent and temperature-dependent magma viscosity. The large-scale convection is assumed to rapidly homogenize the magma, resulting in a characteristic temperature T m.

In cases without magma replenishment, the simulation results for crystal-suspended models show that heat output and the hydrothermal temperature decrease rapidly and that crystallinity reaches 60 per cent in less than 10 a. In crystal-settling models, magma convection may last for decades, but decreasing heat output and hydrothermal temperatures still occur on decadal timescales.

When magma replenishment is included, the magmatic heat flux approaches steady state on decadal timescales, whereas the magma body grows to double its original size. The rate of magma replenishment needed ranges between 5 × 105 and 5 × 106 m3 a⁻1, which is somewhat faster than that required for seafloor spreading but less than that of fluxes to some terrestrial volcanoes on similar timescales. The heat output from a convecting, crystallizing, replenished magma body that is needed to drive observed high-temperature hydrothermal systems is consistent, with gabbro glacier models of crustal production at mid-ocean ridges.

Measuring the Heat Output of Different Lamps

This experiment was intended to measure the way in which different "types" of lamps of the same wattage produce drastically different basking temperatures.

Introduction

One of the basic laws of physics is the law of the Conservation of Energy. This simply states that energy cannot be created or destroyed, it can only be transferred from one form to another. So when a 100watt lamp is switched on, 100 watts of electrical energy is converted to 100watts of light and heat; a 50watt lamp produces a total 50 watts of light and heat, and so on.* However, some lamps are more efficient at producing light than others; this determines how much of that 100 watts is transformed into light, and how much is "wasted" and comes out as heat (very useful, though, if what we want is a basking lamp).

A halogen lamp is a bit better. For every 100 watts you put in, you get about 3.5 watts of light and 96.5 watts of heat.

However, the heat and light from a lamp can be emitted in all directions, or focused on a small area (consider the heat and light you might experience sitting 2ft below a 60 watt frosted "globe" lamp as opposed to a 60 watt narrow beam spot lamp) hence the shape of the lamp, the type of glass surface and the presence or absence of reflectors, such are found inside spot lamps, will also play a major part in determining how hot a basking spot gets directly under any lamp, of whatever wattage.

CALCULATING HEAT REQUIREMENTS

CALCULATION OF POWER REQUIRED

Heating equipment will use one of the following methods for transferring heat to the work-piece.

- Radiation
- Direct Immersion
- Natural or Forced Convection
- Conduction

Normally, it will be obvious from the application which method is to be used. In the case of radiation, power requirements are not normally amenable to calculation. Normally we would advise on this by reference to our experience and data on previous applications. In the case of the other methods of heat transfer, calculations can be made to determine the power required, depending on the following factors:

- Power absorbed by work-piece or material in raising its temperature by the required amount in the required time.
- Power absorbed by container or enclosure for its appropriate temperature rise in the time required.
- Power losses from the equipment (surface losses).

In practice, 2 calculations of power requirements need to be made.

$$\text{A Heating up Kw}\left(A + B + + \frac{C}{2}\right) \quad \text{B Operating Kw}(A + C)$$

These two power requirements may be widely different abd obviously it will be necessary to install whichever is the larger if all the given operating conditions are to be met.

To calculate "A" - power absorbed by material:

- Power absorbed by heating up of material

$$KW = \frac{\text{Kg of mtl heated per hour} \times \text{Specific heat kj/kg} \times \text{Temp rise C}}{3600}$$

Two basic heat energy requirements should be considered in the sizing of heaters for a particular application.

When sizing heaters for a given application, two heat energy calculations should be performed: startup heat and operating heat. Taking these steps before you submit the purchase order can help ensure that the heater you receive will meet the needs of your process.

Startup heat is the heat energy required to bring a process up to operating temperature.

Startup heat requirement calculations that include a material change of state should be calculated in three parts:

- Heat requirement from ambient temperature to change of state temperature.
- Heat requirement during change of state (latent heat).
- Heat requirement from change of state temperature to operating temperature.

Startup heat requirements will include one or more of the following seven calculations, depending on the application.

Wattage required to heat material:

$$W = \frac{\begin{array}{c}\text{Weight of Material (lb)} \times \text{Specific Heat (BT /} \\ \text{Ib°F)} \times \text{Temperature Rise (°F)}\end{array}}{3.412\ \text{BTU / Watt hr} \times \text{Heatup Timer (hr)}}$$

Wattage required to heat container or tank:

$$W = \frac{\text{Weight of Container (lb)} \times \text{Specific Heat (BTU / lb°F)} \times \text{Temperature Rise (°F)}}{3.412\ \text{BTU / Watt hr} \times \text{Heatup Timer (hr)}}$$

$$W = \frac{\text{Weight of Hardware (lb)} \times \text{Specific Heat (BTU / lb°F)} \times \text{Temperature Rise (°F)}}{3.412\ \text{BTU / Watt hr} \times \text{Heatup Timer (hr)}}$$

Wattage required to melt a solid to a liquid at constant temperature:

$$W = \frac{\text{Heat of Fusion (BTU / lb)} \times \text{Weight of Material to be Melted (lb / hr)}}{3.412\ \text{BTU / Watt hr}}$$

Heat of Fusion (Latent Heat). The amount of heat required to change one pound of a given substance from solid to liquid state without change in temperature is termed the heat of fusion.

It requires 144 BTU to change one pound of ice at 32°F (0°C) to one pound of water at 32°F (the heat of fusion of ice being 144 BTU per pound).

A change of state usually is accompanied by a change of specific heat. The specific heat of ice is 0.5 while that of water is 1.0.

To calculate the wattage required to change a liquid to a vapour state at constant temperature:

$$W = \frac{\text{Heat of Vaporization (BTU / lb)} \times \text{Weight of Material to be Vaporized (lb / hr)}}{3.412\ \text{BTU / Watt hr}}$$

Heat of Vaporization (Latent Heat). The amount of heat required to change one pound of a given substance from liquid to vapour state without a change in temperature is termed the heat of vaporization. It requires 965 BTU to change one pound of water at 212°F (100°C) to one pound of steam at 212°F.

To calculate the wattage to counteract liquid surface losses:

$$W = \frac{\text{Total Liquid Sufface Area (ft}^2\text{)} \times \text{Loss Rate Final Temperature (Watts / ft}^2\text{)}}{2}$$

To calculate the wattage to counteract surface losses from container walls, platen surfaces, etc.:

$$W = \frac{\text{Total Sufface Area}(\text{ft}^2) \times \text{Loss Rate Final Temperature}(\text{Watts}/\text{ft}^2)}{2}$$

ENERGY CONSERVATION

Energy conservation is the practice of decreasing the quantity of energy used. It may be achieved through efficient energy use, in which case energy use is decreased while achieving a similar outcome, or by reduced consumption of energy services.

Energy conservation may result in increase of financial capital, environmental value, national security, personal security, and human comfort. Individuals and organizations that are direct consumers of energy may want to conserve energy in order to reduce energy costs and promote economic security.

Industrial and commercial users may want to increase efficiency and thus maximize profit. Unfortunately, we believe that the World has entered an era where fuel prices will continue to increase and place a greater emphasis and urgency on conservation. Electrical energy conservation is an important element of energy policy. Energy conservation reduces the energy consumption and energy demand per capita and thus offsets some of the growth in energy supply needed to keep up with population growth. This reduces the rise in energy costs, and can reduce the need for new power plants, and energy imports. The reduced energy demand can provide more flexibility in choosing the most preferred methods of energy production.

By reducing emissions, energy conservation is an important part of lessening climate change. Energy conservation facilitates the replacement of non-renewable resources with renewable energy. Energy conservation is often the most economical solution to energy shortages, and is a more environmentally benign alternative to increased energy production.

Key to reducing energy usage and costs is in understanding where the energy goes and how it is used.

Alcyum Energy Solutions can undertake a full and thorough review of the utility consumption and usage related to your operations and this will include,

- A complete and comprehensive review of your facilities, with particular focus on all aspects of lagging and insulation designed to retain heat or exclude temperature fluctuations,
- Undertake a review of any previous energy cost reduction programmes and consider their impact to ensure that future recommendations comply with and complement our clients core activities and that there is no duplication of effort,

- Review the electrical distribution system, including input and output voltages, efficiency of distribution boards, examine transformer maintenance procedures and cycles as well as output ratings and conduct a full review of power outages or load restrictions,
- Consider the use of lighting in relation to opera-tional need and demand, and
- Review HVAC systems within the facilities to ensure that these are operating at optimal levels, are being maintained to acceptable industry standards and that they continue to meet with the design requirement.

This energy audit considers every aspect of your operations and will present a full consideration of our findings and a complete listing of our recommendations. These recommendations will not be hollow words but will be fully detailed and will include,

- The features of your operation that need attention relative to their energy consumption,
- Works to be carried out to make these more energy aware or efficient,
- Prioritise these in two main sections, low/no cost projects and those attracting a cost,
- Provide full budget costs for the works to be carried out,
- The provision of a thorough analysis of the anticipated pay back period for the implementation of these recommendations, and
- Present areas that we consider may attract aid funding from the government or other related bodies.

The strategy developed to make power available to all by 2012 includes promotion of energy efficiency and its conservation in the country, which is found to be the least cost option to augment the gap between demand and supply. Nearly 25,000 MW of capacity creation through energy efficiency in the electricity sector alone has been estimated in India. Energy conservation potential for the economy as a whole has been assessed as 23 per cent with maximum potential in industrial and agricultural sectors.

The air-conditioner is the main cause of power consumption increasing during summer period. As the household power consumption is concerned, the air-conditioner plays the major role and the lighting and refrigerators plays the next.

The appliances save energy or not, depend on purchasing, installation, usage, and maintenance. The rule of appliances-purchasing adopts appliances with energy label or high efficiency. Pay attention to maintain in normal time, it can promote efficiency.

- *Air-Conditioner*:

Shut the window and door tightly.

When air-conditioner's setting temperature rises.

Set adequate room temperature.

Clean up air-conditioner's heat exchanger or condenser regularly.

Apply heat-insulated material and sunshade to reduce indoor heat capacity.

Apply highly efficient air-conditioner with high Energy Efficiency Ratio(EER).

- *Refrigerator*:

For the purpose of improving the efficiency of operation and heat dissipation, the location of refrigerators should keep away wall at least 10 centimeters and avoid the source of thermals like ovens and heaters.

Don't put too much stuff inside the refrigerator; keep the 20 per cent space in the chamber so as to let the air circulate easily.

Every time you open the refrigerator, the compressor must operate 10 minutes to recover its state of low-temperature. It would be better to reduce the times you open the refrigerator.

- *Lighting*:

Utilize the natural light sources on lighting system, and install high-efficiency lamps with the HF electronic ballasts.

Manage lighting facilities by districting management system.

Paint the ceilings and walls in favour of reflecting effect with lighter colours.

SHORT TERM MEASURES

- Energy Conservation
  - Bureau of Energy Efficiency operationalized Complete pilot phase of programme for energy efficiency in government buildings and prepare action plan for wider dissemination and implementation.
- Energy audit of government buildings
  - Energy Audit completed for nine govt. buildings.
  - Legal Performance contract agreement, payment security mechanism, bids selection and evaluation criteria provided to all building owners for implementation.
  - Five Building owners have floated tenders.
  - Monitoring and verification of energy savings from March 2007.

- Capacity building amongst departments to take up energy efficiency programmes
  - BEE to train core group members to implement energy efficiency in buildings.

LONG TERM MEASURES

Potential of 23,700 MW assessed by end of XIth Plan

The Thrust Areas:

- Industry specific Task Forces.
- Notifying more industries as designated consumers.
- Conduct of energy audit amongst notified designated consumers.
- Recording and publication of best practises (sectorwise).
- Development of energy consumption norms.
- Monitoring of compliance with mandated provision by designated consumers.

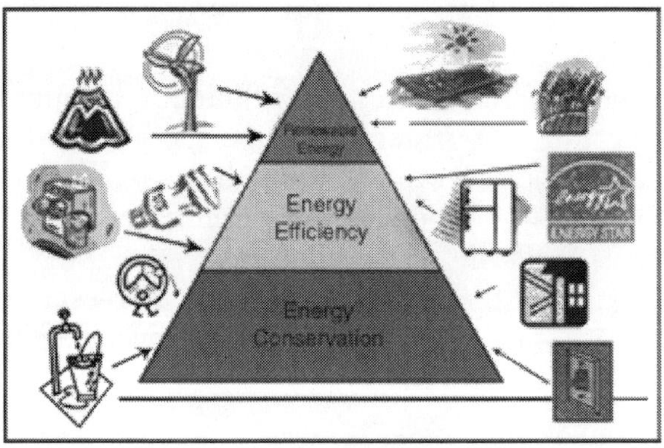

We will be updating this page, especially as we gather information on how community energy efficiency efforts can be funded, and current examples of successful efforts. Please let us know if you have information you believe belongs here.

Good resources for more information on energy conservation and efficiency:

- Energy star
- Energy Ideas Clearinghouse

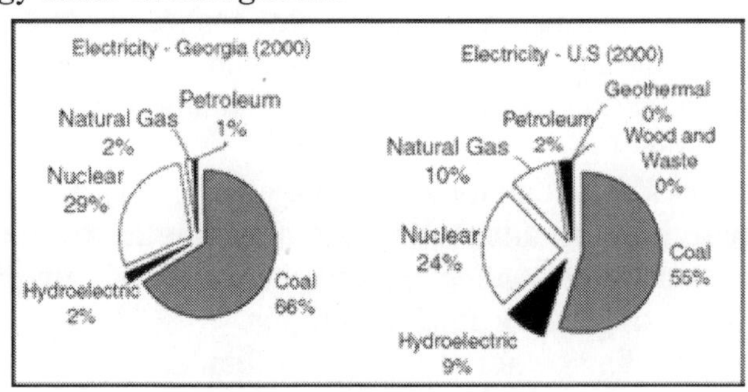

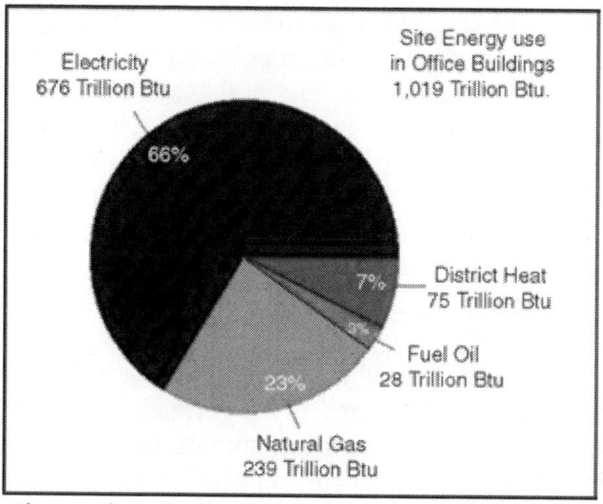

Energy audit studies conducted in several office buildings, hotels and hospitals indicate energy saving potential of 20-30 per cent. The potential is largely untapped, partly due to lack of an effective delivery mechanism for energy efficiency. Government buildings by themselves constitute a very large target market. The Government of India is committed to set an example by implementing the provisions of the EC Act in all its establishments as a first initiative.

HOTEL WASTES

Many things we throw away as waste. But have we even thought of using these profitably? Small- small contributions by each one of us could help in preserving the greens of our planet.

Hotel waste comprises of two components, Biodegradable (Wet) waste and Non- biodegradable (Dry) waste. The wet waste comprises of food, vegetable and non- veg waste whereas the dry waste comprises of plastic bottles, papers, plastic wrappers, HDPE, LLDPE bags etc. Nationally, about 50 per cent of a typical property's waste stream is recyclable, not including food wastes. That means most lodging facilities generate sufficient amounts of recyclable materials to justify recycling. Add conventions and meetings to the mix, and the recycling potential skyrockets. Even for facilities that are smaller or do not serve food, talking with the city or county recycling coordinator can help find new ways to reduce wastes. This fact sheet explains systematic how to start recycling in your facility. It provides a list of questions for potential contractors, identifies materials that can be collected, and suggests ways to design the collection process.

Food waste is recycled into fertilizer, which helps grow rice and vegetables, which find their way back onto dinner tables. These are just a "few examples" of the unwanted items we throw away that become "waste", most of which are destined for disposal at a smelly landfill site! People who live in close proximity to these sites know too well about the smells and odours emitted from these sites and of the vast numbers of scavengers that are attracted to landfill areas such as sea gulls and rats to name just a few!

With landfill sites fast becoming filled to the brim, we are having to develop alternative ways in order to deal with our household wastes. Changes to the current methods of waste disposal will be driven (in part) by environmental pressures, sustainability issues and health and safety requirements, all of which will have affect upon each and every one of us to some degree!

Reducing the amount of wastes you produce is therefore crucial, even if you only start with recycling (it all makes a huge difference). But don't forget you can take it a a stage further, and make yourself (and save) some money along the way! So start today, you having nothing to lose!

Wastes where possible should be reduced at source, which means our manufacturing companies and retailers should be doing their bit to reduce waste as well. Check out the outlets where you shop and ask them about their policies for reducing waste, and what recycling facilities do they have to offer!

With a little thought, the waste being placed into your normal refuse bin, can be reduced to this! So you may be wondering where has all the other waste gone then?

- Paper, glass, metals, plastic containers, tops, boxes and plastic bags can all be disposed of via recyling banks, or kerbside collection schemes.
- Kitchen and green wastes including cardboard can be put into a wormery or a composting unit. 3. Recycle 1. Reduce 2. Reuse.

HOTEL WASTES TREATMENT

From hotels/resorts generally three types of wastewater is generated. Sewage, canteen and laundry wastes. The treatment methodology is decided on the composite wastewater analysis and it depends on:

- Wastewater discharging intermittently from different sections.
- Variation in the volume and characteristics of wastewater from section to section.

Sewage and canteen wastes have mainly BOD, COD and Suspended solids. Laundry waste contains a high amount of dissolved solids. The pretreatment of laundry wastes and other two effluents are done separately and after pretreatment the effluents are mixed and further biological treatment is done.

Canteen Waste Pretreatment System

In pretreatment process mainly suspended impurities are removed. The wastewater coming out from canteen is taken out in to the digester for decomposition of bio-degradable materials and then it is taken in to equalization tank. The detention time in the digester depends upon the characteristics of the influent *i.e.* How much is BOD and Suspended Solids are present in the wastewater. If impurities level are low *e.g.* BOD is around 1200 mg/lit then digester is not required. The water outlet from digester is flown to equalization tank.

Sewage Pretreatment

The raw sewage coming out contains COD, BOD, NH3, and Suspended Solids and sewage flow is introduced to an inlet grit chamber, through a channel equipped with a mechanical screen to remove object and other debris present in sewage stream. Then sewage flows in to a grit chamber to settle grit and high specific gravity materials such as sand etc. This unit is capable of removing grit particles larger than 100 mesh Sp. Gr. of 2.5 and above. The sewage after grit chamber is then flown to equalization tank.

- A method for introduction of sewage pre-treatment in a pipeline infrastructure of a sewage treatment system upstream of a sewage treatment facility of the system and downstream of an untreated sewage discharging facility, said method comprising the steps of:
  - Selecting a site in a pipeline infrastructure of a sewage treatment system between and external to an untreated sewage discharging facility and a sewage treatment facility of the system;
  - Providing a source of biological activity enhancing agent at the selected site, said enhancing agent being an enzyme for increasing the microbial activity in the sewage flow; and
  - Introducing the agent from the source thereof into a flow of untreated sewage at the selected site so as to convert the sewage from an untreated state to a pre-treated state in the pipeline infrastructure upstream of the sewage treatment facility and downstream of said untreated sewage discharging facility.
- The method of claim 1, wherein said site selected is a sewage pumping site including a pump in the sewer pipeline infrastructure and the agent is mixed with the sewage flow either upstream or downstream of said pump.
- A method for introduction of sewage pre-treatment in a pipeline infrastructure of a sewage treatment system upstream of a sewage treatment facility of the system and downstream of an untreated sewage discharging facility, said method comprising the steps of:
  - Selecting a site in a pipeline infrastructure of a sewage treatment system between and external to an untreated sewage discharging facility and a sewage treatment facility of the system;
  - Providing a source of biological activity enhancing agent at the selected site; and

  - Introducing the agent from the source thereof into a flow of untreated sewage at the selected site so as to convert the sewage from an untreated state to a pre-treated state in the pipeline infrastructure upstream of the sewage treatment facility and downstream of said untreated sewage discharging facility, said introducing of said agent being by use of a mixing device interposed in the piping of the pipeline infrastructure at the selected site and receiving the introduced agent from the source thereof and mixing the agent with the sewage flow at the site.
- The method of claim, wherein said providing said agent source includes providing an agent generator and injector at said selected site.
- The method of claim, wherein said agent is an oxygen-bearing gas for changing the sewage flow from an anaerobic to aerobic state.
- The method of claim, wherein said agent is an ozone-bearing gas for depleting the bacterial content of the sewage flow.
- An arrangement for introduction of sewage pre-treatment in a pipeline infrastructure of a sewage treatment system upstream of a sewage treatment facility of the sewage treatment system and downstream of an untreated sewage discharging facility, said arrangement comprising:
  - A selected site in a sewer pipeline infrastructure of a sewage treatment system between and external to an untreated sewage discharging facility and a sewage treatment facility of the sewage treatment system;
  - A source of a biological activity enhancing agent provided at said selected site, said agent being an enzyme for increasing the microbial content of the sewage flow; and
  - Means for introducing said agent from said source thereof into a flow of untreated sewage at said selected site so as to convert the sewage from an untreated state to a pre-treated state in the pipeline infrastructure upstream of the sewage treatment facility and downstream of said untreated sewage discharging facility.
- An arrangement for introduction of sewage pre-treatment in a pipeline infrastructure of a sewage treatment system upstream of a sewage treatment facility of the sewage treatment system and downstream of an untreated sewage discharging facility, said arrangement comprising:
  - A selected site in a sewer pipeline infrastructure of a sewage treatment system between and external to an untreated sewage discharging facility and a sewage treatment facility of the sewage treatment system;

- A source of a biological activity enhancing agent provided at said selected site; and
- Means for introducing said agent from said source thereof into a flow of untreated sewage at said selected site so as to convert the sewage from an untreated state to a pre-treated state in the pipeline infrastructure upstream of the sewage treatment facility and downstream of said untreated sewage discharging facility, said means for introducing said agent including an agent generator at said selected site; and a mixing device interposed in the pipeline infrastructure at said selected site for receiving said agent from said agent generator and mixing said agent with the sewage flow at said selected site.

- The arrangement of claim, wherein said agent is an oxygen-bearing gas for changing the sewage flow from an anaerobic to aerobic state.
- The arrangement of claim, wherein said agent is an ozone-bearing gas for depleting the bacterial content of the sewage flow.
- The arrangement of claim, wherein said selected site is a pumping site in the sewer pipeline infrastructure.
- The arrangement of claim, wherein said pumping site includes a pump and said agent is mixed with the sewage flow upstream of said pump at said pumping station.
- The arrangement of claim, wherein said pumping site includes a pump and said agent is mixed with the sewage flow downstream of said pump at said pumping site.

Laundry Waste Treatment System

Wastewater coming out from laundry is collected in a tank from where it is pumped to a flash mixer in which certain coagulants and flocculants dosing is done for the removal of impurities. The treated water is then transferred to primary clarifier where separated impurities will settle down to the bottom of clarifier by the help of media filled in it. The clear water from top shall be taken in to aeration tank and from bottom sludge shall be transferred to filter press or sludge drawing bed.

Fifty years ago, it seemed OK to discharge untreated wastewater from industrial processes into rivers and lakes. Many believed that our supply of fresh water was unlimited and that it could somehow handle the waste. We also weren't as concerned with the long-term consequences of pollution, neither did we have the available technology to remedy the situation.

Virtually every Canadian municipality today, has adopted similar by-laws, specifying what can and can not be discharged into sanitary sewers and the permissible levels of each contaminant. Pressure from the municipalities and escalating sewer surcharges, which are applied when contaminant levels exceed the by-law maximums, are now making it attractive for commercial laundries to provide their own effective pretreatment programme prior to discharging their wastewater.

Indegrents of Wastewater

Fats, oils and greases (FOG) as well as total suspended solids (TSS), are the major impurities of concern. These impurities are derived from the soils which are removed from clothing as well as from the chemicals which are used. Laundry wastewater may also carry additional impurities, but for the purpose of this article we will address FOG and TSS, the most common contaminants.

Why are High Levels of FOG so Undesirable?

FOG and other organic chemicals are digested, to produce carbon dioxide and water, by sewage bacteria which feed upon them. In this process, these bacteria consume and deplete the dissolved oxygen in the water. If untreated wastewater were to be discharged directly into rivers and streams, it would also deplete the dissolved oxygen and put marine and plant life risk.

A measure of organic water quality contamination is its Biological Oxygen Demand or BOD5. This is a measure of the amount of oxygen wastewater consumes over 5 days, at 20oC during the biological break down of organic contaminants, including FOG. The higher the BOD5level, the more organic contaminants are present in the water

Most municipalities have set limits of 100-150 ppm for FOG (from vegetable or animal sources), 350 ppm for TSS and 300 ppm for BOD5.

Commercial laundries which exceed these limits can have surcharges applied to their water bill; in proportional to the limits exceeded.

For laundries using large volumes of water, this surcharge can be significant, ranging form hundreds to thousands of dollars per month, and so there is a strong economical motivation for abiding by the municipal by-laws.

Why are High Levels of TSS Undesirable?

Undissolved or insoluble matter, floating or suspended in water, imparts a cloudy appearance (turbidity) to it, and is referred to as total suspended solids or TSS.

Aside from its unpleasing esthetic appearance, the main concern with high TSS levels is in its ability to harbour harmful bacteria, such as coliforms. These microorganisms are harmful and can be fatal when ingested. They can readily attach themselves and hide on suspended solids, and are not readily disinfected.

Pretreatment of Water

The topic of wastewater treatment is beyond the scope of this article. Future articles will address other technologies, including Reverse Osmosis,

Ultrafiltration and Nanofiltration. These are technologies which depend on the size of the pores in semi-permeable membranes to filter unwanted impurities out of wastewater, and is carried out under high pressure. A current and very effective new technology for pre-treating laundry wastewater is through the use of a Dissolved Air Floatation Unit (DAF Unit).

Working of DAF Unit

Recall that a large component of the BOD5 in laundry wastewater is due to the presence of fats, oils and greases. Reducing the FOG also lowers the BOD5 level. The economic benefit of using a DAF Unit is in avoiding a double sewer surcharge; one for excess BOD5 and the other for a FOG violation

FOG, being lighter than water has a natural tendency to float to the surface of a wastewater holding tank, from where it can be skimmed off. Since individual FOG droplets are very small and dispersed throughout a large tank of water, a considerable amount of time would be required for most of them to reach and concentrate at the surface. To resolve this problem, the heart of the DAF Unit consists of a compressed air-in-water tank which works as follows:.

Air is sparingly soluble in water under normal atmospheric pressure. However compressing air under high pressure, in a water-containing cylinder, results in a significant amount of the air being physically dissolved. This air enriched solution is then slowly released from the cylinder into the larger wastewater holding tank, and millions of tiny air bubbles come out of solution. A similar phenomena is seen when a soft drink bottle is slowly opened. Hundreds of gas bubbles are released which either adhere to the walls of the bottle or float to the surface.

As the tiny air bubbles rise to the surface, they attach themselves to the dispersed FOG particles, they lift them at an accelerated speed upwards towards the surface of the tank.

Total suspended solids (TSS), being heavier than water, would tend to sediment, within time, to the bottom of the holding tank. However, because many of the tiny air bubbles also surround and attach themselves to each suspended solid particle, they exert the same lifting effect, to the surface. In so doing, the turbidity of the solution is reduced, and so is the risk of paying a 3rd sewer surcharge for violation of TSS maximum levels.

Primary Treatment

Primary Clarifier (Tube Settler)

The mixed wastewater of sewage and canteen is stored in an equalization tank and from here pumped to clarifier for the removal of suspended impurities. In first clarifier removal of SS takes place which is predominantly organic in nature by natural settlement to effect almost 40 per cent reduction in BOD and

80 per cent removal of total suspended solids present in waste water. Poly aluminum chloride is also added in the wastewater flowing into primary clarifier during drought season to reduce BOD up to 60 per cent level.

If the flow is too high then the stream is divided in to some parts and more than one clarifier is installed. If the flow of influent is not very high then only one clarifier is sufficient. Conventional clarifiers require a huge amount of land and the Tube Settlers designed by NUCHEM WEIR are compact and require less space as compared to conventional clarifiers.

We provide PVC tube media in which very higher settling area is available which results in better solid - liquid separation.

The suspended particles in the water, settle on surface of the PVC tubes. Accumulation of the solids make it heavy and cause it to slide by gravity in to the hopper, from where it is removed periodically. The clear water which rises to the top is removed by a weir arrangement. The sludge coming out from the bottom of the clarifier is transferred to filter press or sludge drying bed depends upon the availability of the land or clients preference. Size of the filter press depends upon the characteristics of the wastewater. Clear liquid from top of the clarifier is transferred in to Aeration tank for biological treatment.

Secondary Treatment

Aeration Tank

Treated effluent from primary clarifier is taken in to Aeration Tank where air is made available in to the effluent for further BOD removal. Theoretically 1 kg BOD requires 1 to 1.7 kg oxygen for its decomposition and best source of oxygen available in the nature is air. Since air contains only 23.2 per cent oxygen and density of air is 1.21 kg/m3 so 1 kg BOD needs 6.13 m3 air. But air transfer efficiency is only 10 – 15 per cent in aeration chamber, so net air provided in aeration tank is 40 – 50 m3/ kg of BOD required to be removed.

The selection of the process depends upon the load in the influent and removal percentage required. If BOD load is not more and removal percentage is up to 90 per cent then conventional aeration tank is designed in which aeration is done either through surface aerator or through floating aerator. The aeration can also be done through air diffusers. The selection of the aeration mode depends on the client's interested and also on the input load. This design is called as Activation Sludge

Process in which tank volume is calculated on the basis of F/M ratio and MLSS quantity. In this design maximum 85 per cent BOD of the input value can be removed.

If more space is not available at the site then size of aeration tank is reduced and media of PVC is provided so as the detention time of liquid in tank remains same and oxygen transfer efficiency increased by around four times. In this treatment around 95 per cent BOD of inlet value is possible to remove. The aeration tank is called as SAFF Reactor and in this reactor aeration is done through diffusers and for this purpose T.L.Blower is provided.

In the aeration tank or SAFF Reactor culture is developed by developing bacteria through certain means which reduces BOD. The treated effluent is then transferred to Secondary Settling Tank for sludge-liquid separation.

Secondary Settling Tank

In secondary settling tank solid separated from water in aeration tank is separated out. In this tank artificial surface is created with the help of PVC tube media. The media is kept at an angle which creates a sliding surface for sludge settling. The media has very high surface area which helps the sludge separation from water with a very high speed The bottom of this tank is also at a certain angle, generally 55 - 60 degrees which is helpful for sludge sliding towards bottom.. The suspended particles in the water, settles on the surface of the PVC tubes. Accumulation of the solids make it heavy and cause it to slide by gravity in to the hopper, from where it is removed periodically. The clear water which rises to the top is taken out by weir arrangements.

Maximum amount of impurities gets removed here. In fact this impurity is decomposed BOD/SS. From the bottom of Secondary Settling Tank activated sludge is taken out and a portion of sludge is recycled back to aeration tank and rest of the sludge is thrown out or can be used as a fertilizer for plants.

If treated water is to be used for horticulture then it can be passed through DMF/ ACF only. For reuse of treated water in certain processes like cooling water/ chilled water make up, toilet flushing, ground water recharging etc. then it has to be treated further by chemical methods.

Chemical Treatment System

A chemical treatment system of the present invention injects a chemical solution into a process. The chemical treatment system comprises a chemical tank containing the chemical solution. A pump is disposed to provide a dosage of the chemical solution from the tank to the process. A sensor and a controller are disposed in a closed loop with the process and the pump to vary in real time the dosage of the chemical solution provided by the pump based on a condition of the process sensed by the sensor and communicated to the controller.

The treated sewage water is treated for chemical treatment by further treatment to reduce phosphates, hardness, alkalinity, suspended matters,organics and remaining nitrogens by processing in a clariflocculator followed by lime softening clarifier, chlorination system and pressure sand filter.

The treated sewage water will be supplied clariflocculator for the removal of phosphate and suspended solids. Hardness and silica are removed in softening clarifier by adding lime and polyelectrolyte under high pH condition. The pH adjustment chamber is also employed to adjust pH. In this process Sulphuric acid is added to water to the pH range of 7.5 – 8.0.The chlorination is envisaged to oxidize residual organics BOD and it reduces to less than 2 ppm.

The need for chemical treatment depends on the quality of the water supplied to the facility and the types of equipment in service at the facility. There is no one treatment programme or system that is right for all facilities or systems within the facilities. The chemical treatment examples are based on the facility being supplied with water either from a municipal supply system or from a well system dedicated to the facility. The water supplied to the facility generally meets drinking water standards and is used to supply potable water and process water systems within the facility.

Applications: The systems for which treatment practices are discussed as follows.

- Well water delivered to facility domestic and industrial water reservoirs.
- Closed-loop recirculating water systems (chilled water, recirculating cooling water, and hot water heating).
- Open recirculating water systems (cooling tower spray water or recirculating cooling water in an open cooling tower loop).
- Steam boiler system (makeup water, feedwater, and steam and condensate).

Water supply disinfection: Although the water supplied to the facility is already drinking water quality, additional disinfection may be required to control the growth of biological contaminants, such as algae, in the potable and industrial water reservoirs where long-term storage may provide conditions for growth. This additional disinfection may be direct treatment of the water supplied to the facility, treatment of a recirculating stream at the reservoirs, or a combination of both. Operator involvement is limited to testing the water to determine the amount of treatment required, adjusting the pump stroke and/ or the hypochlorite solution strength to obtain the desired dosage, and keeping an adequate supply of hypochlorite solution in the local storage tank.

Process water systems: Process water refers to systems, such as chilled water systems, hot water heating systems, and recirculating water equipment cooling systems. The three primary reasons that process water chemical treatment may be required are to control corrosion, scale formation, and the growth of biological agents. Because corrosion and scale control chemicals can change the pH of the circulating water stream, the pH of a system may also require monitoring and adjustment. Process water streams may be closed-loop systems or open systems.

- In closed loop systems, there are negligible losses from or additions into a known volumesystem. Once the initial volume is chemically treated, the quality of the circulating fluid needs to be monitored on a regular basis and additional chemicals added as required to maintain recommended residual concentrations of treatment chemicals. When chemical treatment of a closed-loop water circulating system is required, the chemicals are usually introduced into the system by means of a pot feeder. The chemical treatment can be accomplished as the system is filled or during normal operation of the system using a pot feeder in a bypass loop.

- In cold service closed-loop systems, the system may only need to have chemical treatment when the system is filled initially and any time the system has been open for maintenance. Cold service recirculating systems are usually treated to prevent corrosion from dissolved oxygen. Scale formation is usually not a problem in cold systems.
- In warm or hot service closed-loop water circulating systems, regular monitoring and chemical additions may be required to prevent corrosion from dissolved oxygen and scale formation from precipitation of minerals in the water.

- In open recirculating cooling water systems there is constant loss from the system due to evaporation and a constant addition of makeup water into the system which constantly changes the quality of the recirculating stream. Also, as water evaporates from the system, impurities in the water are left behind which causes an increase in the concentration of these impurities. These impurities are generally referred to as total dissolved solids. Open systems typically control total dissolved solids by blow down from the system. Additionally, the methods used to reduce the temperature of open recirculating water streams allow oxygen, which is a primary cause of corrosion, to be entrained in the recirculating stream.
  - This constant change in the system quality may require frequent water quality monitoring along with the frequent addition of chemicals to control corrosion, scale formation, and growth of biological agents. Some combinations of chemicals used may also change the pH of the system significantly which will require pH monitoring and adjustment. If an open system requires chemical treatment, treatment programme options range from the operator periodically sampling the water and making slug additions of chemicals into the basin to a continuous water quality analyzer controlling the operation of metering pumps which inject controlled doses of chemicals into the circulating stream to maintain a uniform water quality.
  - A typical automated open-loop water quality monitoring and

control system has a stream passes through a water quality analyzer which has probes that monitor pH and conductivity (a measure of total dissolved solids). The pH meter controls a metering pump that injects a pH adjustment solution (usually an acid) into the circulating stream. The conductivity meter controls the operation of the blowdown valve. A signal from a water meter in the makeup waterline controls the corrosion inhibitor metering pump. A timer in the water quality analyzer activates the biological growth control metering pump. Some automated systems may have a corrosion sensing probe, rather than a water meter, to control the corrosion inhibitor metering pump. A likely alternate to the fully automated system is metering pumps controlled by timers. Based on a periodic water sample, the operator sets the timers and adjusts the metering pumps to provide the desired level of chemical treatment for the system.

The general purposes of chemical treatment include:

- Removal of suspended solids (turbidity) from water
- pH adjustment
- Removal of dissolved material

The main treatment components of FII chemical treatment packages include:

- pH adjustment and control
- Coagulation/ Flocculation
- Precipitation
- Clarifications

Other chemical treatment processes include:

- Ion exchange
- Water softening
- Chemical stabilization
- Disinfection

The obvious disadvantage of chemical treatment systems is that they consume chemicals. In addition, even if they are effective in rendering the waste non-infectious, the products of the chemical reactions they undergo are present in the waste, and may pose problems of their own. However, chemical treatment systems are convenient, and may be suitable in some situations, particularly when small quantities of waste are involved.

One of the most common constituents of chemical treatment systems is chlorine, either in the form of sodium hypochlorite solution (common bleach), or as the more powerful (and correspondingly more hazardous) gas, chlorine dioxide.

These compounds are relatively cheap and effective. However, in the course of reacting with organic compounds, they tend to form objectionable byproducts such as chloroform and other persistent toxins.

The chlorine compounds work by "oxidizing" (stripping electrons from) organic compounds, including the constituents of pathogenic microorganisms. The original "oxidizer" is, of course, atmospheric oxygen. Although it is, in fact, a fairly powerful oxidizing agent, ordinary oxygen is not harmful to, andis in fact essential for the survival of, many organisms including most of the pathogens in medical waste. However, when oxygen (02) is converted to ozone (03), a much stronger oxidizer, it becomes toxic to most life forms. Ozone can readily be generated by passing an electric arc through ordinary oxygen gas. When used in a medical waste treatment system, ozone acts as an effective sterilizer, without the tendency to generate the types of by-products found with chlorine compounds.

The major problem encountered with ozone systems is the need to avoid exposure to anyone in the vicinity of the treatment system, since ozone is highly injurious to lungs.

Alkaline agents are also used in medical waste treatment, either in highly corrosive form (sodium hydroxide, or lye), or in somewhat milder form (calcium oxide, or quicklime). Alkali tends to hydrolyze (decompose) proteins, among other effects. Apart from the cost of the reagents, the major disadvantage is the risk of contact, since alkaline solutions damage skin and lungs.

Pressure Sand Filter

The treated water from treated water pit is then pumped to Pressure Sand Filter for further removal of suspended impurities. The Pressure Sand Filter consists of pebbles, gravels along with the bed of quartz sand. The above said materials are kept in a layer form water passes downward through a filter bed of sand etc.,trapping and accumulating suspended. After a fixed period of operation backwashing of filter is done and waste water is sent to equalization tank.

The treated water from Effluent Treatment Plant will be under the limit of Pollution Control Board standards.

The treated water will be suitable for horticulture or for disposal in to the drains. For reuse of treated water in the process, installation of Reverse Osmosis Plant can also be done through which product water of very fine quality can be achieved and reject of the plant can be used for irrigation.

NUCHEM WEIR has the technology for further treatment of the treated water so that it can be reused in the process. For reuse of treated water in the process, installation of Reverse Osmosis Plant can also be done through which product water of very fine quality can be achieved and reject of the plant can be used for irrigation. The product water from Reverse Osmosis Plant will be of WHO Standard for drinking water. Alternatively treated water can be purified by D M Plant/ Softeners also for the use in cooling water, chilled water makeup,etc.

Reverse Osmosis System

Diffusion is the movement of molecules from a region of higher concentration to a region of lower concentration. Osmosis is a special case of diffusion in which the molecules are water and the concentration gradient occurs across a semipermeable membrane. The semipermeable membrane allows the passage of water, but not ions (*e.g.*, Na+, Ca2+, Cl) or larger molecules (*e.g.*, glucose, urea, bacteria). Diffusion and osmosis are thermodynamically favorable and will continue until equilibrium is reached. Osmosis can be slowed, stopped, or even reversed if sufficient pressure is applied to the membrane from the 'concentrated' side of the membrane.

Reverse osmosis occurs when the water is moved across the membrane against the concentration gradient, from lower concentration to higher concentration. To illustrate, imagine a semipermeable membrane with fresh water on one side and a concentrated aqueous solution on the other side. If normal osmosis takes place, the fresh water will cross the membrane to dilute the concentrated solution. In reverse osmosis, pressure is exerted on the side with the concentrated solution to force the water molecules across the membrane to the fresh water side.

Reverse osmosis is often used in commercial and residential water filtration. It is also one of the methods used to desalinate seawater. Sometimes reverse osmosis is used to purify liquids in which water is an undesirable impurity (*e.g.*, ethanol).

The reverse osmosis process depends upon a semi-permeable membrane through which pressurized water is forced. Reverse osmosis, simply stated, is the opposite of the natural osmosis process of water. Osmosis is the name for the tendency of water to migrate from a weaker saline solution to a stronger saline solution, gradually equalizing the saline composition of each solution when a semi-permeable membrane separates the two solutions.

In reverse osmosis, water is forced to move from a stronger saline solution to a weaker solution, again through a semi-permeable membrane. Because molecules of salt are physically larger than water molecules, the membrane blocks the passage of salt particles.

The end result is desalinated water on one side of the membrane and a highly concentrated, saline solution of water on the other side. In addition to salt particles, this process will remove a select number of drinking water contaminants, depending upon the physical size of the contaminants. For this reason, reverse osmosis has been touted as an effective drinking water purification method.

Reverse osmosis (RO) was the first cross flow membrane separation process to be widely commerciallised. RO removes virtually all organic compounds and 90 to 99 per cent of all ions. Large selection of reverse osmosis membranes are available to meet varying rejection requirements.

RO can meet with most water standards with a single pass system and the highest standards with the double pass system. RO rejects 99.9+ per cent of viruses, bacteria and pyrogens. Pressure,on the order of 200 to 1000 psi(13.8 to 68.9 bar), is the driving force of the RO purification process. It is much more energy efficient compare to heat driven purification (distillation) and more efficient than the strong chemicals required for Ion Exchange. No energy incentive phase changes required.

Pros and Cons: Reverse osmosis is a valuable water purification process when mineral-free water is the desired end product. Most mineral constituents of water are physically larger than water molecules. Thus, they are trapped by the semi-permeable membrane and removed from drinking water when filtered through a reverse osmosis system. Such minerals include salt, lead, manganese, iron, and calcium. Reverse osmosis will also remove some chemical components of drinking water, including the dangerous municipal additive fluoride.

Although reverse osmosis does extract several contami-nants from drinking water, its removal capabilities are not ideally suited to the challenges of the municipally treated water that the overwhelming majority of people receive. Municipal water contains such contaminants as chlorine and volatile organic chemicals (VOCs). Because these contaminants are physically smaller in size than water, the semi-permeable membrane cannot prohibit them from passing through with the water. Thus, they remain in drinking water.

Reverse osmosis, also, by removing alkaline mineral constituents of water, produces acidic water. Acidic water can be dangerous to the body system, causing calcium and other essential minerals to be stripped from bones and teeth in order to neutralize its acidity. Trace elements of minerals were intended to be in water; their removal leaves tasteless, unhealthy drinking water.

Reverse osmosis, although it is less wasteful than distillation, is still an incredibly inefficient process. On average, the reverse osmosis process wastes three gallons of water for every one gallon of purified water it produces.

SYSTEM OF DISPOSAL OF HOTEL WASTE

At present Hotel waste generated by small restaurants is disposed off directly by the hotels at nearby collection spots. The substantial quantity of food waste dumped at these collection spots gets mixed with all the other kinds of dry and wet waste and gives an ugly look to the collection spots with lot of dirt and stink.

In case of large four and 5 star hotels, the hotel waste is disposed off directly by the hotels through MCGM or through private contractors to the dumping ground.

MCGM provides a service of directly lifting hotel waste from the small hotels in some wards such as A, B, H west, M West ward etc.

MCGM charges Trade Refuse Charge (TRC) to the hotels for the waste generated by the hotels. The TRC is charged in multiples of license fees which is directly based on the area of the hotel and the grade. The grade one hotels are generally bars and permit rooms which do peak business during evening hours. The waste generated by the restaurants with bars and permit rooms is much less as compared to that generated by the food restaurants. However the TRC charged for the bars and restaurants is much higher than that charged for the ordinary restaurants which generate much more quantity of waste.

As per our observations of the hotel waste generated by hotels in a few wards, around 70 to 75 per cent of the hotel waste is biodegradable and gets mixed with all the other type of waste when dumped at the collection spots. Also the waste which is collected directly by the MCGM/private contractors gets mixed with all the other type of non- biodegradable waste at the dumping ground.

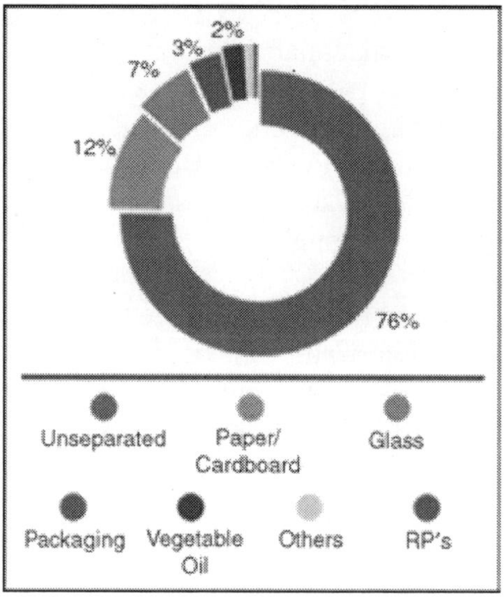

EQUIPMENTS USED IN HOTEL WASTE

The following are the major equipments used in RO Plants:

Feed Inlet Valve

This valve is used to stop the feed water flow whenever the plant is shut down.

Booster Pump

This pump is used for boosting the pressure and pumping the raw water to dual media filter/activated carbon filter.Booster pumps can be used to provide additional pressure to the flow of water. It may sometime reach at 50 psi. Generally, Booster pump can be used for electric purpose. It acts as a perfect irrigation controller. The tank here plays a role of a reservoir and stabilizes the pressure. You might have seen different hand pumps around, these hand pumps can be called as booster pumps. The main function of booster pump is to pull the water and bring it to the surface. However, advanced booster pumps have the capacity to increase the flow of the water.

Booster pumps are also used in cleaners. The use of booster pumps in a cleaner helps the cleaner to perform a pressurized cleaning. There are different types of boosters in the market, and their uses are different. Booster pumps can be used to pump air these are called diesel booster pumps, and an electric booster pump is used for electric models.

Dual Media Filter/Activated carbon Filter

These filters are used for removing the residual organic matters,suspended solids etc. in feed water.

Cartridge Filter

The cartridge filter is used to remove the turbidity up to 5 micron from the feed water.

Micron filters are used to remove the particulate matter that could damage the high pressure pump or may cause device plugging.

High Pressure Pump

Centrifugal pumps are used for providing RO feed pressure in brackish water system. They are less complex than positive displacement pumps. A back pressure valve,sized for about 105 of total flow is used to fine tune the system by the recirculating the excess flow when the pump capacity is greater when than that needed to supply the permeate.

Chemical Dosing System

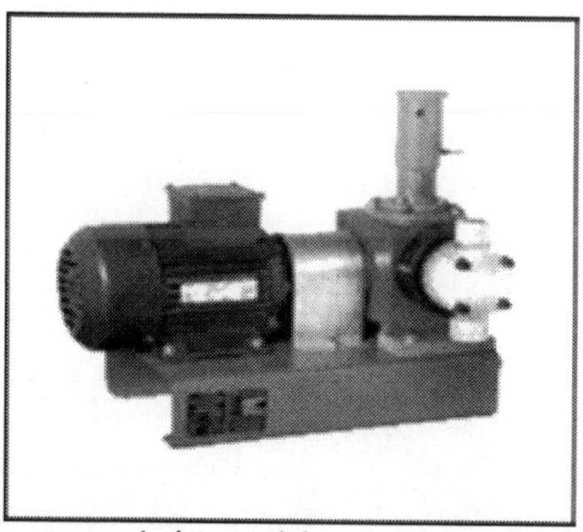

- *Acid Dosing system*: Acid addition has two tasks in pretreatment to prevent scaling and to reduce the rate of Fe ++ oxidation. Sulphuric Acid/ Hydrochloric Acid is used for pH adjustment.

- *Antiscalant Dosing System*: In theory various comme-rcially available inhibitors can be used to prevent CaCO3 scaling. When using an inhibitor, several factors must be considered.

Toxicity (with respect to potable water and reject disposal)

Pollution (disposal of brine reject stream)

Chemical compatibility with permeations.

Cost effectiveness.

Most of the inhibitors are in meta stable state and delay scale deposits. Thus when plant shut down occurs, provisions must be made to flush the super saturated solutions from the permeations. S.H.M.P. Is approved scale inhibitor. Doses of SHMP various around 5 ppm.

- *Chlorine Dosing System*: Chlorination is the process used to disinfect water and to destroy pyrogen and control microorganisms. Hydrochloride dosing set provides the sterilizing and oxidising properties of chlorine solution. In general, the dosage ranges from 1 ppm to over 10 ppm. The chlorinated water should have a chlorine residual of 0.1 to 10 ppm.
- *Sodium bi sulphite dosing System*: This chemical is normally used to dechlorinate feed water. The dosage rate is 1.4 times of commercial sodium bi sulphite rate per part per million of chlorine residual.
- *pH Correction System*: Adjustment of pH in the product water may be necessary before it can be used. For these caustic/ soda ash dosing is provided. The exact quantity of the caustic/soda ash required to be dosed is decided at the time of commissioning of the plant.

Suggested Action Points for MCGM

Management of waste generated by all the 3,4 and 5 star hotels and restaurants generating over one tonne of waste by themselves: These hotels can look at options of in-situ composting, installation of small biomethanation plants in the premises etc.

At present, hotel Orchid, Rhodas and Lotus suites are manging their waste quite well and can set an example for other hotels.. MCGM should enforce in-situ management of waste generated by these hotels.

Direct collection of waste generated by hotels my MCGM and its localized disposal: MCGM should look at direct collection of hotel waste and set up zone wise processing facilities (either composting or biomethanation. MEDC is evaluating various technologies for biomethanation and developing a business model. The report will be ready in a couple of months). This will substantially reduce the transport cost as well as the load on the dumping grounds. The public collection spots will also get less amount of garbage.

Some methods for management of Hotel Restaurant and Club food waste could be as follows:

Bio Sanitizer by Excel Industries: Excel Industries Ltd. supplies machines of capacity 500kg, per day, 1 tonne per day and 3 tonnes per day machines along with biosanitizer. This machines can crush the food waste to $1/3^{rd}$ of the original volume and odourless compost produced can be used as manure after curing. (Details can be available with Excel Industries).

Biomethanation: Biomethanation Plants of capacities 100 -500 kg per day can be installed in the premises of hotels if adequate space is available. Gas generated can be used for cooking.

Composting/Vermicomposting: Options of composting/vermicomposting could be explored.

INCINERATOR

DEFINITION

The term *incinerate* means to burn something until nothing is left but ashes. An incinerator is a unit or facility used to burn trash and other types of waste until it is reduced to ash. An incinerator is constructed of heavy, well-insulated materials, so that it does not give off extreme amounts of external heat. The high levels of heat are kept inside the furnace or unit so that the waste is burned quickly and efficiently. If the heat were allowed to escape, the waste would not burn as completely or as rapidly.

One function of an incinerator is to dispose of trash or waste effectively, eliminating the high cost of having waste hauled away and deposited elsewhere, such as piling even more rubbish atop existing landfills. Incinerators also serve to keep dangerous materials from finding their way to landfills where they can harm people, including those that work in such facilities. Another benefit is the fact that an incinerator can produce power in the process of waste burning, though not all incinerators harness that power.

Since not only power but also smog and air pollution are byproducts of incineration, some people feel that an incinerator is a poor alternative to other waste disposal methods. They believe it is simply a trade off, exchanging land waste for smog. However, an incinerator can dispose of an incredible amount of solid waste when utilized properly, which proves to many people that it is the most efficient waste disposal process. Aside from reducing the sheer quantity of solid waste by roughly 90 per cent, an incinerator can also be used to manage certain materials that cannot be disposed of properly by simply dumping them in another location due to issues of public health and safety. The extreme temperatures produced by an incinerator can obliterate certain biohazards, as well as other toxic materials which are found in medical and hazardous waste.

Other dangerous and harmful materials can also be broken down in an incinerator, such as confiscated drugs, bio-weapons, and contaminants. The use of an incinerator, as well as all other processes by which waste is disposed of, is strictly regulated to protect our health and the environment.

Incineration is a waste treatment technology that involves the combustion of organic materials and/or substances.[1] Incineration and other high temperature waste treatment systems are described as "thermal treatment". Incineration of waste materials converts the waste into incinerator bottom ash, flue gases, particulates, and heat, which can in turn be used to generate electric power. The flue gases are cleaned of pollutants before they are dispersed in the atmosphere.

Incineration with energy recovery is one of several waste-to-energy (WtE) technologies such as gasification, Plasma arc gasification, pyrolysis and anaerobic digestion. Incineration may also be implemented without energy and materials recovery.

In several countries there are still expert and local community concerns about the environmental impact of incinerators. In some countries, incinerators built just a few decades ago often did not include a materials separation to remove hazardous, bulky or recyclable materials before combustion. These facilities tended to risk the health of the plant workers and the local environment due to inadequate levels of gas cleaning and combustion process control. Most of these facilities did not generate electricity.

Incinerators reduce the mass of the original waste by 80-85 per cent and the volume (already compressed somewhat in garbage trucks) by 95-96 per cent, depending upon composition and degree of recovery of materials such as metals from the ash for recycling. This means that while incineration does not completely replace landfilling, it reduces the necessary volume for disposal significantly. Garbage trucks often reduce the volume of waste in a built-in compressor before delivery to the incinerator. Alternatively, at landfills, the volume of the uncompressed garbage can be reduced by approximately 70 per cent[citation needed] with the use of a stationary steel compressor, albeit with a significant energy cost. In many countries simpler waste compaction is a common practice for compaction at landfills.

Incineration has particularly strong benefits for the treatment of certain waste types in niche areas such as clinical wastes and certain hazardous wastes where pathogens and toxins can be destroyed by high temperatures. Examples include chemical multi-product plants with diverse toxic or very toxic wastewater streams, which cannot be routed to a conventional wastewater treatment plant.

Waste combustion is particularly popular in countries such as Japan where land is a scarce resource. Denmark and Sweden have been leaders in using the energy generated from incineration for more than a century, in localised combined heat and power facilities supporting district heating schemes. In 2005, waste incineration produced 4.8 per cent of the electricity consumption and

13.7 per cent of the total domestic heat consumption in Denmark. A number of other European Countries rely heavily on incineration for handling municipal waste, in particular Luxemburg, The Netherlands, Germany and France.

TYPES OF INCINERATORS

An incinerator is a furnace for burning waste. Modern incinerators include pollution mitigation equipment such as flue gas cleaning. There are various types of incinerator plant design: moving grate, fixed grate, rotary-kiln, fluidised bed.

The burn pile is one of the simplest and earliest forms of waste disposal, essentially consisting of a mound of combustible materials piled on bare ground and set on fire.

Indiscriminate piles of household waste are strongly discouraged and may be illegal in urban areas, but are permitted in certain rural situations such as clearing forested land for farming, where the stumps are uprooted and burned. Rural burn piles of organic yard waste are also sometimes permitted, though not asphalt shingles, plastics, or other petroleum products

Burn piles have the potential to spread uncontrolled fires, if for example wind blows burning material off the pile into surrounding combustible grasses or onto buildings. As interior structures of the pile are consumed, the pile can shift and collapse, spreading the burn area. Even in a situation of no wind, small lightweight ignited embers can lift off the pile via convection, and waft through the air into grasses or onto buildings, igniting them.

The burn barrel is a somewhat more controlled form of private waste incineration, containing the burning material inside a metal barrel, with a metal grating over the exhaust. The barrel prevents the spread of burning material in windy conditions, and as the combustibles are reduced they can only settle down into the barrel.

The exhaust grating helps to prevent the spread of burning embers. Typically steel 55-gallon drums are used as burn barrels, with air vent holes cut or drilled around the base for air intake. Over time the very high heat of incineration causes the metal to oxidize and rust, and eventually the barrel itself is consumed by the heat and must be replaced.

Private burning of dry cellulosic/paper products is generally clean-burning, producing no visible smoke, but the large amount of plastics in household waste can cause private burning to create a public nuisance and health hazard, generating acrid odors and fumes that make eyes burn and water.

The temperatures in a burn barrel are not regulated, and usually do not reach high enough or for enough time to completely break down chemicals such as dioxin in plastics and other waste chemicals. Plastics and other petroleum products must therefore be separated and sent to commercial waste disposal facilities.

Private rural incineration is typically only permitted so long as it is not a nuisance to others, does not pose a risk of fire such as in dry conditions, and the fire is clean-burning, producing no visible smoke. People intending to burn waste may be required to contact a state agency in advance to check current fire risk and conditions, and to alert officials of the controlled fire that will occur.

Moving Grate

Control room of a typical moving grate incinerator overseeing two boiler lines

The typical incineration plant for municipal solid waste is a moving grate incinerator. The moving grate enables the movement of waste through the combustion chamber to be optimised to allow a more efficient and complete combustion. A single moving grate boiler can handle up to 35 metric tons (39 short tons) of waste per hour, and can operate 8,000 hours per year with only one scheduled stop for inspection and maintenance of about one month's duration. Moving grate incinerators are sometimes referred to as Municipal Solid Waste Incinerators (MSWIs).

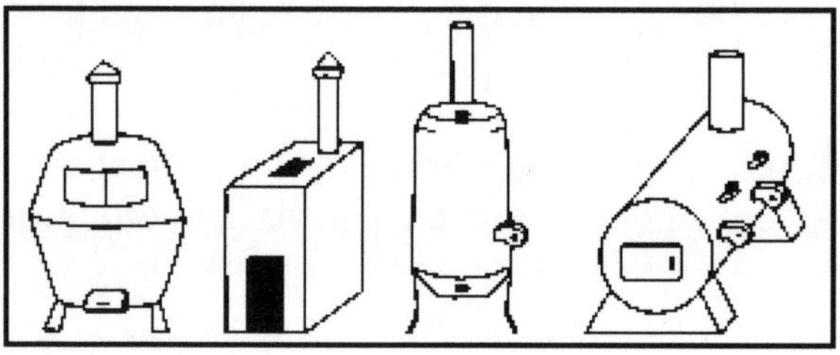

The waste is introduced by a waste crane through the "throat" at one end of the grate, from where it moves down over the descending grate to the ash pit in the other end. Here the ash is removed through a water lock.

Municipal solid waste in the furnace of a moving grate incinerator capable of handling 15 metric tons of waste per hour. The holes in the grate elements supplying the primary combustion air are visible. Part of the combustion air (primary combustion air) is supplied through the grate from below. This air flow also has the purpose of cooling the grate itself. Cooling is important for the mechanical strength of the grate, and many moving grates are also water cooled internally.

Commercial or industrial incinerators:

- Usually specific or 'tailor-made'
- More consistant waste stream
- Higher temperatures may be necessary
- Standards for destruction of hazardous waste are set at those that will destroy pcb's (polychlorinated biphenols).

Municipal incinerators:

- More common

- Less consistent waste stream
- Pre-treatment (shredding, drying, etc.) Is usually necessary
- Batch or continuously loaded

Secondary combustion air is supplied into the boiler at high speed through nozzles over the grate. It facilitates complete combustion of the flue gases by introducing turbulence for better mixing and by ensuring a surplus of oxygen. In multiple/stepped hearth incinerators, the secondary combustion air is introduced in a separate chamber downstream the primary combustion chamber.

According to the Waste Incineration Directive, incineration plants must be designed to ensure that the flue gases reach a temperature of at least 850 °C (1,560 °F) for 2 seconds in order to ensure proper breakdown of organic toxins. In order to comply with this at all times, it is required to install backup auxiliary burners (often fueled by oil), which are fired into the boiler in case the heating value of the waste becomes too low to reach this temperature alone.

The flue gases are then cooled in the superheaters, where the heat is transferred to steam, heating the steam to typically 400 °C (752 °F) at a pressure of 40 bars for the electricity generation in the turbine. At this point, the flue gas has a temperature of around 200 °C (392 °F), and is passed to the flue gas cleaning system. At least in Scandinavia scheduled maintenance is always performed during summer, where the demand for district heating is low. Often incineration plants consist of several separate 'boiler lines' (boilers and flue gas treatment plants), so that waste can continue to be received at one boiler line while the others are subject to revision.

Fixed Grate

The older and simpler kind of incinerator was a brick-lined cell with a fixed metal grate over a lower ash pit, with one opening in the top or side for loading and another opening in the side for removing incombustible solids called clinkers. Many small incinerators formerly found in apartment houses have now been replaced by waste compactors.

Rotary-kiln

The rotary-kiln incinerator is used by municipalities and by large industrial plants. This design of incinerator has 2 chambers: a primary chamber and secondary chamber. The primary chamber in a rotary kiln incinerator consist of an inclined refractory lined cylindrical tube. Movement of the cylinder on its axis facilitates movement of waste. In the primary chamber, there is conversion of solid fraction to gases, through volatilization, destructive distillation and partial combustion reactions. The secondary chamber is necessary to complete gas phase combustion reactions

The clinkers spill out at the end of the cylinder. A tall flue gas stack, fan, or steam jet supplies the needed draft. Ash drops through the grate, but many particles are carried along with the hot gases. The particles and any combustible gases may be combusted in an "afterburner". A diagram of a rotary-kiln incinerator can be found here.

Fluidized Bed

A strong airflow is forced through a sandbed. The air seeps through the sand until a point is reached where the sand particles separate to let the air through and mixing and churning occurs, thus a fluidised bed is created and fuel and waste can now be introduced. The sand with the pre-treated waste and/or fuel is kept suspended on pumped air currents and takes on a fluid-like character. The bed is thereby violently mixed and agitated keeping small inert particles and air in a fluid-like state. This allows all of the mass of waste, fuel and sand to be fully circulated through the furnace.

Specialized Incineration

Furniture factory sawdust incinerators need much attention as these have to handle resin powder and many flammable substances. Controlled combustion, burn back prevention systems are essential as dust when suspended resembles the fire catch phenomenon of any liquid petroleum gas.

Use of Heat

The heat produced by an incinerator can be used to generate steam which may then be used to drive a turbine in order to produce electricity. The typical amount of net energy that can be produced per tonne municipal waste is about 2/3 MWh of electricity and 2 MWh of district heating. Thus, incinerating about 600 metric tons (660 short tons) per day of waste will produce about 17 MW of electrical power and 1200 MWh district heating each day.

Pollution

Incineration has a number of outputs such as the ash and the emission to the atmosphere of flue gas. Before the flue gas cleaning system, the flue gases may contain significant amounts of particulate matter, heavy metals, dioxins, furans, sulfur dioxide, and hydrochloric acid. In a study the Solid Waste Authority found that, for same amount of produced energy, incineration plants emitted fewer particles, hydrocarbons and less SO2, HCl, CO and NOx than coal-fired power plants, but more than natural gas fired power plants. According to Germany's Ministry of the Environment, waste incinerators reduce the amount of some atmospheric pollutants by substituting power produced by coal-fired plants with power from waste-fired plants.

HOT WATER BOILERS

A hot water boiler is an enclosed container that allows heat to be transmitted into water till the time it becomes heated water. The hot water is then effectively utilized for transferring the heat to where it is needed. A hot water boiler is filled with water, unlike the steam boiler.

However, like the steam boiler, hot water boilers have many add-ons to function effectively. The presence of aquastat serves a two-fold objective. It monitors the temperature in which the boiler runs, and offers a low-voltage transformer and relay to control the circulator.

A majority of commercial buildings, manufacturers and businesses employ hot water boilers. Water is heated to dispersing temperatures, characteristically 140-180°F, and generally put back about 20°F lower.

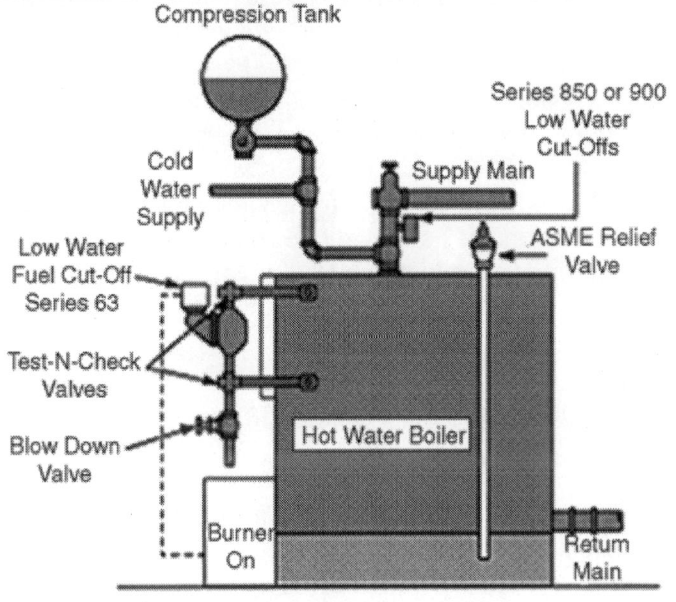

Hot Water Boiler

These structures are called "closed loop," with nominal fresh water make-up. Hot water boilers are favored since they generally do not call for operators or complex water chemistry. As they function at lower temperatures, hot water boilers can perform at greater fuel-conversion efficiencies than steam boilers.

Some of the characteristic features of a hot water boiler include low water fuel cutoff and a safety valve. Low water fuel cutoff dries up the supply of fuel to the burner during low water conditions in the boiler. The low water fuel cut ff is positioned 2" to 6" beneath the boiler water level.

Low water fuel discontinues operations using an electric probe or a float sensor. When the sensor displays a low water state, a contact to the main burner control circuit unlocks and blocks the fuel.

Low water fuel cutoffs should be checked regularly based on usage or necessities. If a low water condition is not correctly gauged there are chances for the boiler to overheat. Under these circumstances boilers are likely to be damaged for good. Safety valves are the most significant devices on a boiler. They unbolt to vent pressure that climbs over the maximum boiler operating pressure.

DESCRIPTION

It is only in large hotels and public institutions that a special provision is made for heating the water which is so necessary for the various purposes required, such as for supplying baths, lavatories, sinks, and for other domestic purposes, and in some instances for radiators and coils for heating the various corridors or rooms.

In ordinary mansions and private dwelling-houses it is usual for the boiler or water-heater to be attached to, and form an integral part of, the kitchen range or cooking-stove.

Figure is a sketch representing a front view of an open range, such as is generally used in the kind of houses above referred to, and which has a large fire surface in front, before which joints of meat, game, etc, can be hung for roasting. In the sketch, A is a side oven sometimes placed as shown, and used for baking pastry, etc, in.

Where no provision is made for supplying hot water to other places in the house it is usual to have a large boiler, sometimes made of cast and sometimes of wrought iron, placed at the back of the fire and extending the whole length of it.

Where this, which is commonly called a low-pressure boiler, is used, a draw-off tap is usually fixed as shown at D. A small-sized feed-cistern with a ball-valve and the necessary cold-water supply pipe is fixed in a convenient position, and a pipe connection made between the feed-cistern and the boiler.

Figure is a sketch showing how this is done. At E is shown a bag in the connecting pipe, made to prevent the water circulating back into the feed-cistern, making the contents of that hot. But for this bag, or trap as it is sometimes called, the water in the feed-cistern would get very hot and give off steam to a very inconvenient extent.

This bag, under certain conditions, must be made rather deep. When a large fire is kept up and not much water drawn from the boiler the water will expand in bulk, with the result that although a circulation may not be set up between the boiler and feed-cistern, yet the water will ebb and flow, so to speak, between them, and so raise the temperature of that in the feed-cistern.

In some cases the boilers have tops bolted down to them and a hole cast in the top, over which is placed a loose cover. When the water in the boiler is so hot as to give off steam it will escape through the loose cover, the latter making an unpleasant clattering noise the whole of the time the steam is escaping. To prevent this noise it is usual to fix a steam or vent pipe from the boiler, as shown at F, Figure.

The top end of this pipe is generally carried up the chimney-flue a few feet, some of the escaping steam passing upwards, but a great deal condenses and falls down on to the fire, sometimes bringing soot with it.

This is very objectionable, especially where cooking has to be done over the fire. Cases have occurred where the steam pipe, when fixed as described, has had to be altered and continued to a place out-of-doors, or turned into a condensing-chamber.

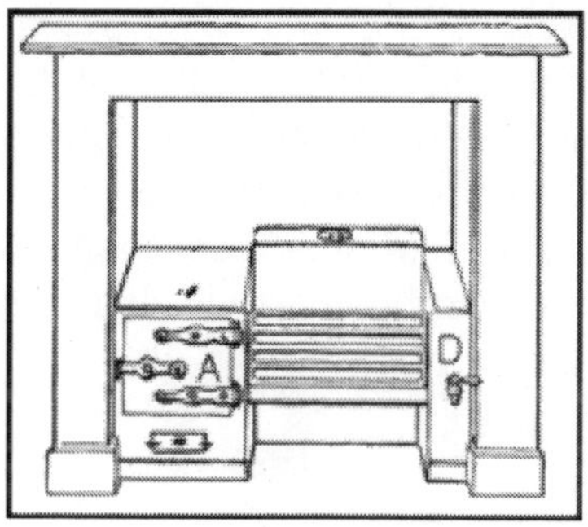

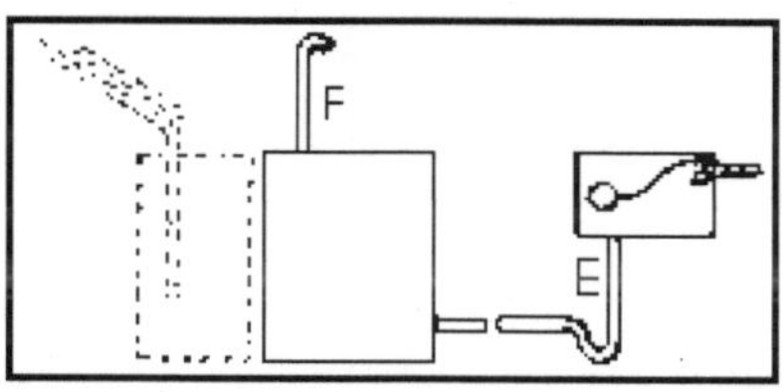

Where the boiler under consideration has been of wrought iron, with a manhole bolted or screwed on tight, the steam or vent pipe is indispensable. Water would not run into the boiler if it was air-bound, and when steam was generated it would force the water back into and overflow the feed-cistern.

Figure is a sketch showing an arrangement sometimes met with, but not by any means to be recommended. In the sketch, G is a cold-water cistern supplying the boiler, H, and also the cold-water draw-off tap, J.

In a case that the writer had to alter, the work was fixed as shown. From appearances it was seen (and was confirmed by report) that originally only one pipe was fixed to supply the boiler and also the cold-water tap over the sink. Whenever the kitchen fire was alight a considerable quantity of warm water had to be run to waste before cold water could be drawn at the tap, J.

As it was found that hot water passed from the boiler to the cold-water cistern, which was about 40 feet (forty feet) awa), the writer introduced an ordinary feed-cistern at L, so as to break the continuity of the feed pipe to the boiler. At the same time the expansion pipe, K, had the top end lowered so that if the water in the boiler got very hot and expanded it would overflow and run to waste, instead of forcing its way back into the feed-cistern. The tap was fixed over the scullery-sink, and was the only means of drawing hot water from the boiler. In spite of the alterations made the job was a poor one, and the system is not to be recommended for anyone to adopt.

When repairing or altering work fixed some years ago, one often finds a low-pressure boiler and feed-cistern as shown at Figure and a coil of lead, sometimes iron, pipe inside the boiler, one end of the coil being connected with a pipe leading from a cold-water cistern fixed on an upper floor, and the other end with a pipe leading up to a bath or sink. By this means cold water is simply passed through a reservoir of heated water, and in its passage absorbs and takes away a certain amount of heat. This system is not a good one and is now very rarely practised. One of the greatest objections is the coil has to be removed each time the boiler is cleaned out. Because of this the boiler does not get cleaned so often as it should be, and consequently soon wears out. When the coils are made of iron, oxidation takes place inside and outside at the same time, and they soon corrode.

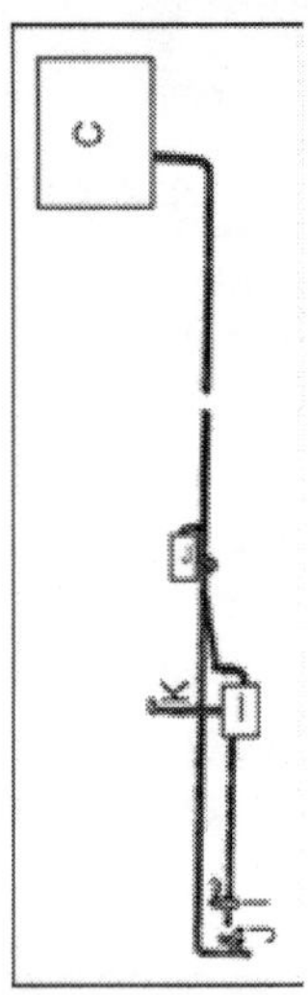

A great many kitchen ranges of modern construction have two boilers at the back of the open fire, the large one, as shown by firm lines in above figure and a smaller one, as shown by dotted lines. The former is called the low-pressure boiler, the draw-off cock being generally as shown at D, Figure. The other one is called the high-pressure boiler, and is connected by means of circulation pipes with a hot-water cistern or cylinder fixed near or at some higher place in the building so that hot water may be drawn at the sinks, baths, etc, on the various floors.

A great many hot-water engineers now omit fixing the two boilers in smaller houses, and arrange for the high-pressure boiler to provide all the hot water that is required. In clubs, hotels, and some of the largest mansions, the low-pressure boiler is fixed and fitted up slightly different, and is used to generate steam to be used for cooking purposes.

In some cases where very large fires are used, say 6 or 7 feet long, so that several joints of meat can be roasted at the same time, the fire lays against the iron boiler, and that is found sufficient to heat the water, but in smaller ranges a flue is constructed to pass beneath and up the back side of the boiler so as to get a larger heating surface. It is always necessary, when flues are fixed, to have dampers so as to regulate the draught.

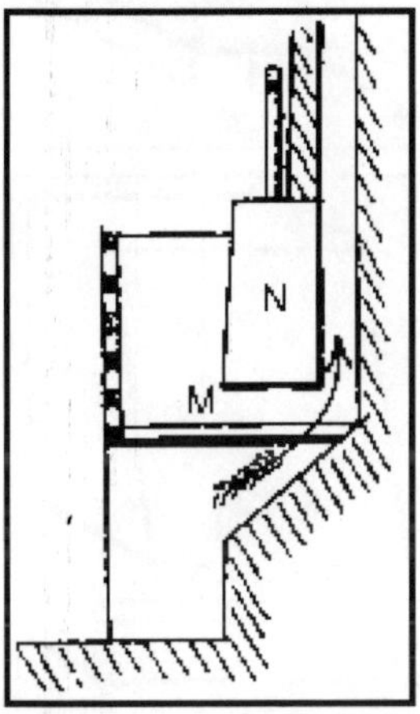

In some cases the fire-bars are continued beneath the boiler, as shown in figure above, at M but the writer has often found it necessary to put a dead-plate over that part immediately under the boiler to prevent cold air instead of heat passing up the flue behind. This cold-air draught is denoted by an arrow.

The shape of the boiler for open ranges is generally as shown at Nin above figure, that being an end view, but for a close range, or what is commonly called a "kitchener," a boiler, technically named a "boot-boiler," is used. This is shown at Figure. A manhole for cleaning out and other purposes is generally placed at P, but the best makers have another manhole at Q.

The reader will, no doubt, notice that from the manhole, P, access cannot very well be had to clean the toe of the boiler where most of the fur accumulates, and which it is necessary to remove at intervals of time. The boiler, Figure, has fire-bricks placed as shown at r, r, leaving an open space for the heat from the fire to pass up the back flue.

A great many boilers are now made and used as shown at Figure, a flue being made in the boiler itself. These, sometimes called saddle-boilers, are bedded on a solid base of fire-bricks.

A few boilers have a tube through them as shown at Figure, the fire passing through the tube and then up an ordinary flue behind the boiler. Where the kitchen fire has been expected to provide or heat sufficient water for a very large house, a double boot-boiler has sometimes been fixed. This is shown at Figure shown. The fire lays between the two feet of the boiler, and an under and back draught is provided for, as shown.

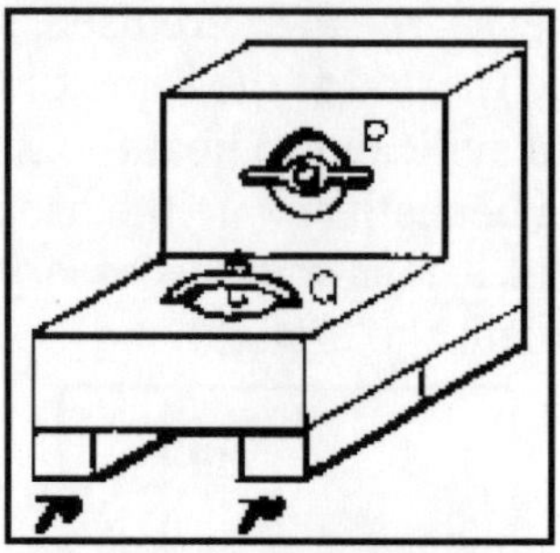

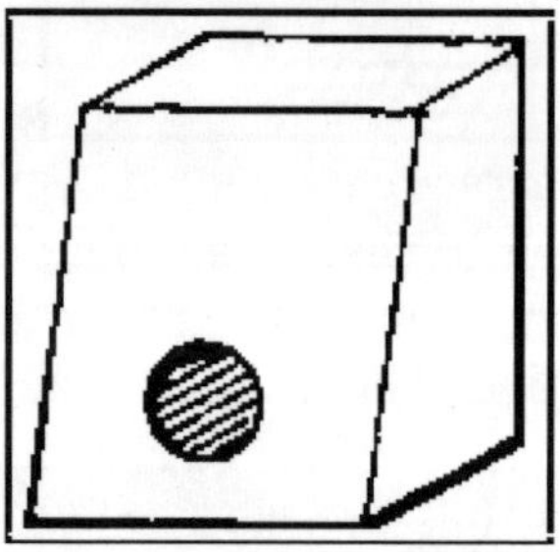

In some cases water is circulated from a boiler fixed in a "hot plate." This hot plate sometimes has ovens also, and may be described as a horizontal kitchener. The shape of the boiler is usually as shown at Figure, the fire being in the centre at X.

There are a great many other-shaped boilers used, but the few illustrated are sufficient for our present purpose. A great many of them are rivetted together, but this last few years the welded boilers have come more into general use.

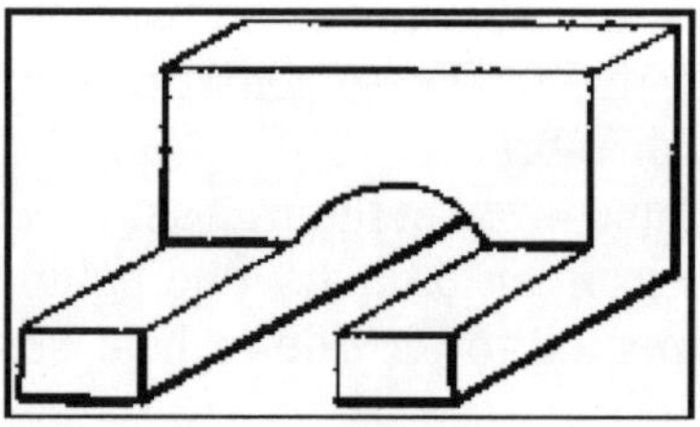

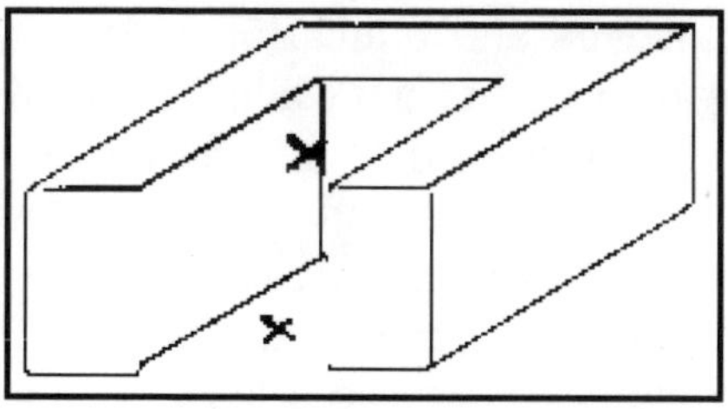

SOLAR HEATING SYSTEM

BACKGROUND

In just one second, the Sun gives off 13 million times the energy that is generated by all the electricity consumed in one year in the country.

Only one millionth of the Sun's energy reaches Earth, but this scant amount would be more than sufficient to meet the energy requirements of our entire planet. The relative difficulty in extracting energy from the Sun, when compared to systems that derive energy from fossil fuels or nuclear power, has hindered its development as a widespread source of energy. On a smaller scale and in many experimental projects, however, solar energy has proven highly effective in producing both electricity and heat.

Solar energy was first explored for electrical purposes in the 1950s, when the need for continuous electric power generation on space satellites spawned the development of a solar cell in the Laboratories. Even today, though, the best silicon solar cell converts sunlight to electric power with only 18 per cent efficiency. Still, experiments have utilized sun-generated electricity with great success. One highly visible project focusing on solar power is the annual international solar-powered automobile race.

Solar energy has proven more effective and has been more widely utilized for both water and space heating and cooling systems. As a water heater, solar energy is most commonly used to heat swimming pools.

For space heating, two main types of systems are used. A passive solar heating system admits solar energy directly into a building through large windows facing south (in the northern hemisphere) and directly heats the space within (this is known as direct gain and is also referred to as the greenhouse effect) or through a wall or roof that absorbs the solar radiation, stores the resulting heat, and transfers the heat into the building (this is known as indirect gain).

A passive system may also utilize an absorber and storage components (such as a rock bed) that are not a part of the building, but are contained in their own separate chamber. This is known as an isolated-gain system.

DEFINITION

Solar heating was once considered the realm of tree-huggers and hippies, but as technology improves and education abounds, more families and businesses are realizing the benefits of installing a solar heating system in their buildings. Solar heat, or heat from the sun, can be harnessed in a variety of ways to cut consumers' heating costs, and create a renewable source of energy that has less of an impact on the environment. A solar heating system certified by the U.S. Department of Energy's Solar Rating and Certification Corporation (SRCC) could also increase a home's value. In some locations, energy companies may buy some of the harnessed energy, actually making money for the homeowner.

Most solar heating systems utilize some form of a solar panel. A panel is placed on the house or property and collects the sun's energy, which is then transferred using an individually customized system to heat the building, depending on the build of the solar panel model. Solar heaters can be simple or complex, and there are so many varieties that it would be tough to cover them all. Some systems, especially those using liquids to contain solar energy, are suited for hot climates only, where freezing temperatures are not a factor. Quite a few solar heating systems are made for all environments.

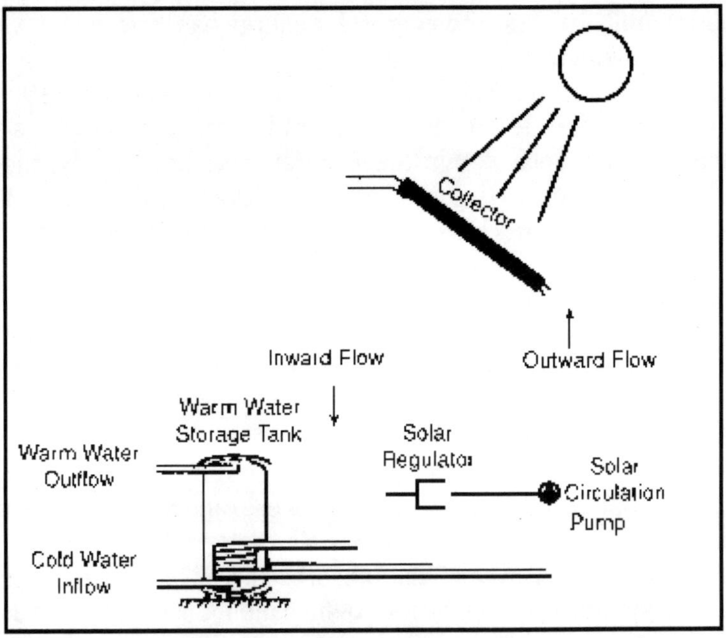

A solar heating system is designed to be maintenance-free, and a solar heating system is a fairly easy do-it-yourself project. Panels are easy to install, and a solar heater requires very little afterthought once installed. Almost always, a solar heating system is designed to last for the life of the building, so while the initial investment may cost as much as $5,000 US Dollars (USD), the initial investment eventually pays for itself in utility bills that can be cut by as much as 40 per cent per year. In addition to do-it-yourself plans, many companies also offer full installation plans that offer more guidance. Many governments support solar heating system programmes, and grants may be available to pay for the installation in private homes or businesses. Building codes and regulations vary by location, so it is best to speak with a local government official to figure out if installing a solar heating system is acceptable for the individual consumer's geographic location. It is also advisable to speak with local energy providers to find out if they offer discounts or energy buy-back programmes for consumers who use a solar heating system.

Two circuit indirect systems with controlled circulation are most predominant in Germany. These use heat-transfer fluid that is transported by pumps to the hot water storage tank.

Once there, the solar heat is transmitted from the heat transfer fluid to the potable water through a heat exchanger. In order to protect solar heating systems from freezing damage, there is a water-antifreeze mixture in the circulation pipes, and, due to separate circuits, the heat-transfer fluid and the domestic water do not mix. The heated potable water can then flow to the hot-water faucets. In comparison, one circuit systems heat water directly in the collector (usually in countries without danger of freezing).

In thermosiphon systems the regulator and the solar circulation pumps are not necessary because of convection: The solar radiation heats the heat-transfer fluid, its density then decreases as its temperature increases. The fluid becomes lighter and rises inside the circulation pipes. Therefore, a pump is not necessary. In order for such a system to function, however, the water tank must be installed above the collector.

SOLAR HEAT CIRCULATION

Within the solar heat circulation, heat is transported from the collector to the hot water storage tank. In order to minimize heat loss, the distance from the collector to the tank should be as short as possible. For systems in one or two family homes, copper pipes with a circumference of 15 mm to 18 mm are enough to guarantee an optimal transportation of heat. The pipes are sufficiently insulated with 30 mm of insulation. For pipes with a circumference of 30 mm, the insulation should have at least the same thickness as the pipe. The insulation must be able to withstand high temperatures, and the outdoor section has to be UV- and weather-resistant. The following materials are used as insulation: mineral wool, polyurethane pipe wrappers, and foam rubber.

The prevalent flow rate in small solar heating systems amounts to 30 to 50 liters per hour per square meter of collector surface. The solar circulation pump has to be able to guarantee this rate of flow. As a general rule, conventional pumps with an electric input between 40 W and 80 W suffice. Also, the pump should always be installed in the colder reflux of the solar circulation system. In this way the pump will not be exposed to high temperatures during operation.

Finally, stop valves are mounted in front of and behind the pump, so that the entire system does not have to be emptied when replacing a defective pump.

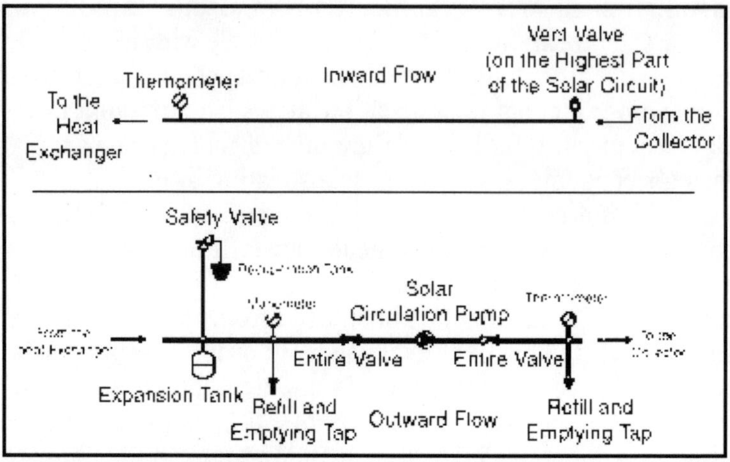

The typical operating pressure of solar heating systems, which can be controlled by a manometer, lies at approximately 4 bar. The safety valve should open at an approximately 0.3 bar triggering pressure. With a recuperation tank, the heat-transfer fluid can be captured and then fed back into the solar circuit through one of the refilling taps. Thermometers fitted in forerun and reflux are used to check the system's operation. To prevent heat loss out of the tank because of insufficient solar radiation or at night due to convection (the heat-transfer fluid cools in the cold collector, and through the force of gravity, then circulates towards the storage tank) a rebound valve is mounted in the outward flow. The expansion tank keeps the pressure in the system stable and takes up the volume difference of the heat-transfer fluid that is caused by the temperature difference. For safety reasons, the volume of the expansion tank has to be sufficiently large. It should be able to take up the entire volume of heat-transfer fluid. The vent valve serves to ventilate the solar circuit after it has been filled with heat-transfer fluid. It is to be mounted on the highest part of the solar circuit.

Bibliography

A D Khurana.: *Handbook of Catering, Hospitality and Tourism*, Mohit Publication, Delhi, 2008.

A Jayakumar.: *Food Security Management: A Comparative Study*, Anmol Publication, Delhi, 2007.

A Mohamed Abdullah.: *Food Security and Gender Inequality*, Abjiheet Publication, Delhi, 2008.

Agatha Christie.: *At Bertram's Hotel*, HarperCollins Publication, Uttar Pradesh, 2003.

Alex Polizzi.: *Alex Polizzi's Little Black Book of Hotels*, Quadrille Publication, London, 2010.

Anil Kathuria.: *Hotel Industry*, Sonali Publication, Delhi, 2008.

B K Chakravarti.: *Hotel Management*, APH Publication, Delhi, 2008.

Banwari Lal Raheja.: *Beverage Management in Hotels and Marketing*, Arise Publication, Delhi, 2006.

Basudeb Guha-Khasnobis, Shabd Acharya. S and Benjamin.: *Food Security : Indicators, Measurement and the Impact of Trade Openness*, Oxford University Press, Delhi, 2008.

D.K. Aggarwal.: *Housekeeping Management*, Aman Publication, Delhi, 2006.

Dennis Rumley and D. Gopal.: *Globalisation and Regional Security: India and Australia*, Shipra Publication, Delhi, 2007.

Dinesh Tomar.: *Management of Hotel and Catering Industry*, Ankit Publication, Delhi, 2011.

Fleur Barrington.: *1001 Little Housekeeping Miracles*, Carlton Publishing Group, London, 2009.

Gajendra Singh.: *Food for All : An Assessment of Food Security in Indian Context*, MD Publication, New Delhi, 2007.

Jagmohan Negi and Gaurav Manoher.: *Hotels Resorts and Restaurants Planning Designing and Constructions : A Facility Planning*, Kanishka Publication, Delhi, 2013.

Jagmohan Negi, Gaurav M.J., Ritushka and Suniti.: *Housekeeping Operation and Management : Procedure and Techniques*, Kanishka Publication, Delhi, 2011.

Kumar, Bimal Kapoor : *Tourism and Hotel Industry*, Murari Lal and Sons, Delhi, 2007.

L.K. Sharma.: *Hotel and Catering Management*, Surendra Publication, Delhi, 2012.

Lal, Banwari Raheja : *Beverage Management in Hotels and Marketing*, Arise Publication, Delhi, 2006.

O'Connor, M. Hitz.: *Information and Communication Technologies in Tourism*, Springer-Verlag Publication, 2003.

Otto Kleppner.: *"Advertising Procedure"*, Prentice-Hall Publication, 1966.

Percy K Singh.: *HRM in Hotel and Tourism Industry : Existing Trends and Practices*, Kanishka Publication, Delhi, 2008.

Pradeep Chaturvedi.: *Food Security in South Asia*, Concept Publication, New Delhi, 2002.

Pragati Mohanty.: *Hotel Industry and Tourism in India*, APH Publication, Delhi, 2008.

R. P. Saxena.: *Hotel Management : Food And Food Services*, Centrum Press, Delhi, 2010.

Suchi Garg.: *Fundamentals of Hotel Housekeeping*, Alfa Publication, Delhi, 2006.

Sunil Sharma.: *Managing Hotel and Tourism Operations*, Akansha Publication, Delhi, 2005.

Tarun Bansal.: *Hotel Engineering*, Aman Publication, Delhi, 2011.

Tarun Bansal.: *Hotel Facility Planning*, Oxford University Press, Delhi, 2010.

Vacca.: *Guide to Wireless Network Security (With CD)*, Springer, 2003.

Vijay Kaushik.: *Management and Functions of Housekeeping*, Book Enclave, Jaipur, 2006.

Index